SCHOOL SPIRIT

PIERRE HUYGHE   DOUGLAS COUPLAND

ENCOUNTERS

My name is Kelly Harding.
I was a junior at John Glenn Secondary, Rancho Las Palmas, California.
I died on my birthday, April 14, 1984, the day I turned sixteen. That day the weather was overcast with clouds the colour of ashes. At 2:36 PM Pacific Daylight Time the last thing I saw was that sky, drifting south from Los Angeles, polluted with unleaded exhaust fumes, radio waves and dead dreams.

***

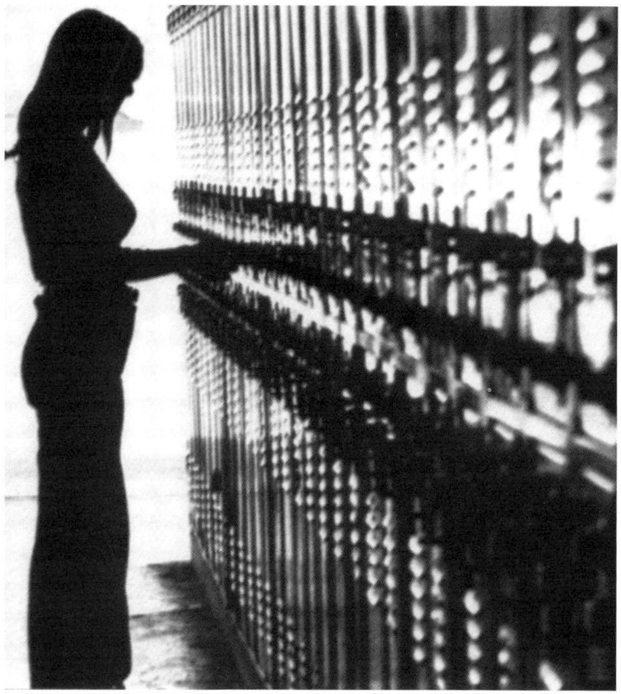

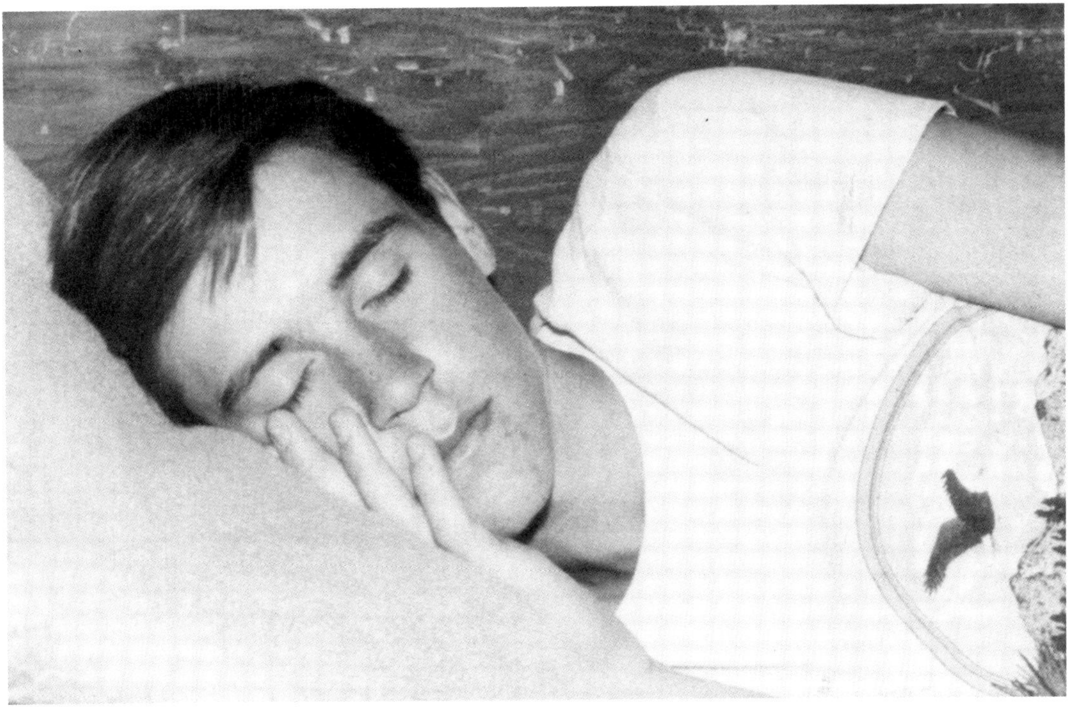

I Won't grow up

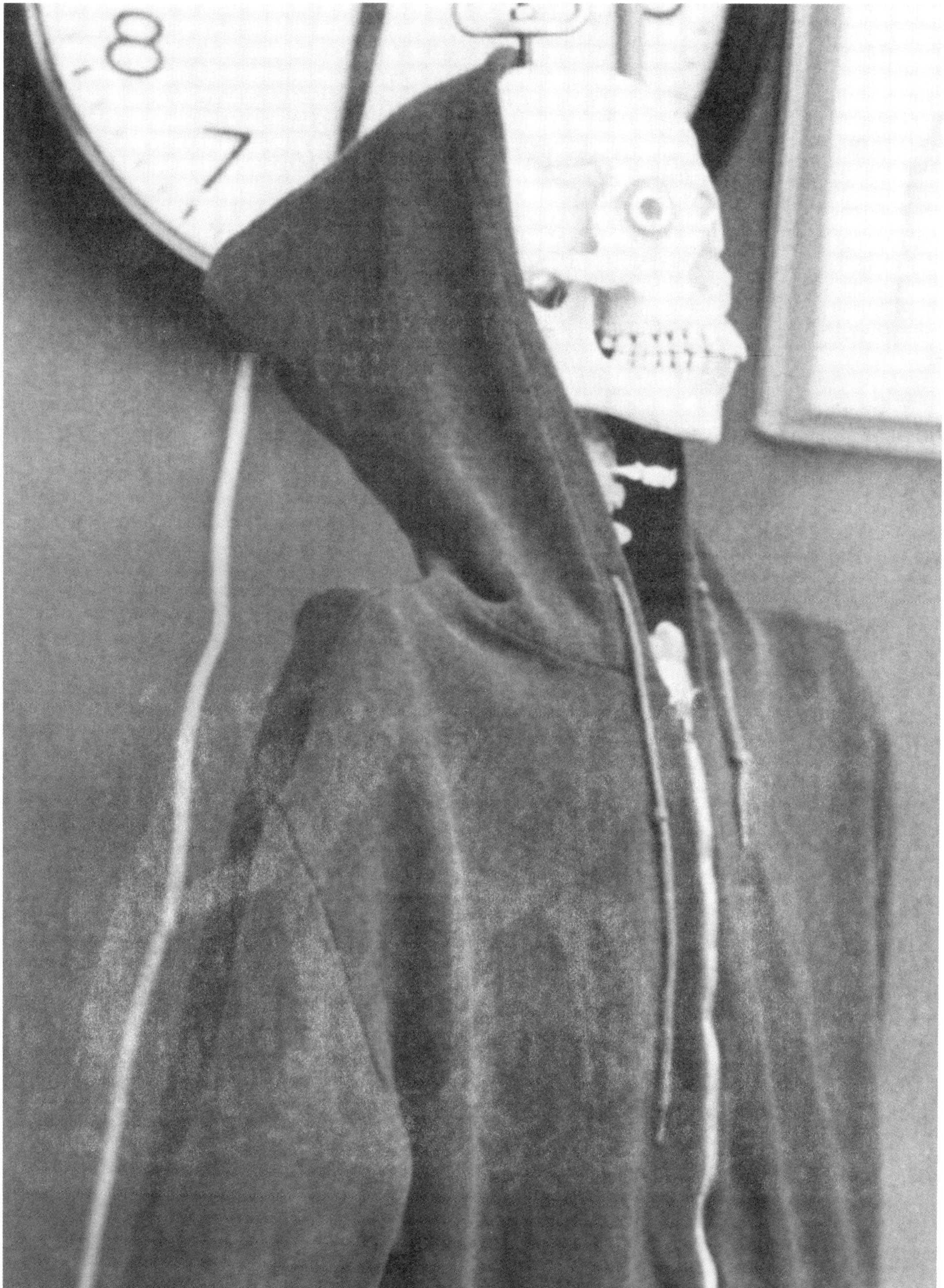

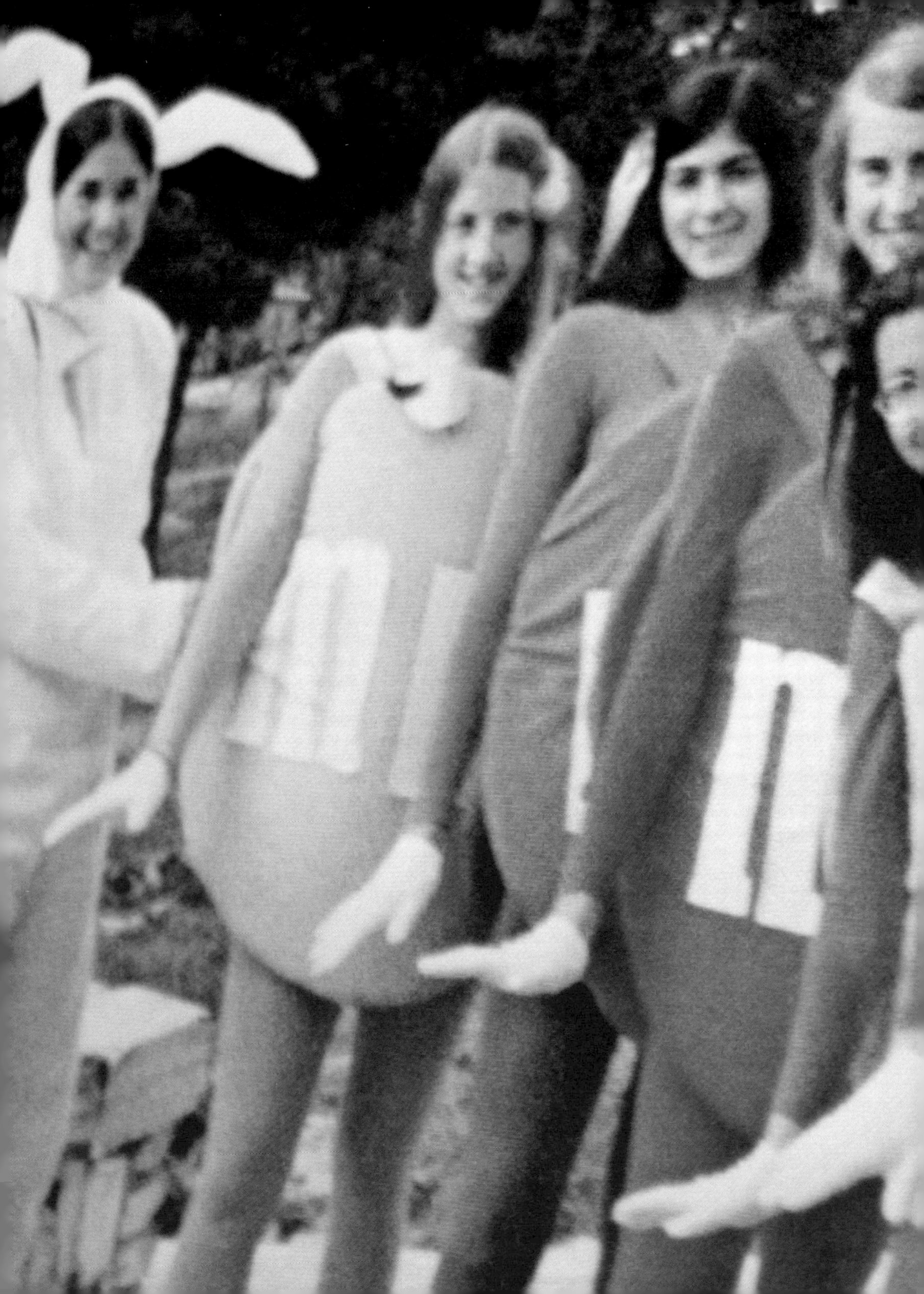

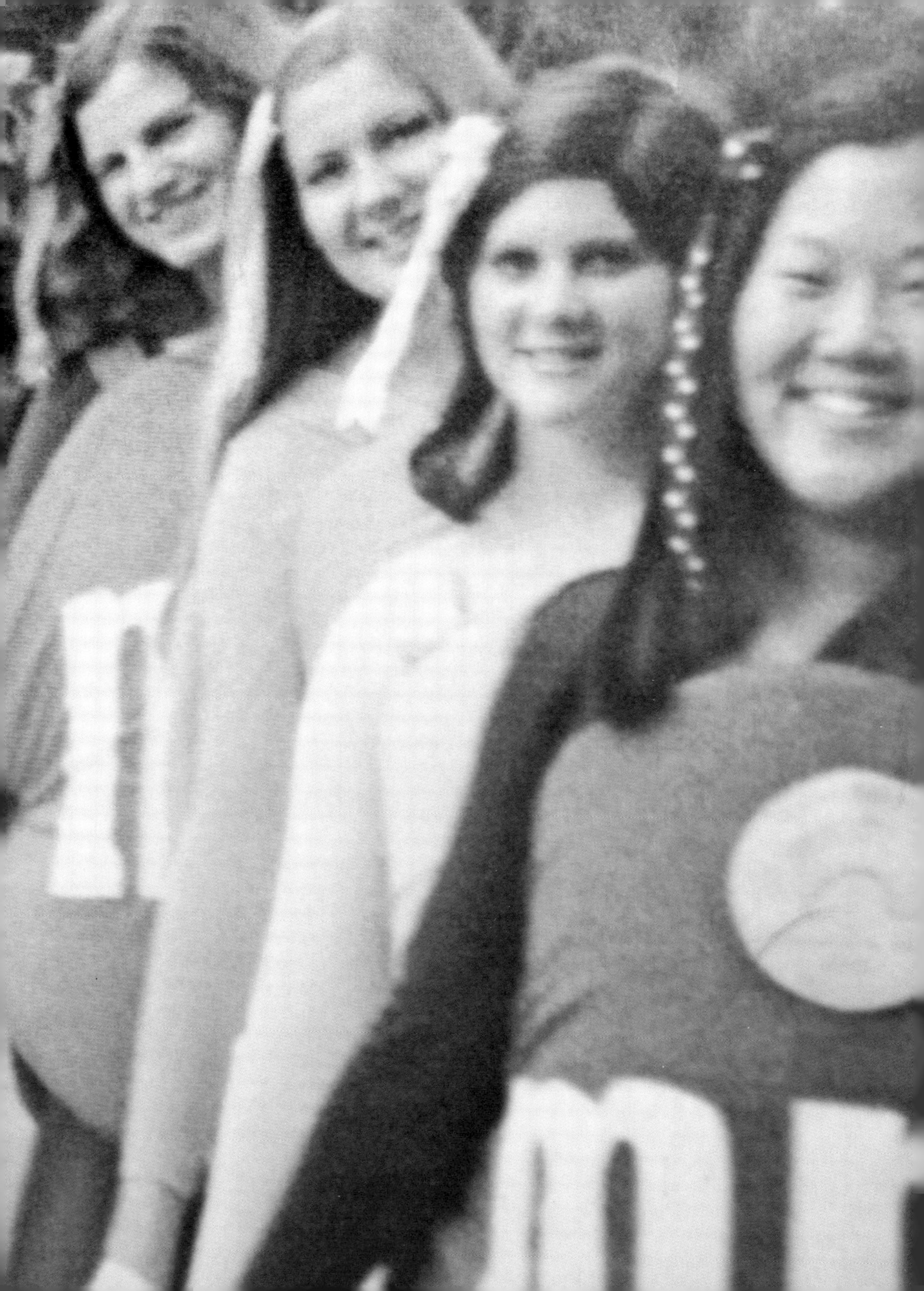

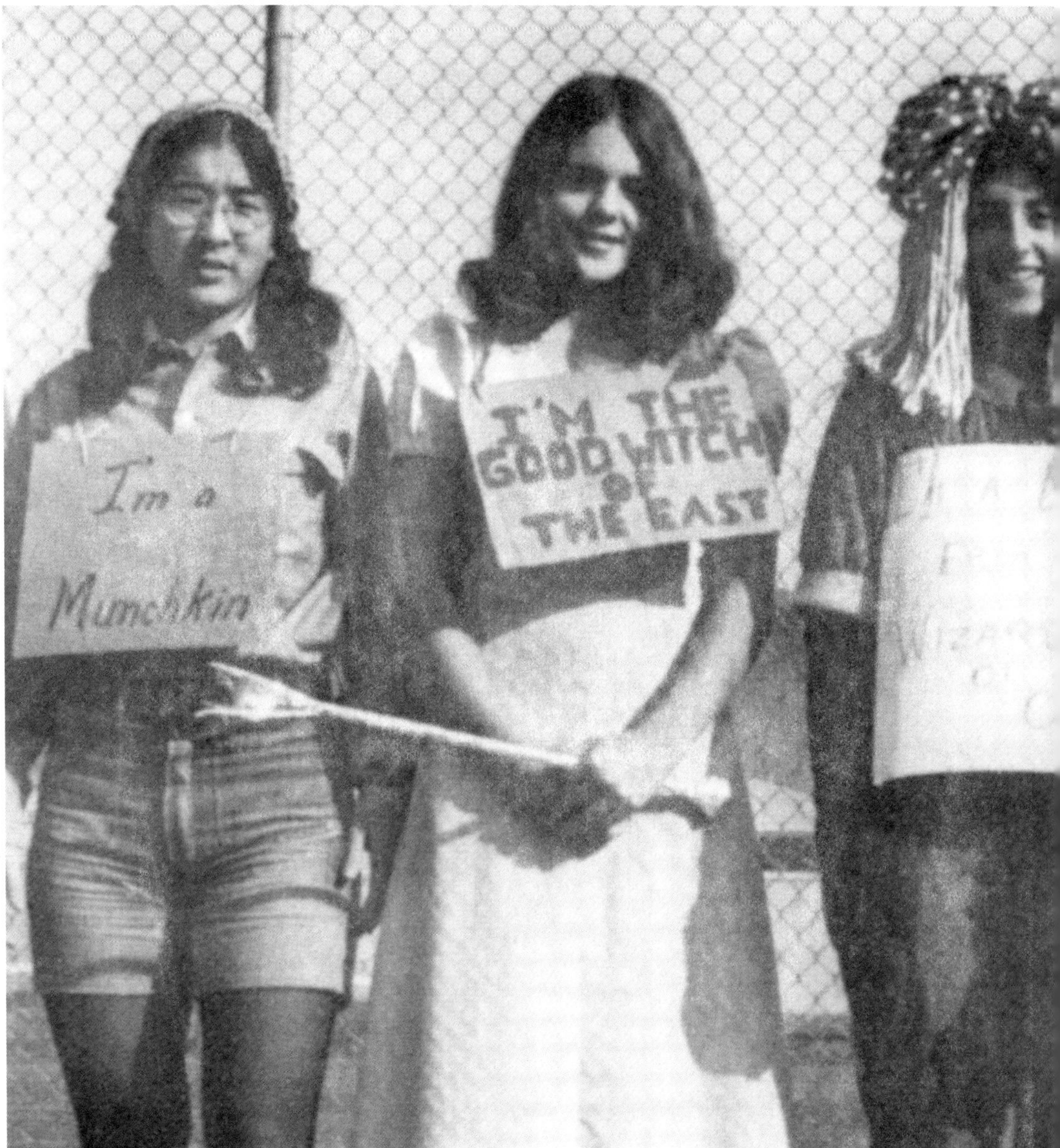
I'm a Munchkin
I'M THE GOOD WITCH OF THE EAST

UNIMAGINATION

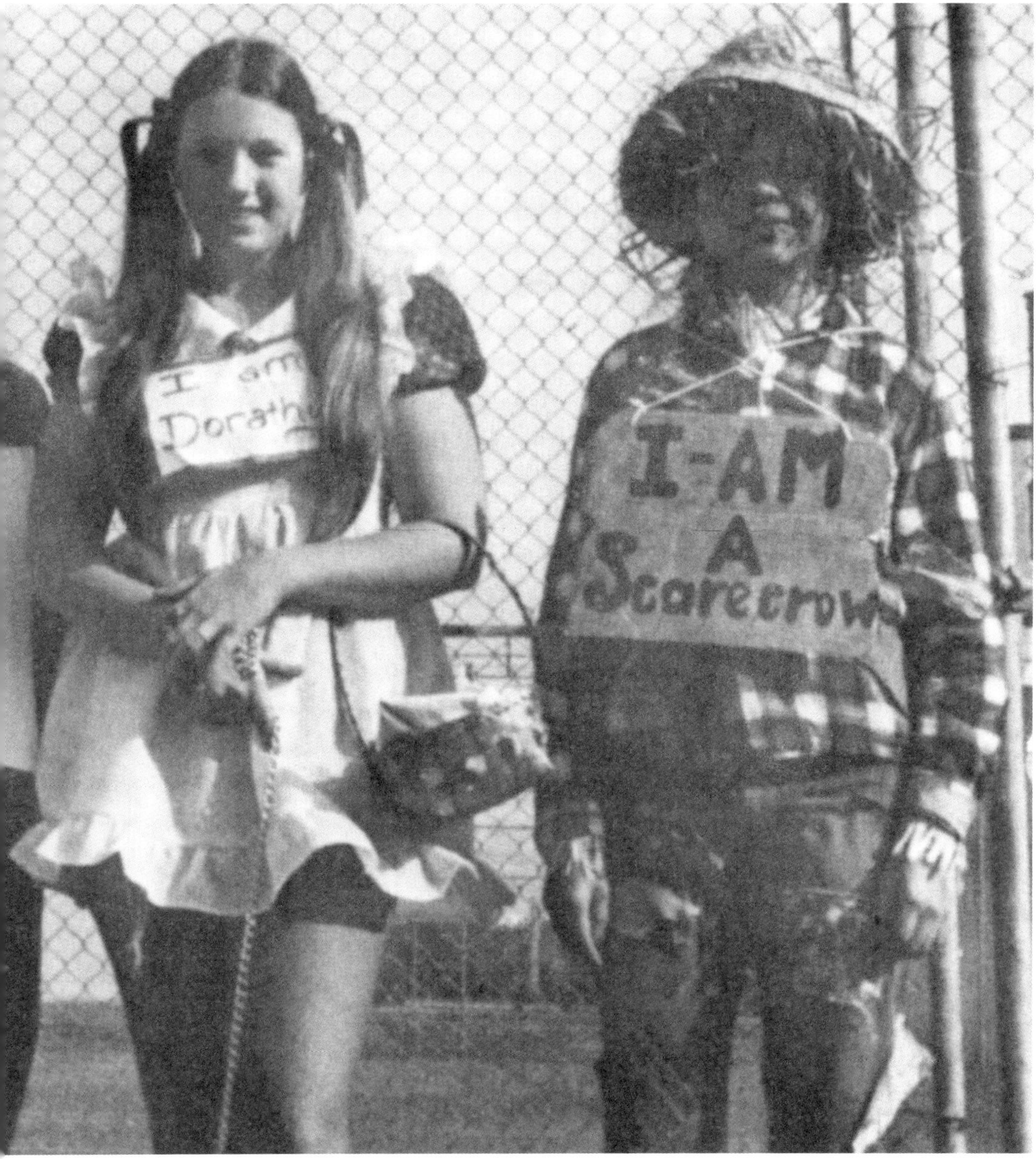

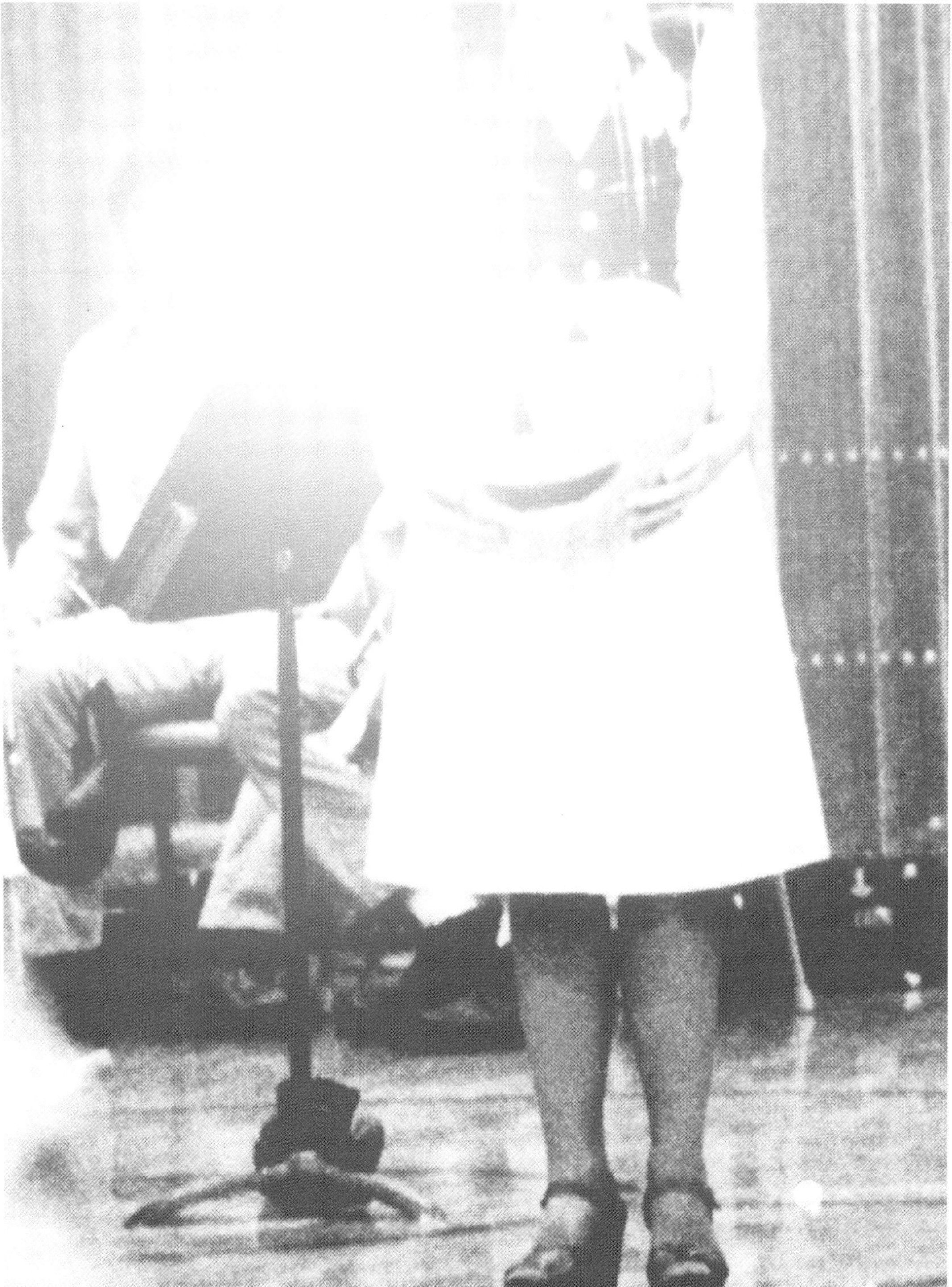

HILLARY...

WHERE DO I BEGIN?
BIZARRE LOVE TRIANGLES
HIGHWAY CLOVERLEAFS
THE COOKIE MONSTER.
THANKS FOR OUR DEEP
SPIRITUAL TALKS.

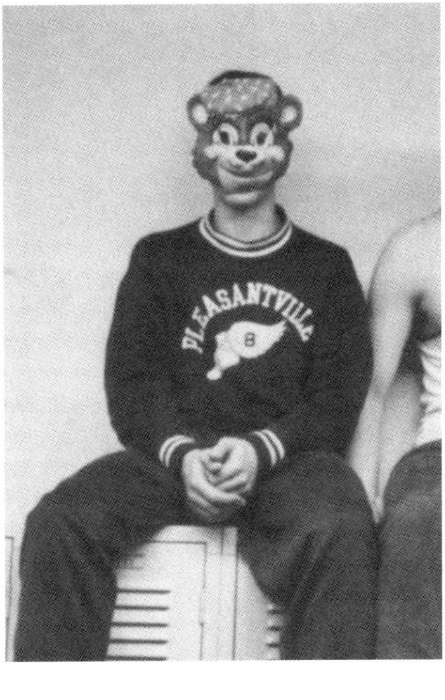

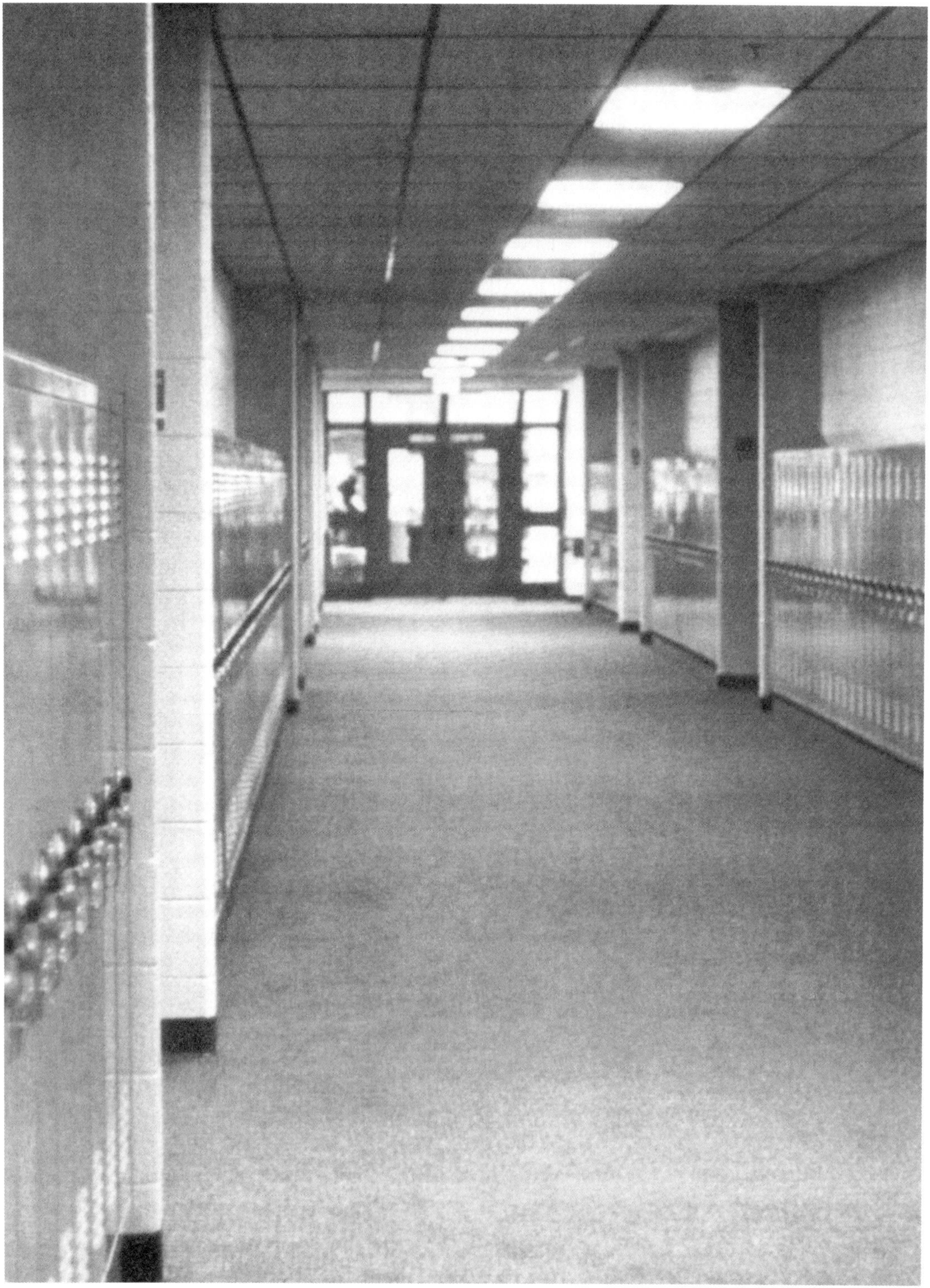

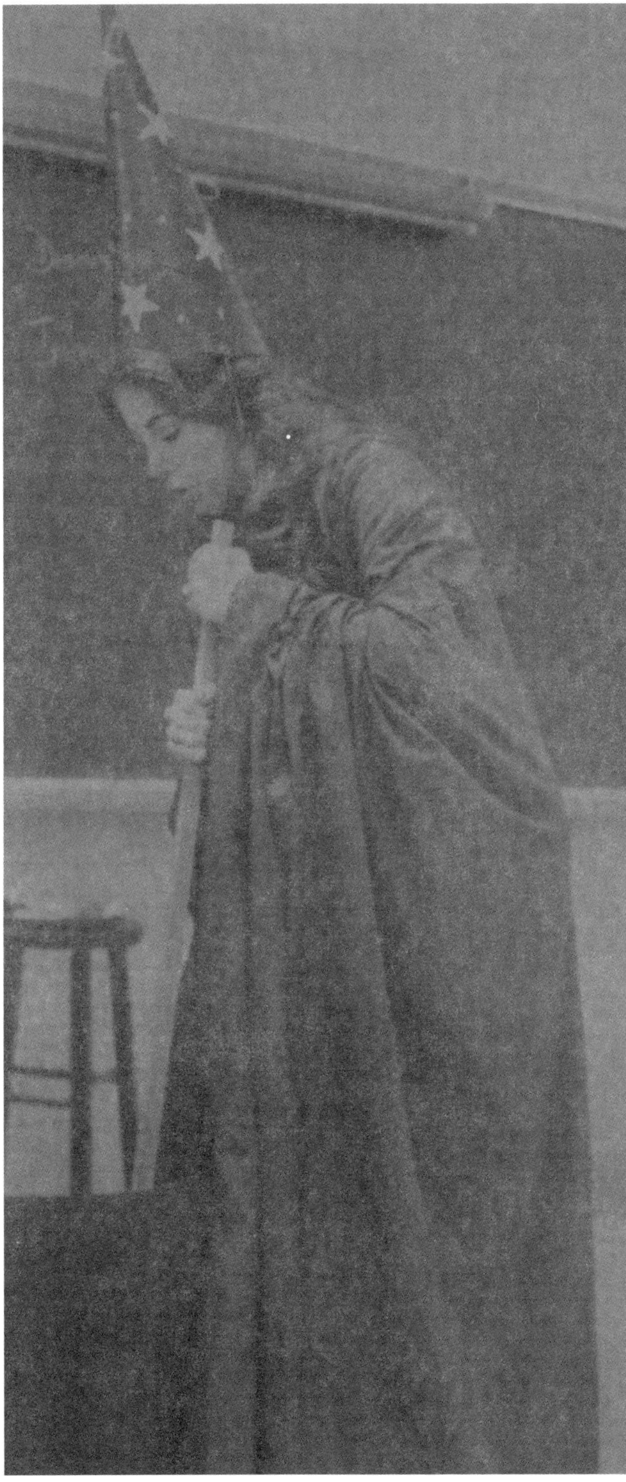

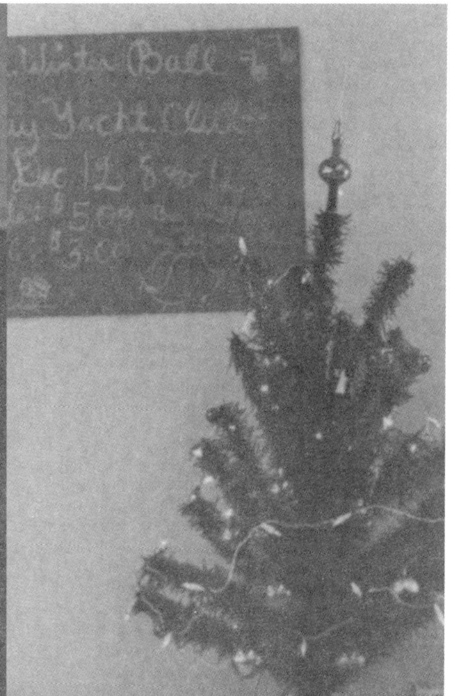

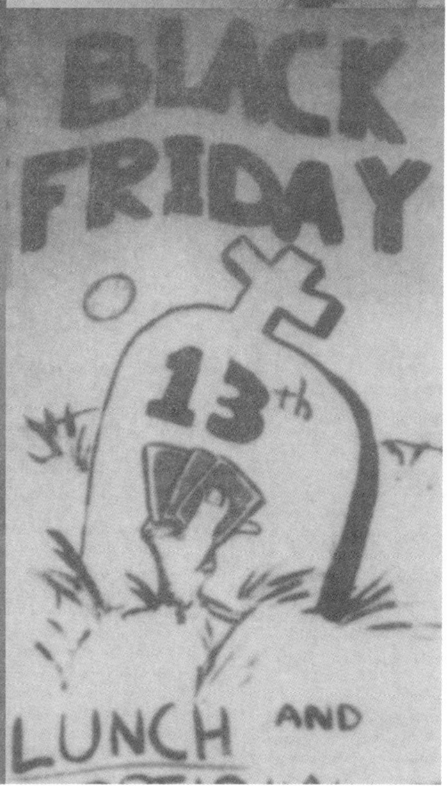
BLACK
FRIDAY
13th
LUNCH AND

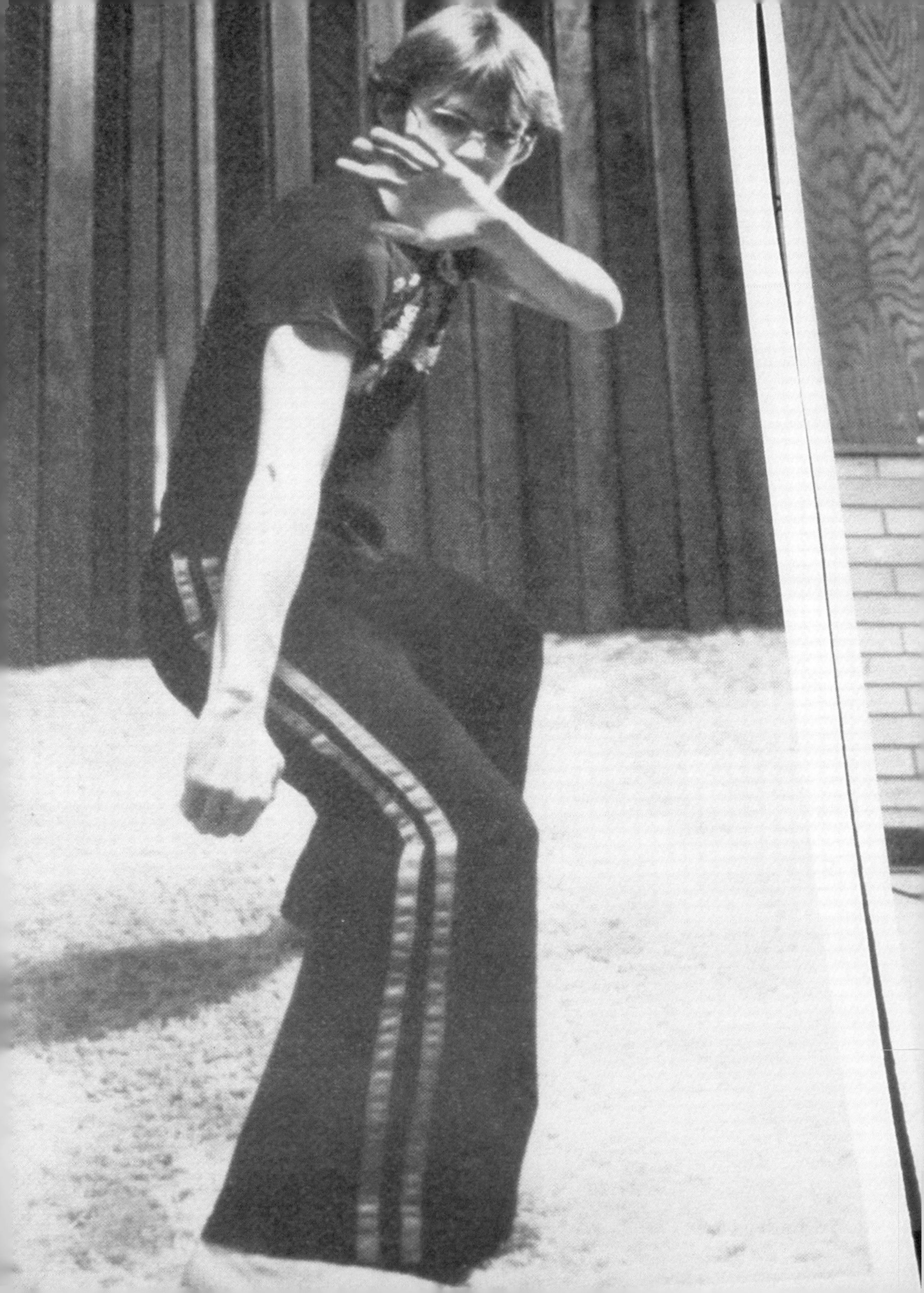

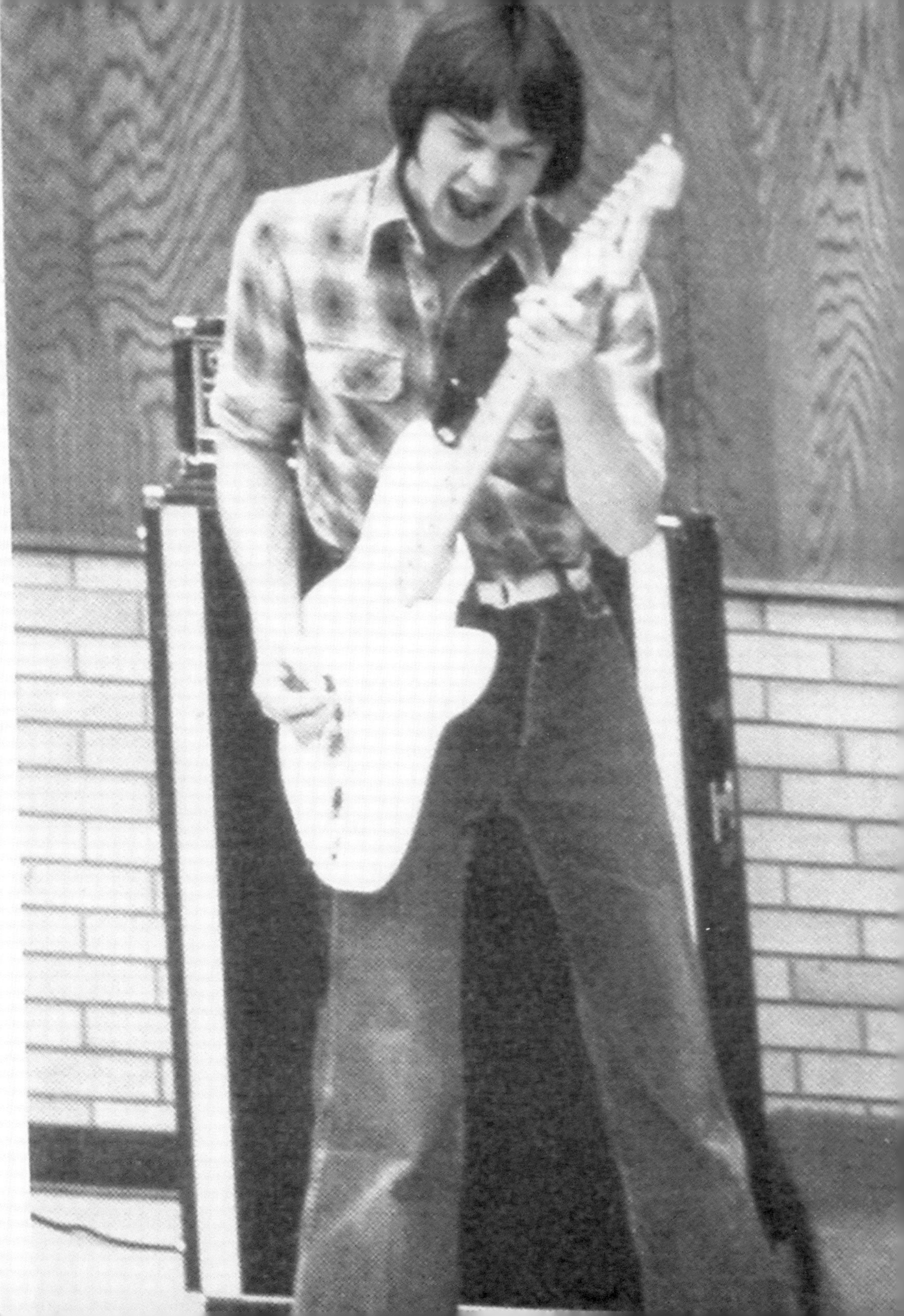

I died during the afternoon gym class. We were playing soccer, and after kicking the ball to my friend Tracy, I slipped and fell on the muddy grass, and the fall triggered an aneurysm: a small clot of blood that had been lurking in my brain waiting for me to do something like slip and fall. I was already dead before I was carried back into the school's front hallway, where they placed my body beneath a mural of several helmeted bears crushing other small animals – the school's team was called the Bears. The light on my face came from the team's trophy case, fluorescent and yellow, but as I said, by that point I was already died. I'd seen the clouds.

***

As my body was carted away from the building on a gurney, somehow I —or my spirit or whatever it is I am—was consigned to remain here in the high school, and I didn't at first know why. But the situation didn't frighten me. I just knew that I wasn't trapped in the school forever—or for eternity—or whatever word you use once you no longer use the word, 'future.' I was trapped in the school until I learned things I might have learned differently had I lived longer.

* * *

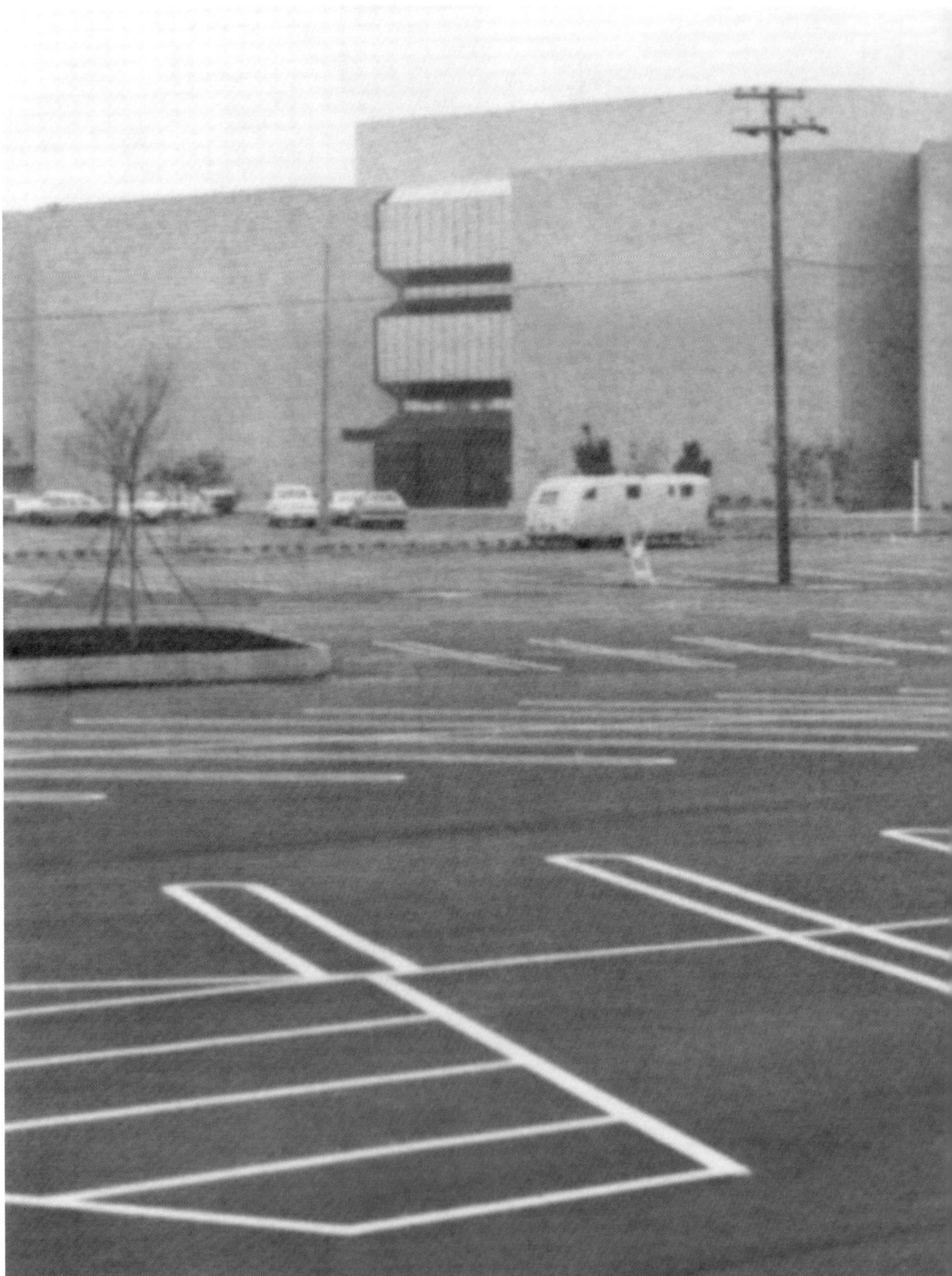

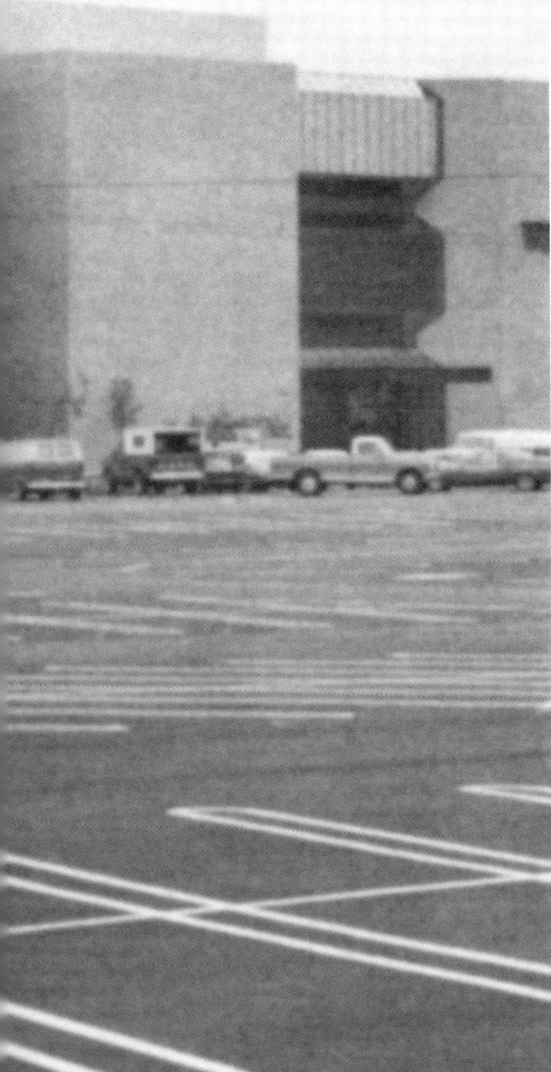

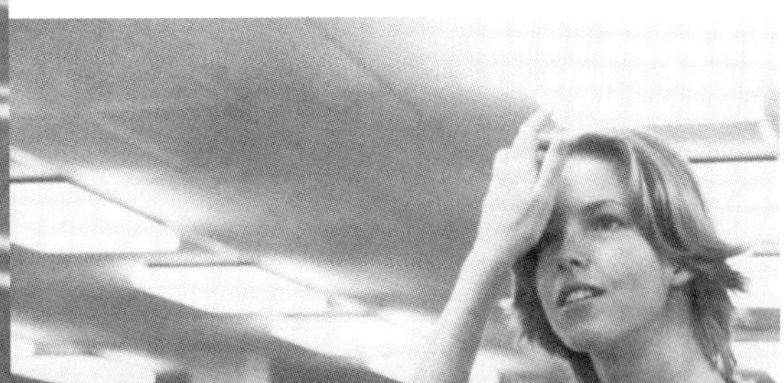

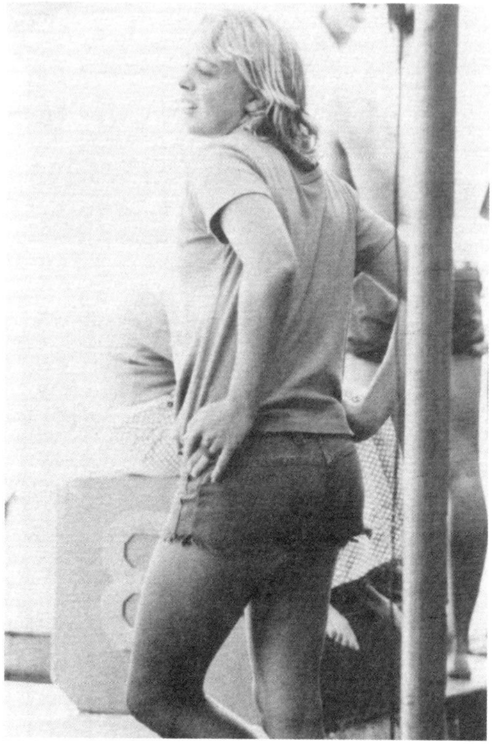

WHEN THE FLOWER DIES,
SO DOES LOVE.

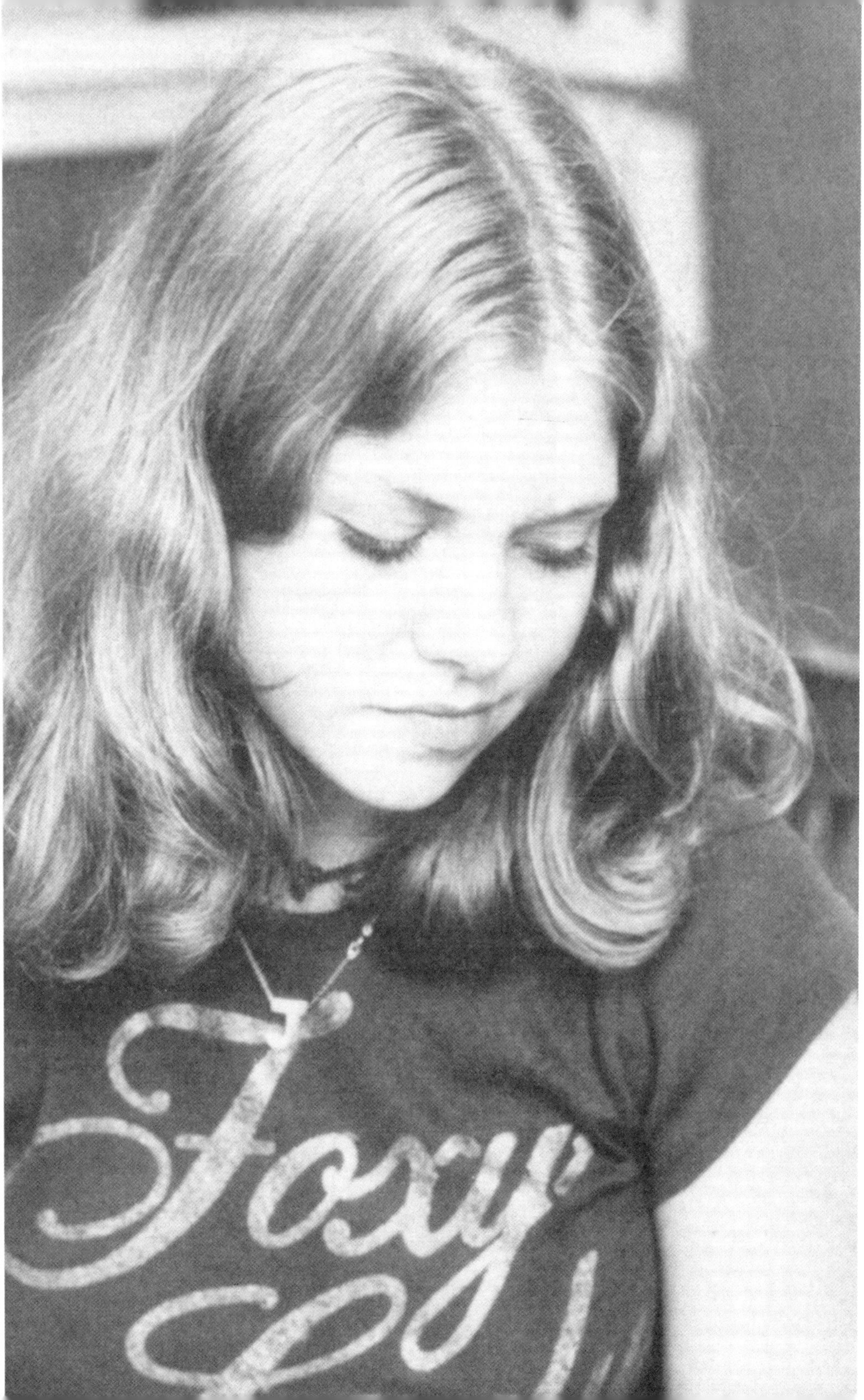
Foxy

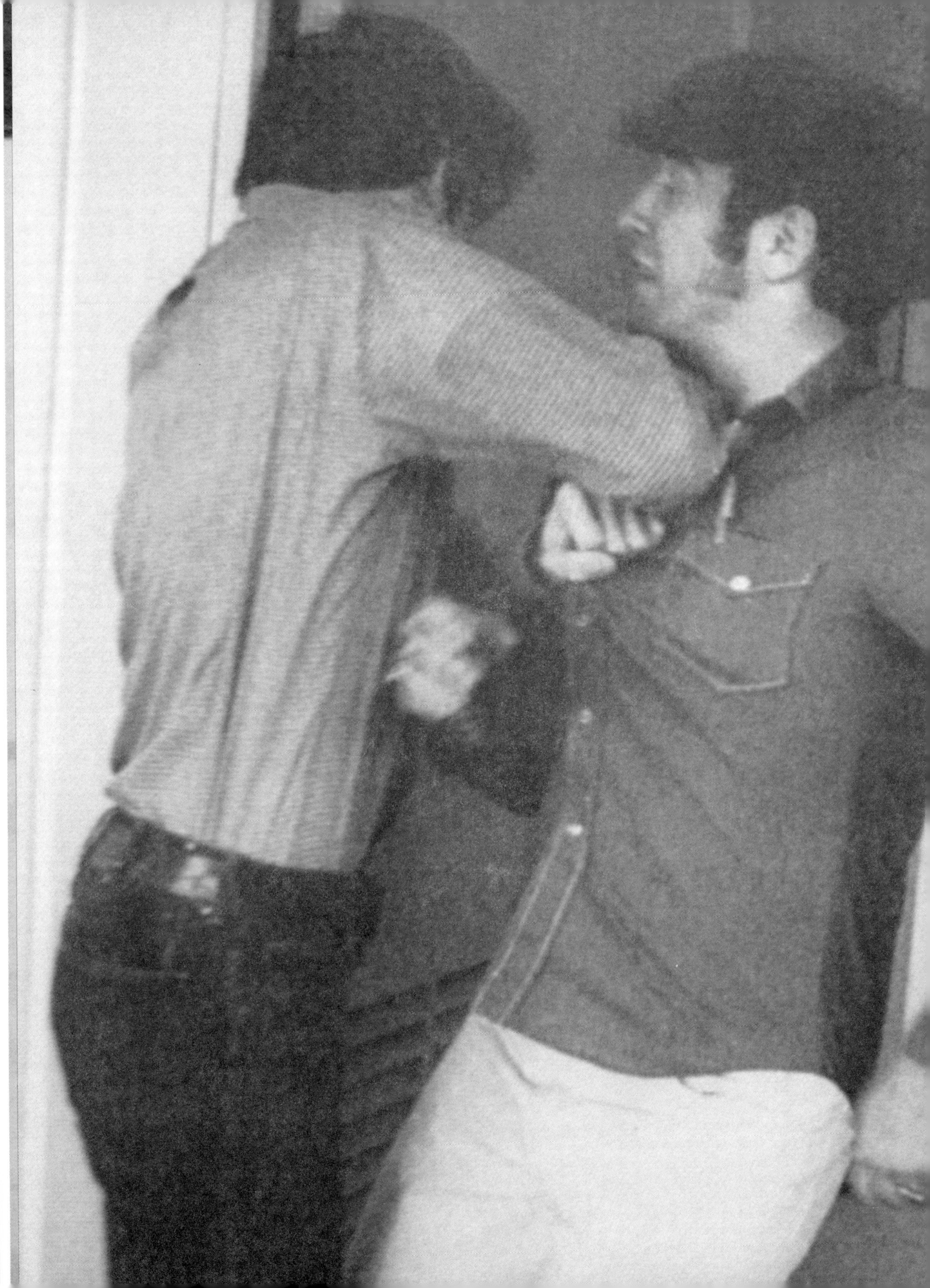

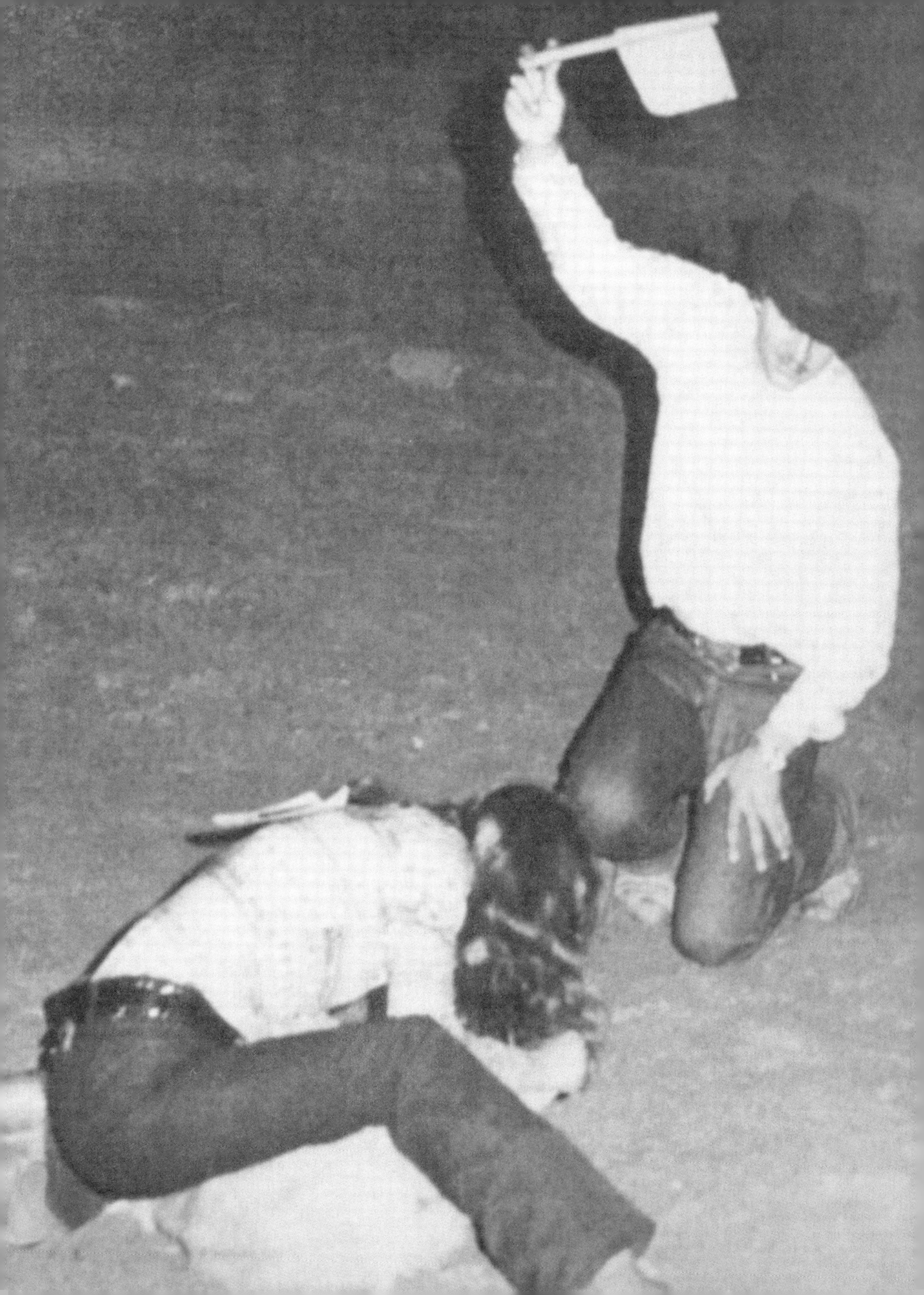

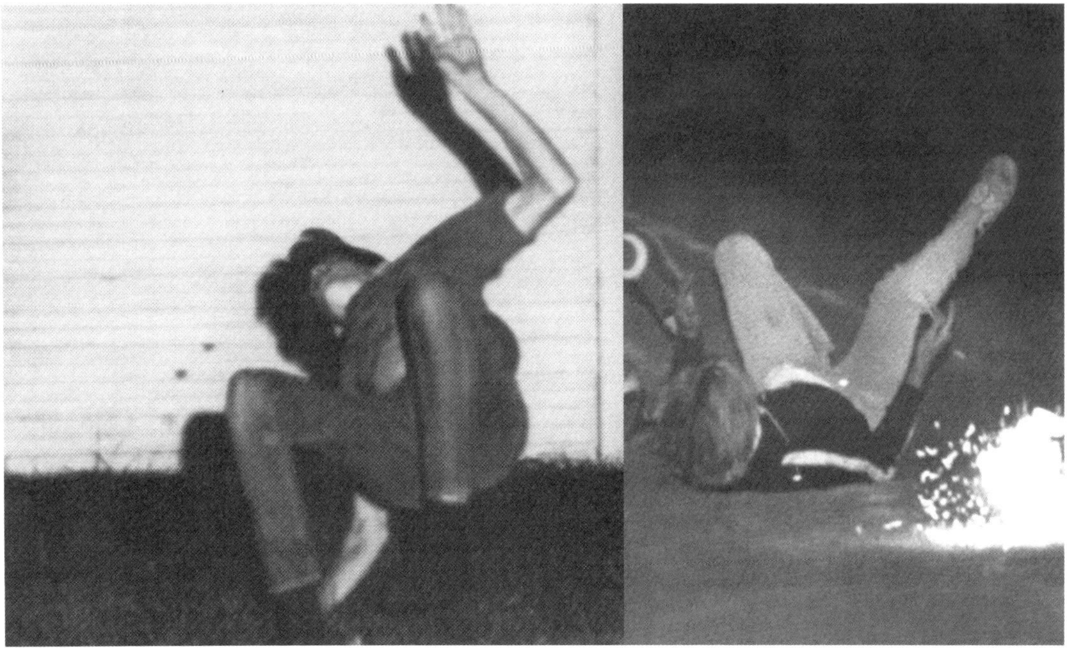

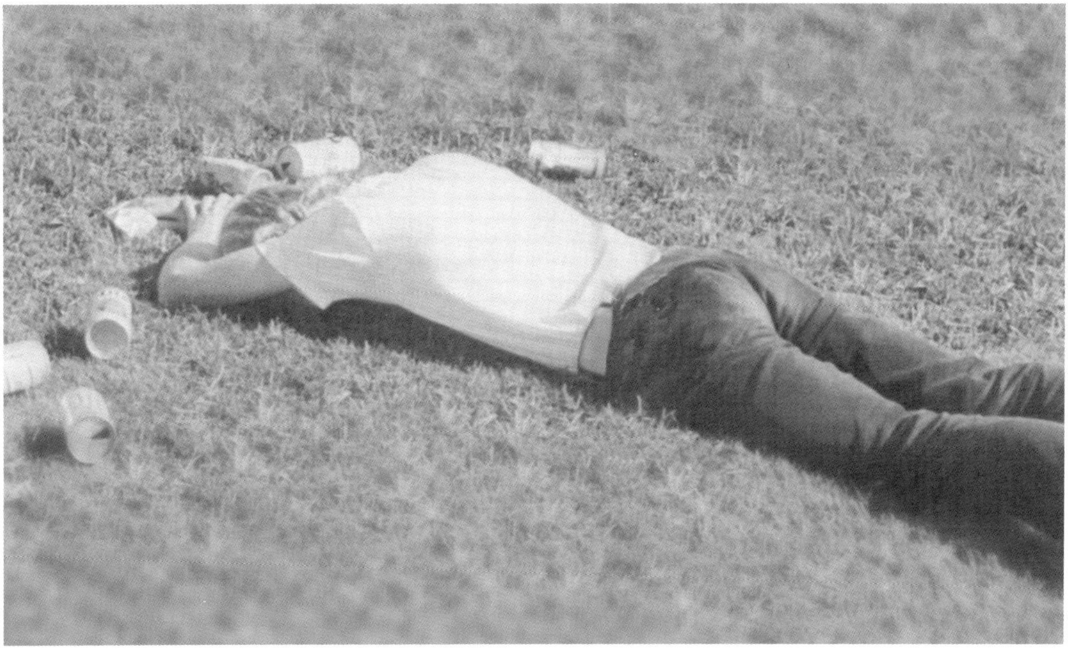

TO LISA
A GOOD FRIEND, THROUGH GOOD TIMES
AND THE BAD, AND I'M SO SORRY
FOR THE BAD TIMES.
Y.F.A.
SUZI

I've been dead going on two decades now, and I think my time is soon up. And I'm not the only dead person in the school, either. There are other undeads like myself roaming the hallways, but I'm unable to communicate with them, but we're all aware of each other. We are, however, allowed to visit each other's schools.

* * *

High schools, I have learned, are like people – the things that make them different are trivial compared what they have in common. They're like Chinese food. Or pizza.

* * *

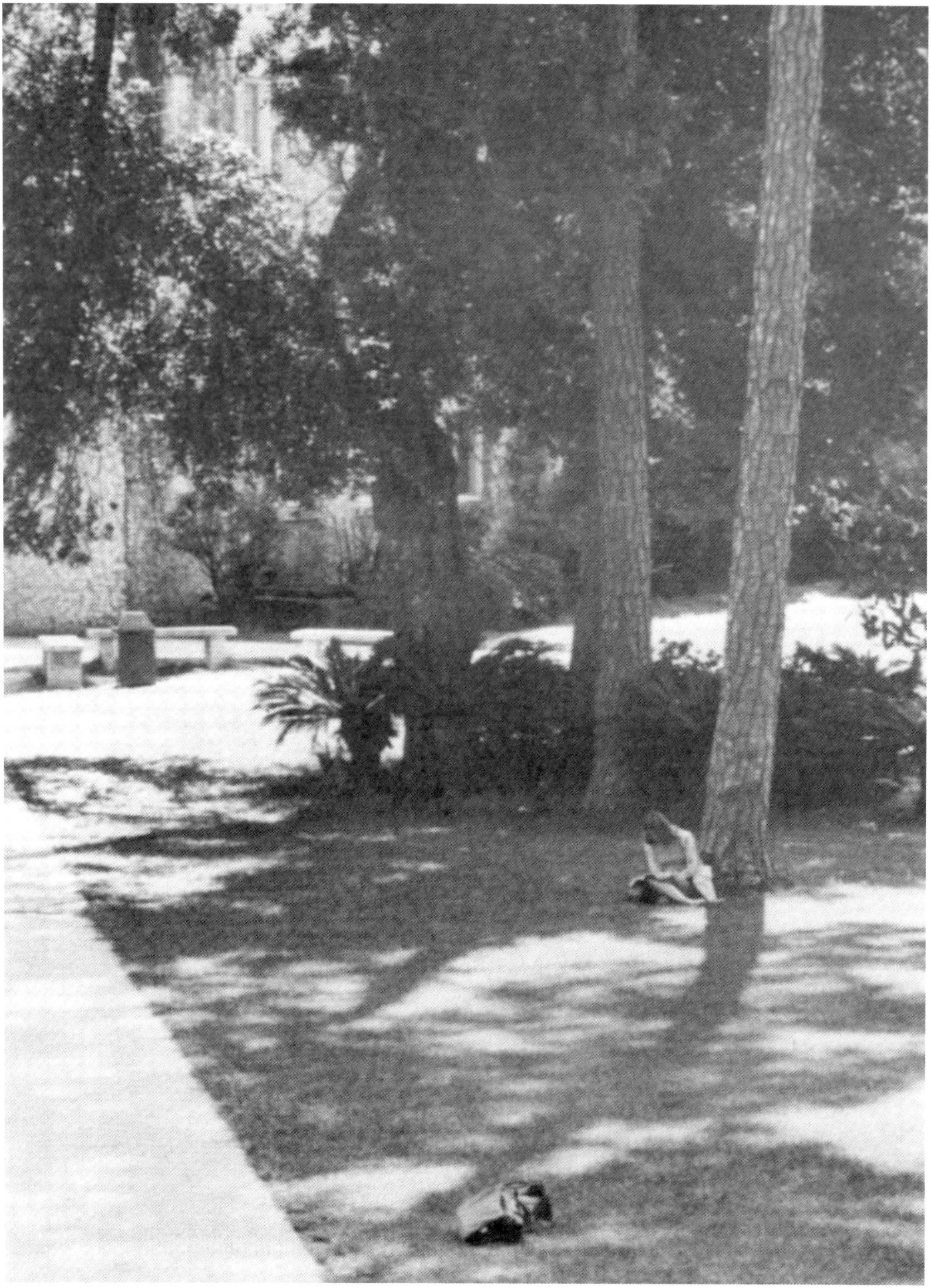

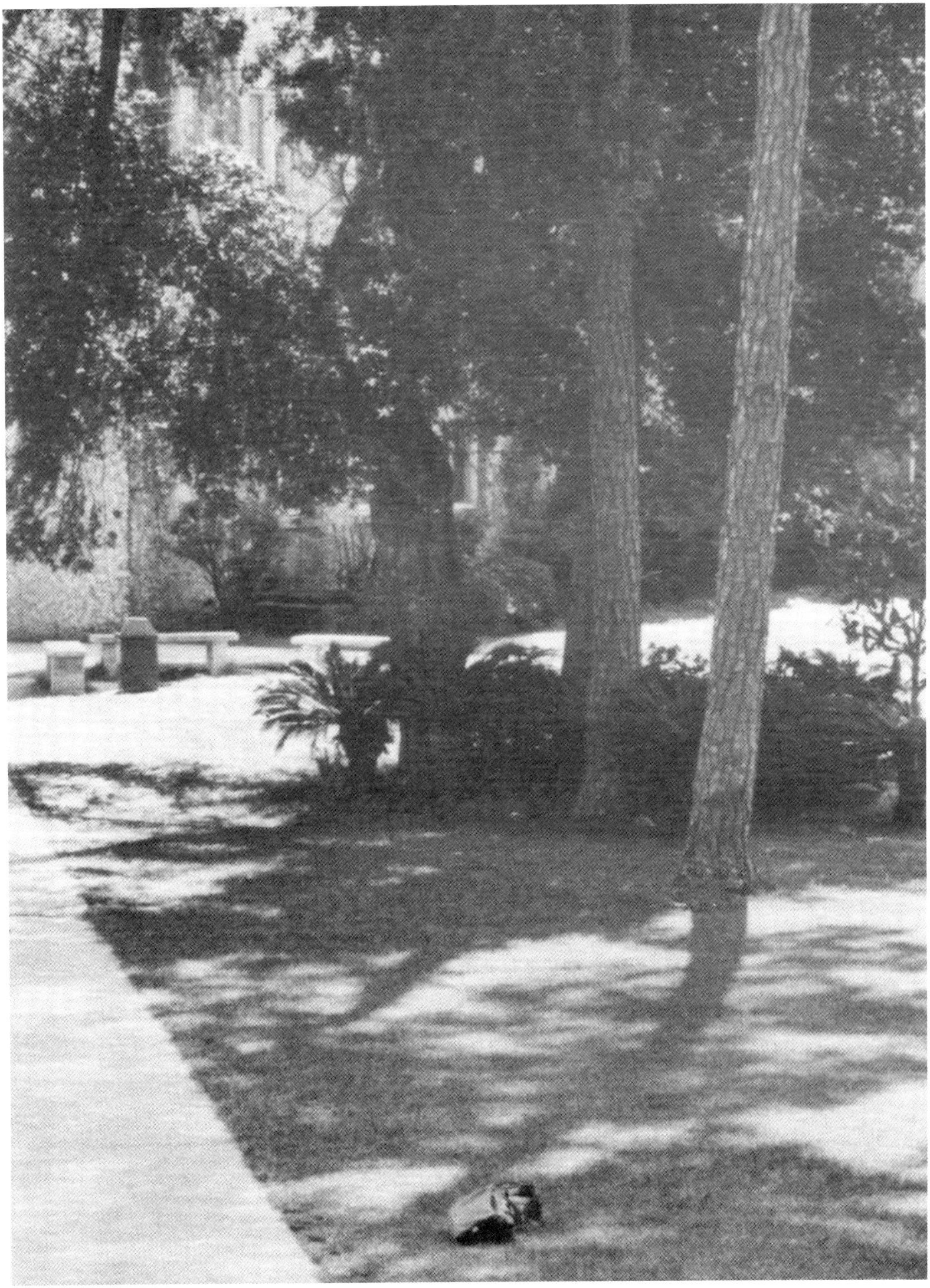

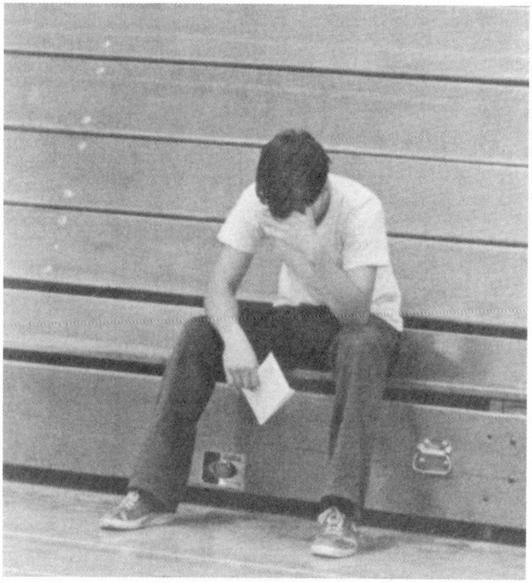

DAVE,

YOU PROBABLY DON'T EVEN KNOW WHO I AM BUT I ALWAYS KNEW WHO YOU WERE

DEE.

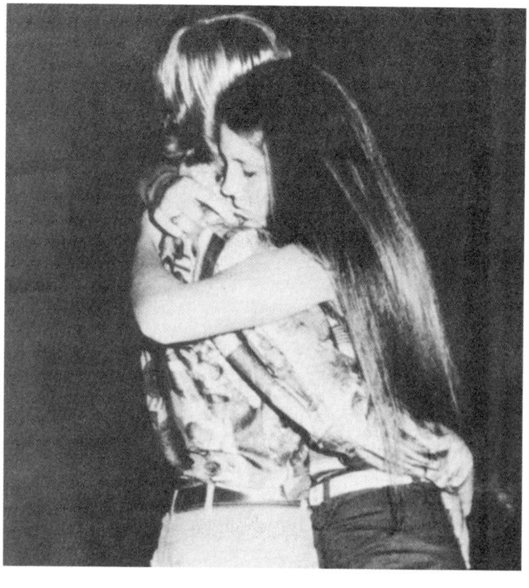

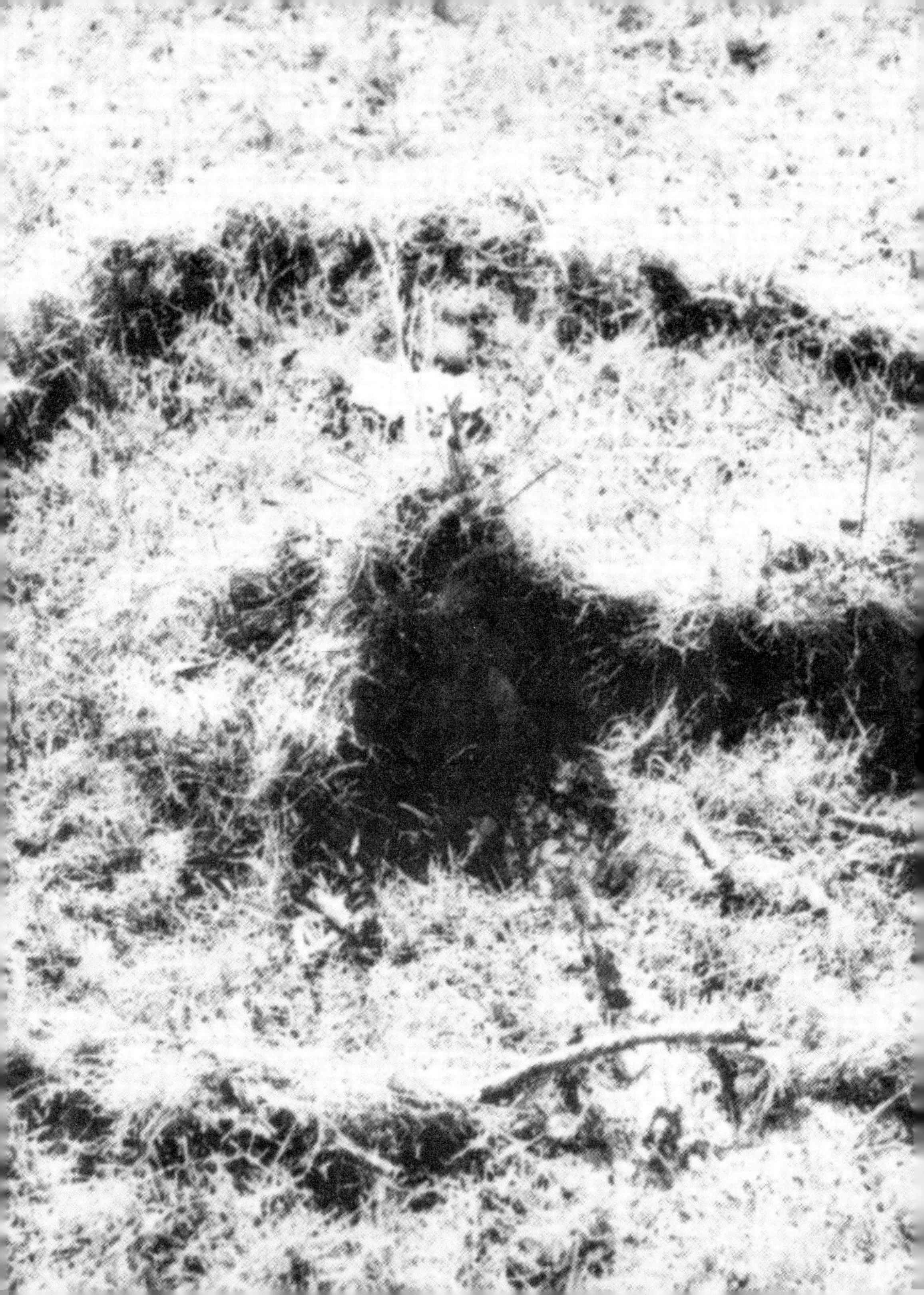

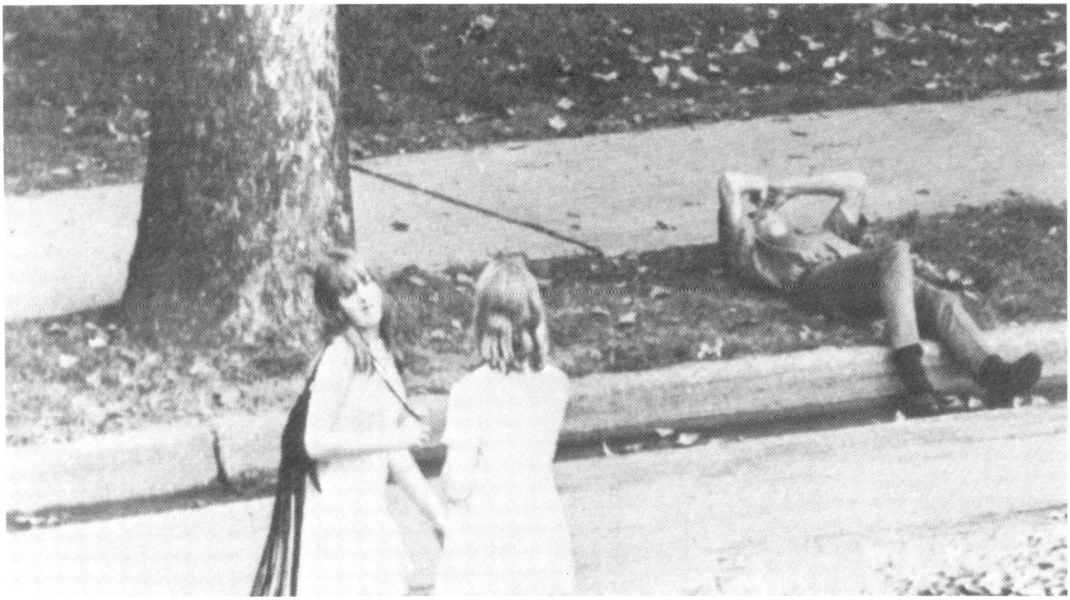

MOM & DAD,
YOU GUYS ARE THE WORLD TO ME AND I LOVE YOU BOTH SO MUCH. THANKS FOR ALL THE SACRIFICES YOU MADE FOR ME AND I'M SORRY I DIDN'T LIVE UP TO YOUR EXPECTATIONS. I'LL TRY HARDER IN THE FUTURE, AND THAT'S A PROMISE.

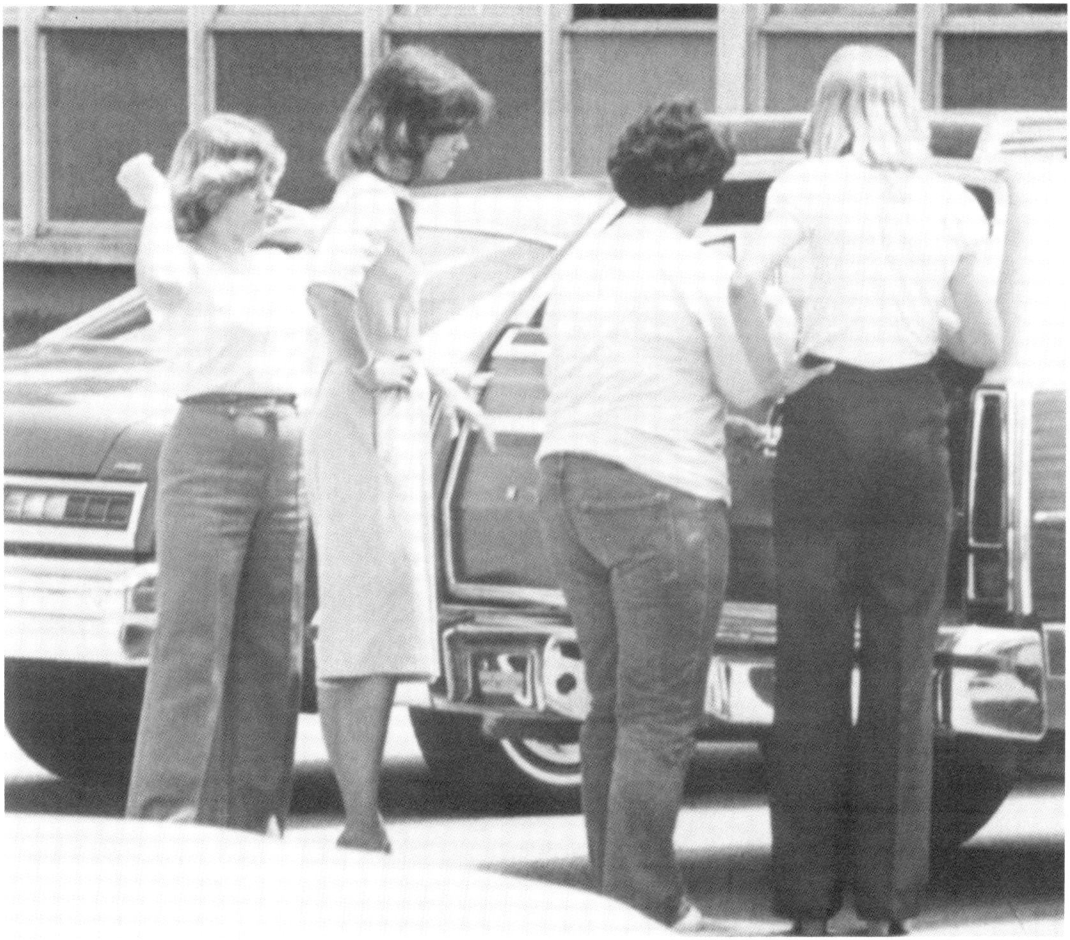

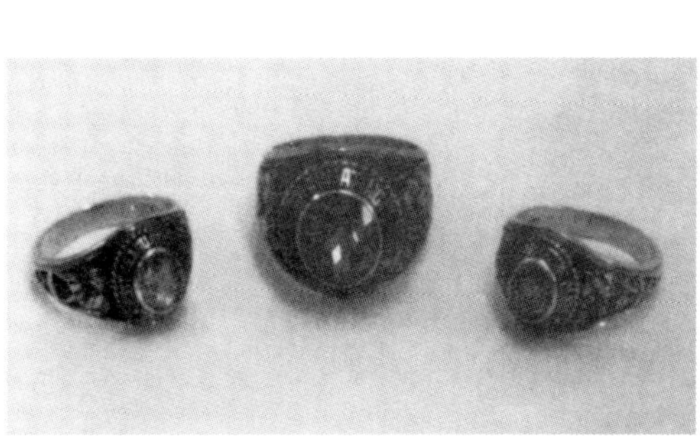

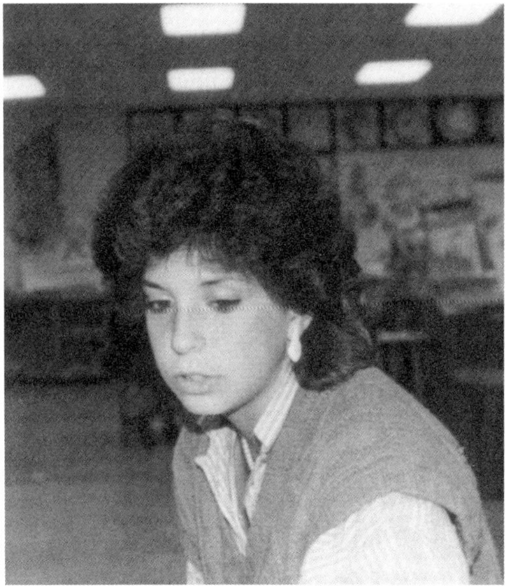

BITTER!
BITTER!
BITTER!

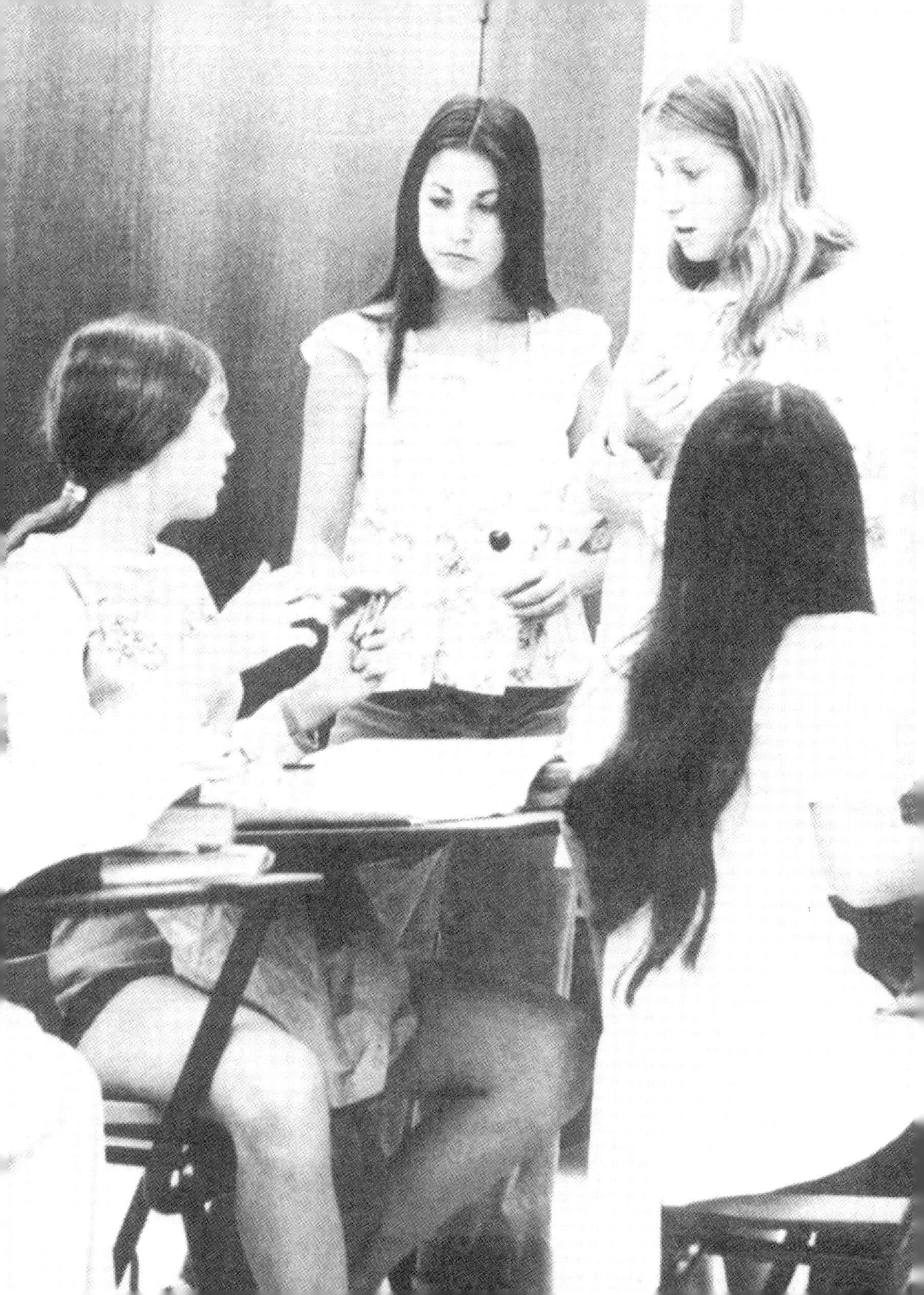

LAURIE,

I'M SORRY FOR THE THINGS I'VE DONE IN THE PAST THAT HURT YOU I DON'T KNOW WHY YOU STUCK BY ME.

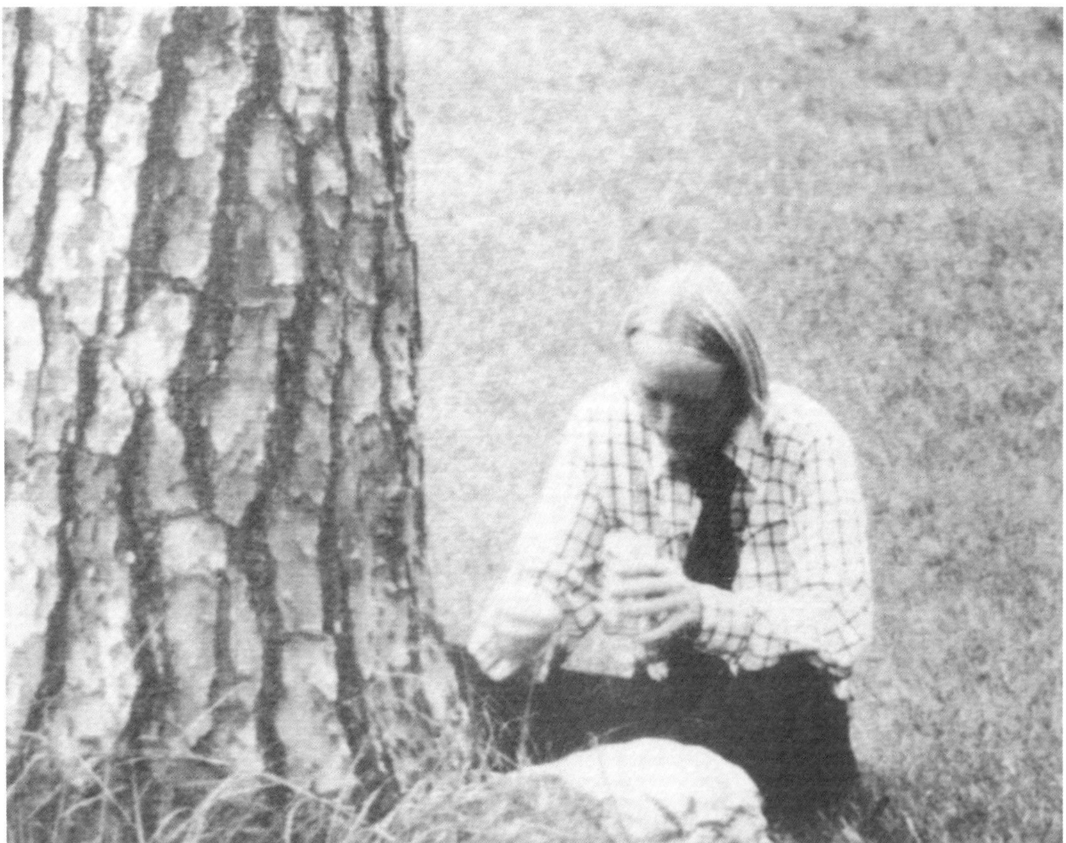

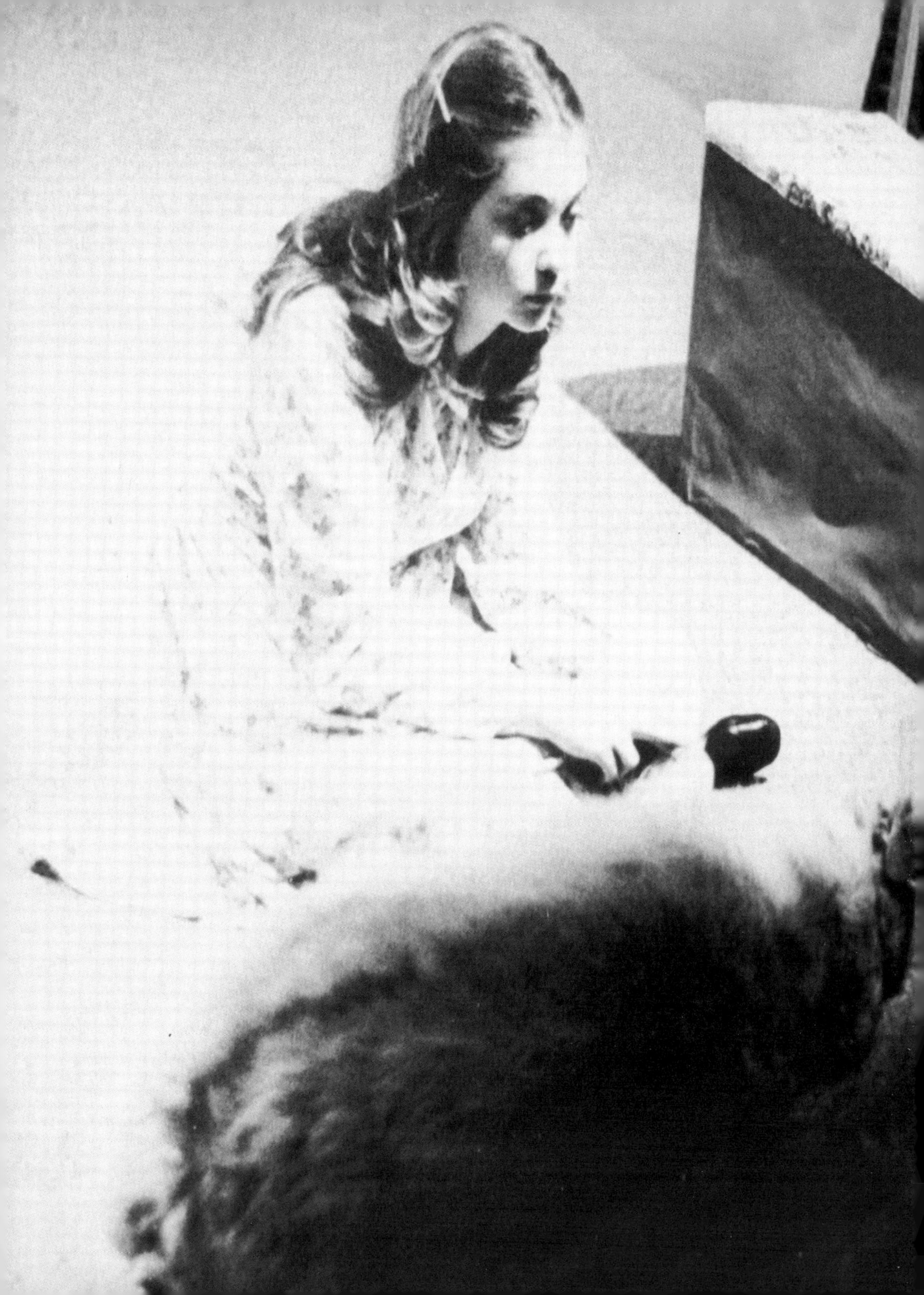

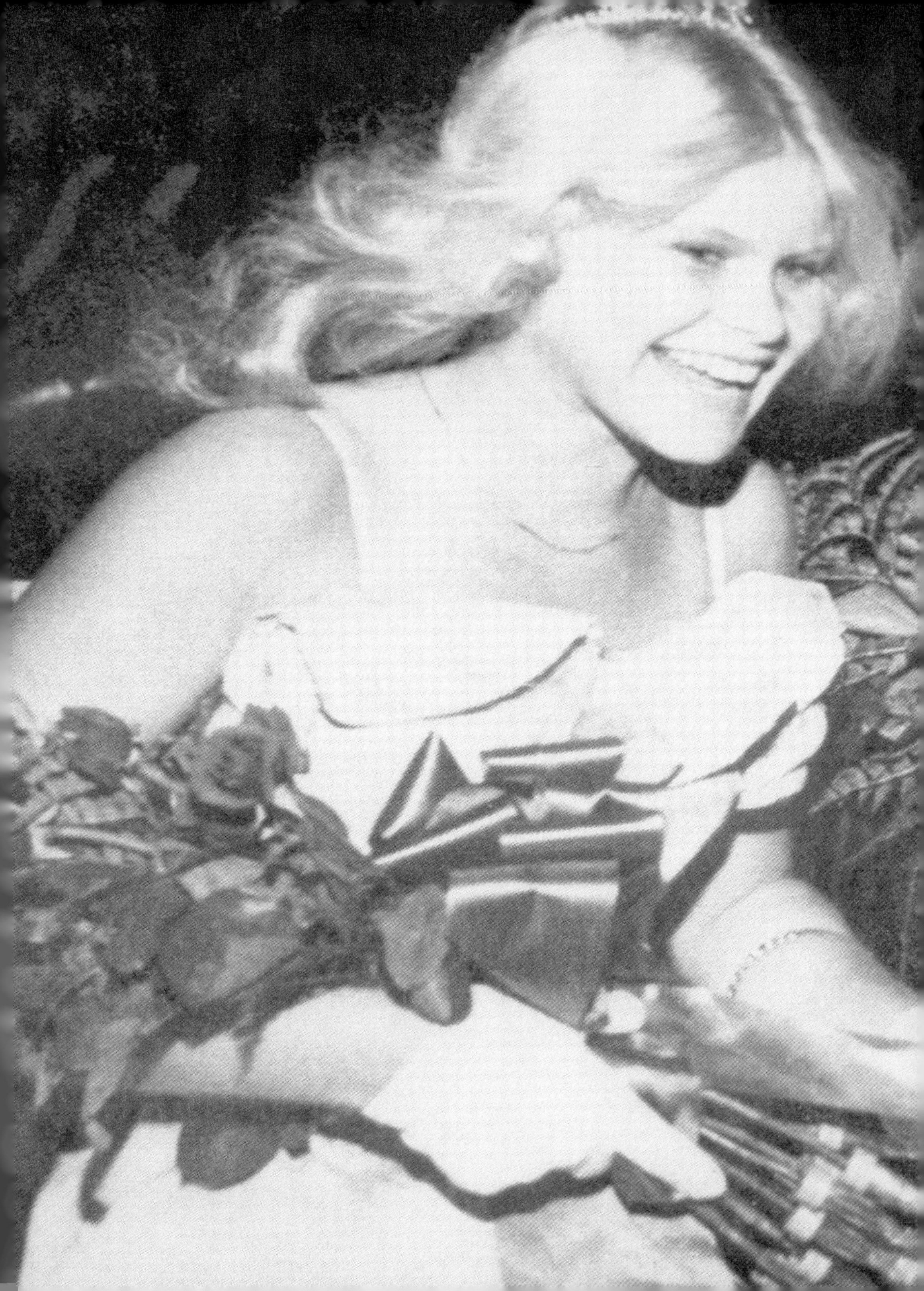

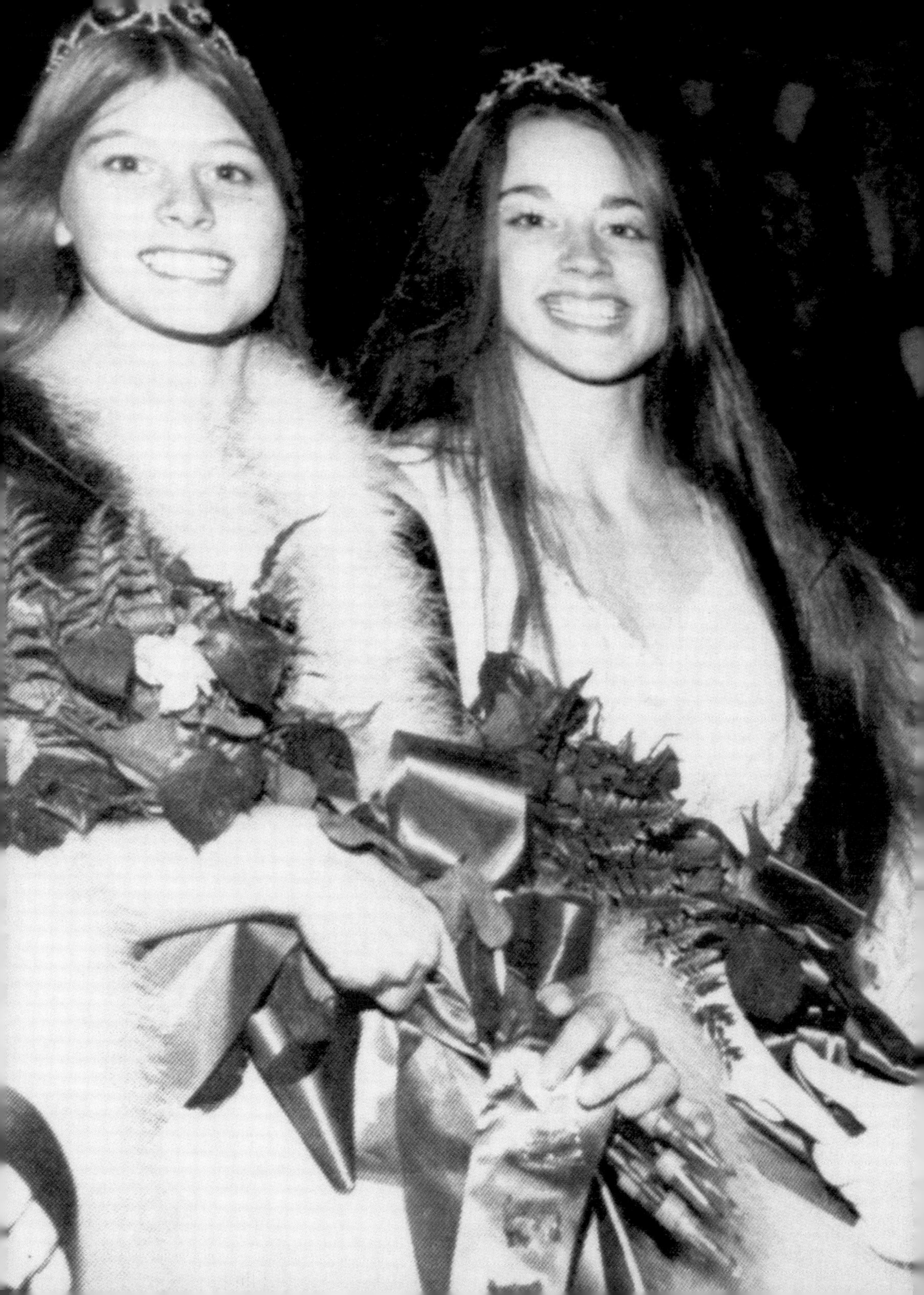

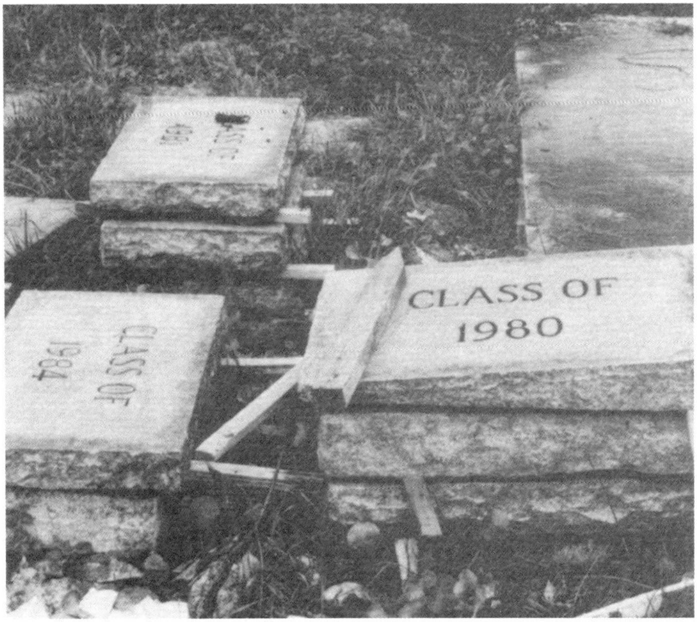

SUSAN,
FRIENDS FOREVER
FRIENDS 4EVER
SANDY

I USED TO BE LOST IN THE SHUFFLE.
NOW I SHUFFLE ALONG WITH THE LOST.

MOST LIKELY TO SUCCEED
MOST AMBITIOUS
BEST ALL AROUND
MOST CHEERFUL
MOST THOUGHTFUL
BIGGEST PARTIER
NICEST EYES
MOST MUSICAL
CLASS CLOWN
BIGGEST FLIRT
CRAZIEST
MOST TALKATIVE
BEST DRESSED
SHYEST
MICEST LEGS
MOST ARTISTIC
CLASS COUPLE
CUTEST
SKI BUMS
SHORTEST
TALLEST
NICEST SMILES
MOST MISUNDERSTOOD
MOST DOWN TO EARTH

BEING NICE
IS STUPID

FUN IS
FOR IDIOTS
AND
BABIES

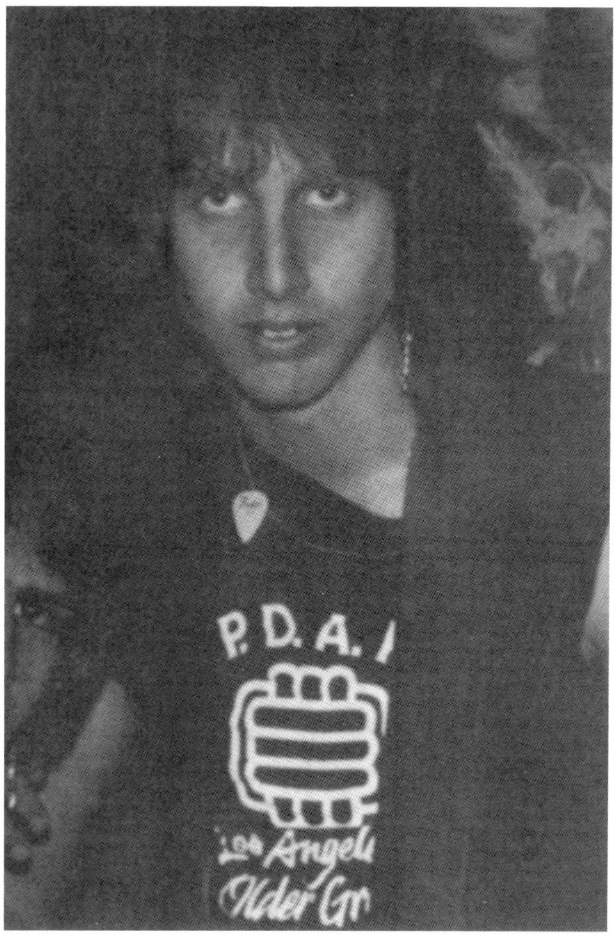
P. D. A.

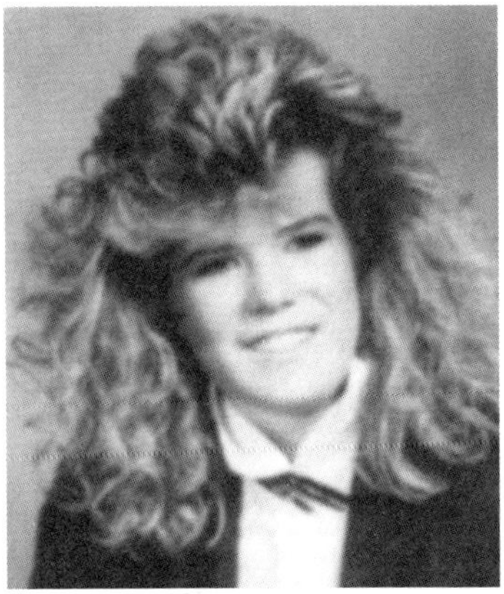

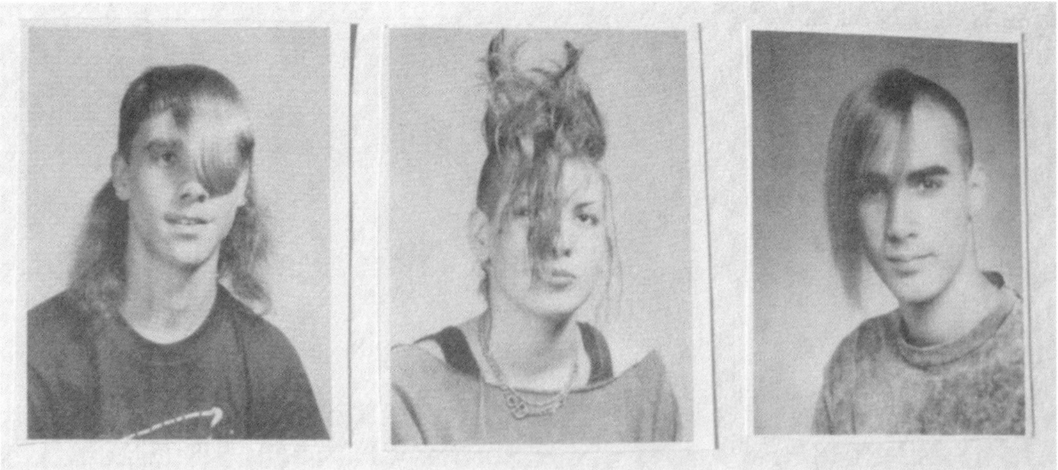

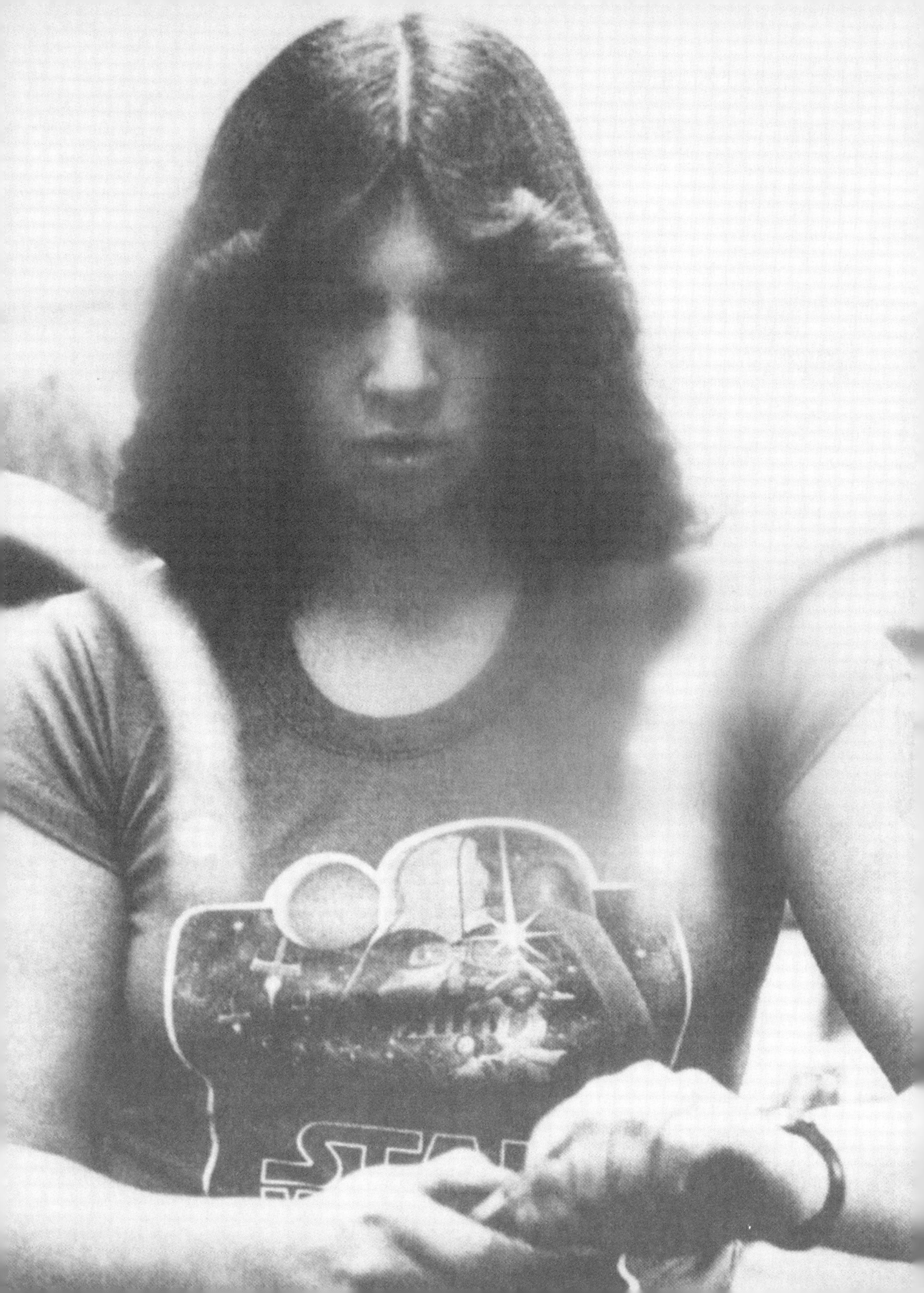

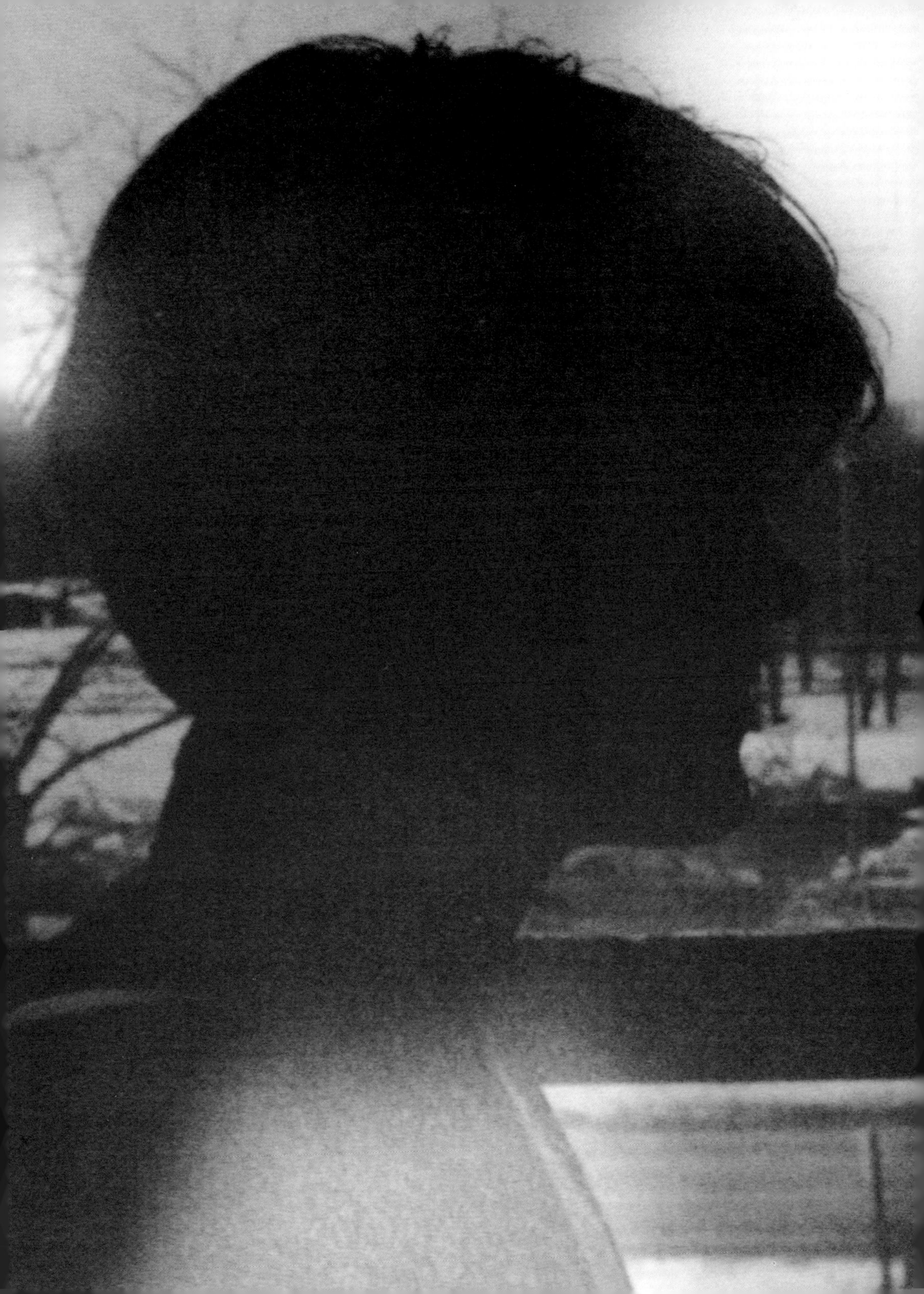

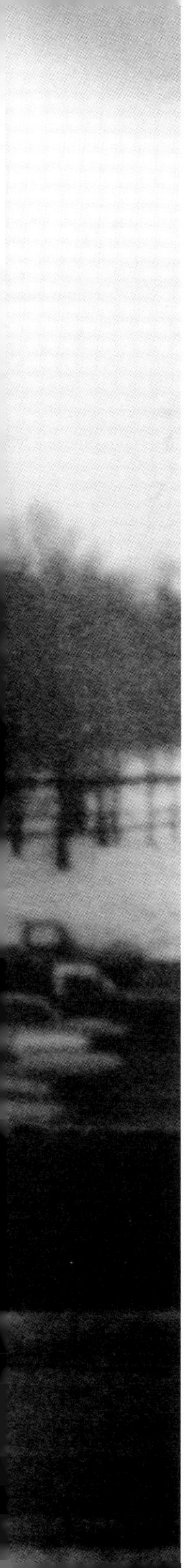
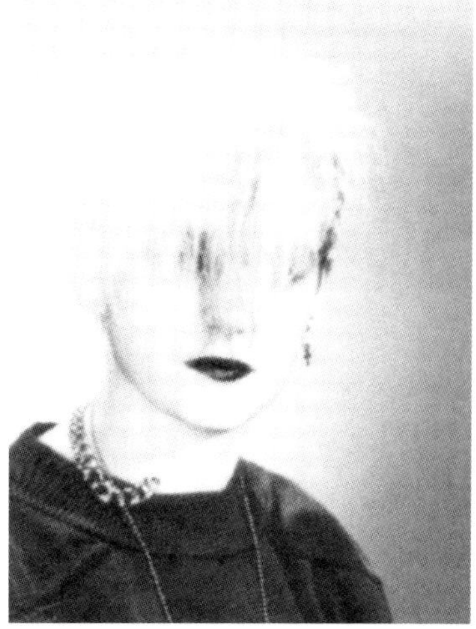

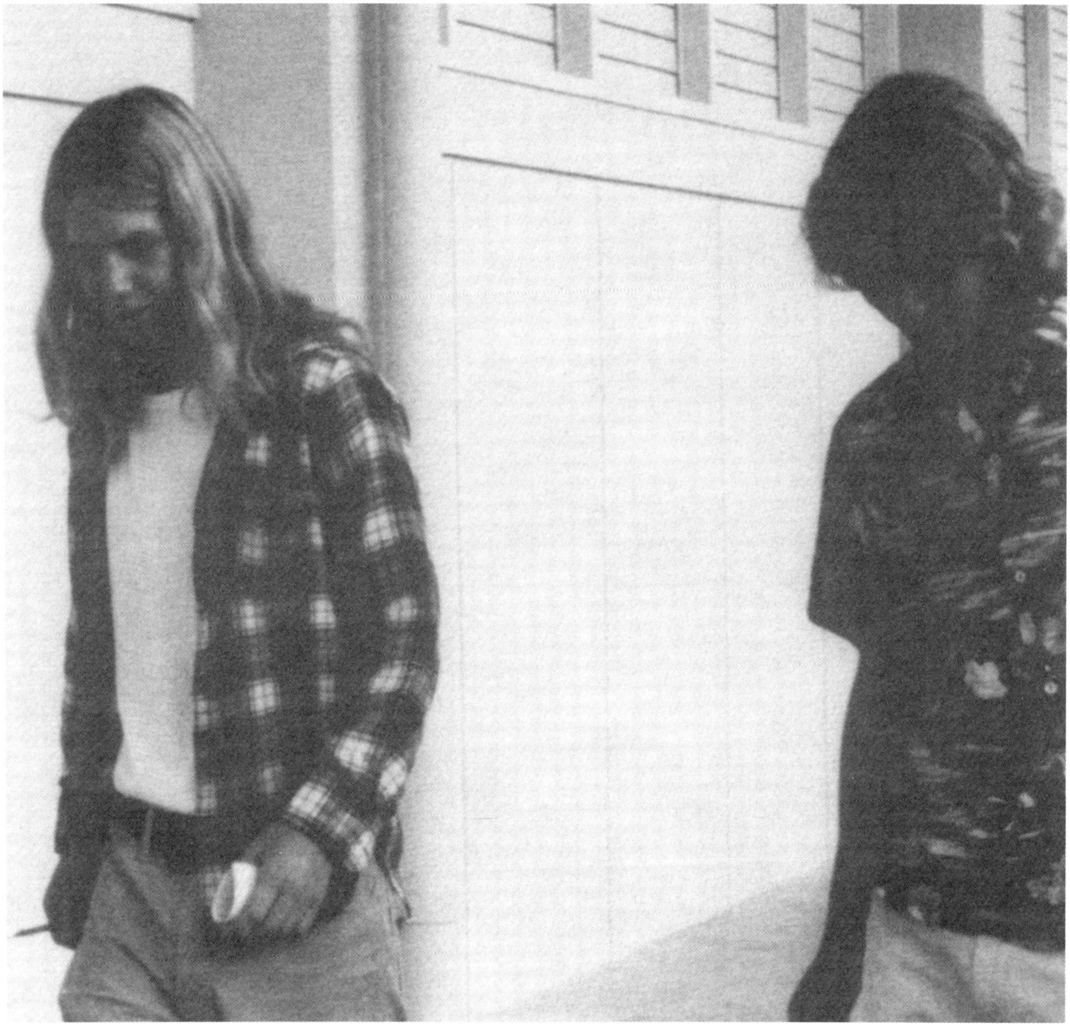

IF YOU LOVE SOMETHING, SET IT FREE.
IF IT DOESN'T, HAVE IT HUNTED DOWN AND SHOT.

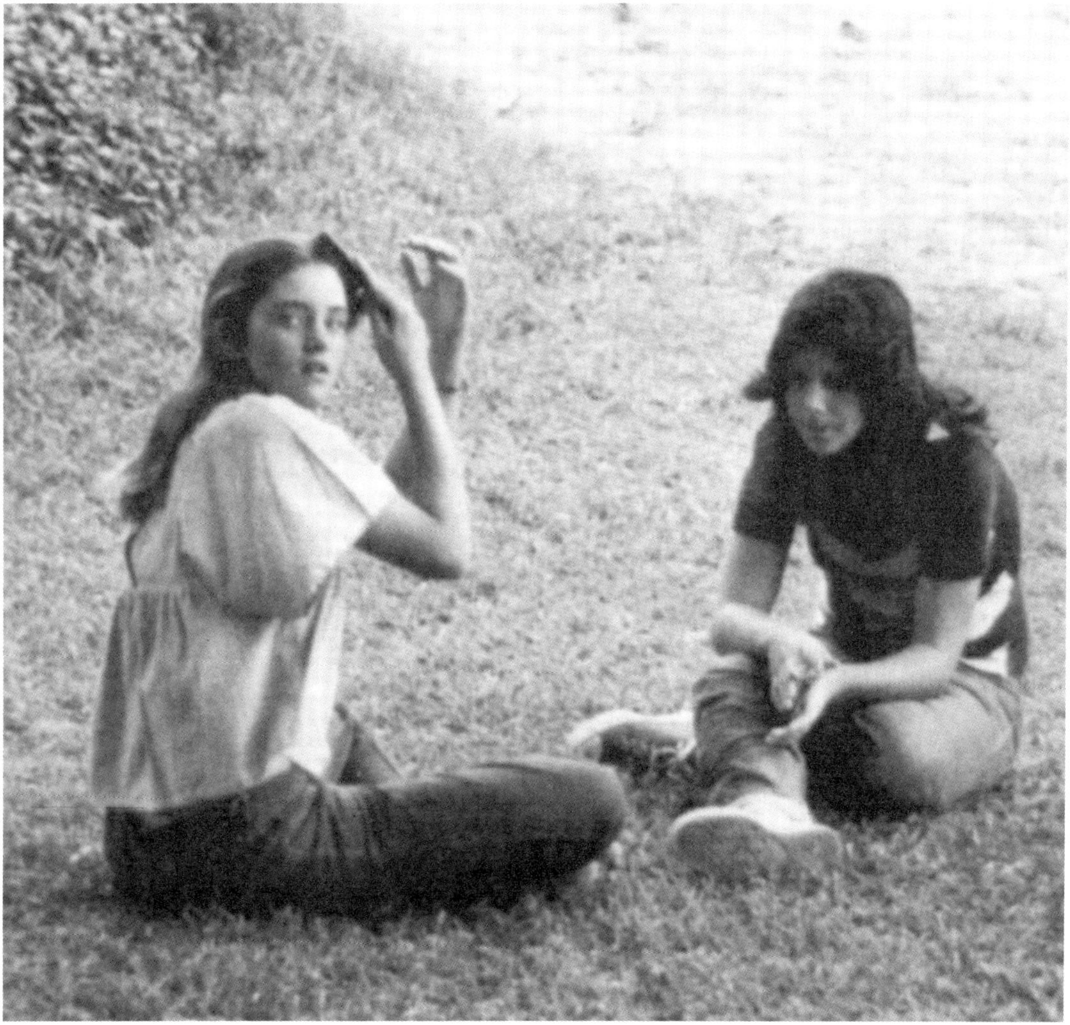

IF YOU LOVE SOMETHING, SET IT FREE.
IF IT COMES BACK TO YOU, IT IS YOURS.
IF IT DOESN'T, THEN IT NEVER WAS.

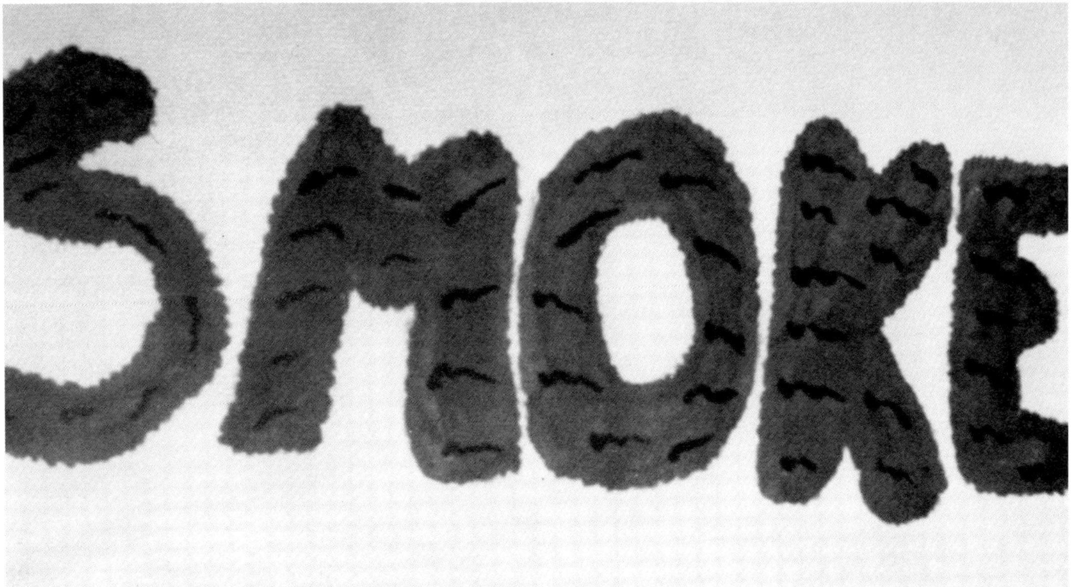
SMOKE

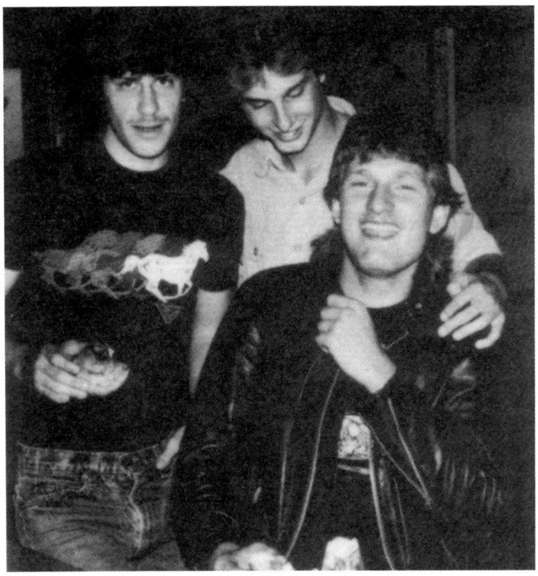

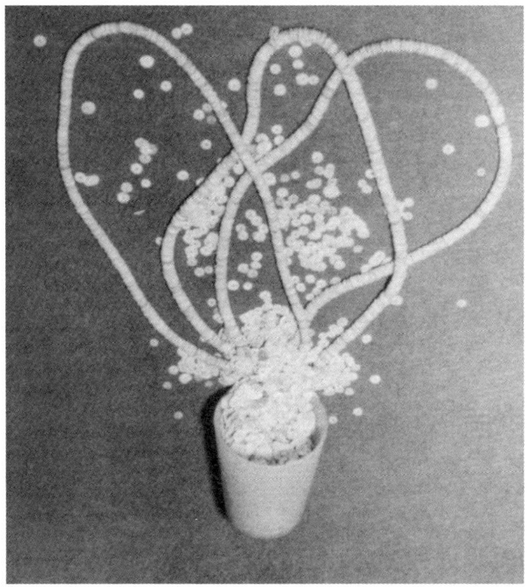

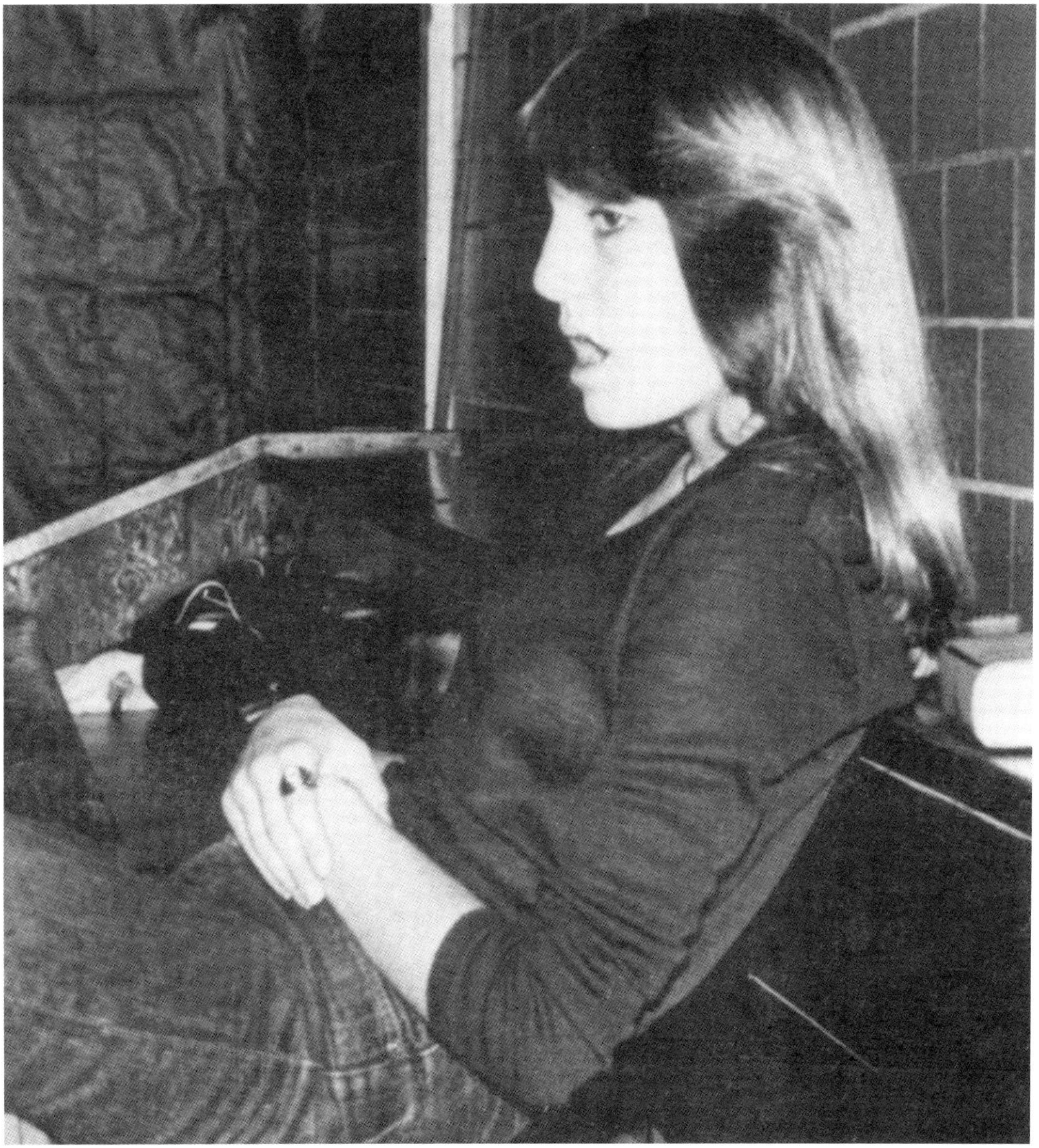

CAROL...

YOU BORN AGAIN QUEEN. AFTER ALL OF THOSE MIND/BODY CONFLICTS I'M SURPRISED WE'RE BOTH STILL EVEN SLIGHTLY SANE.

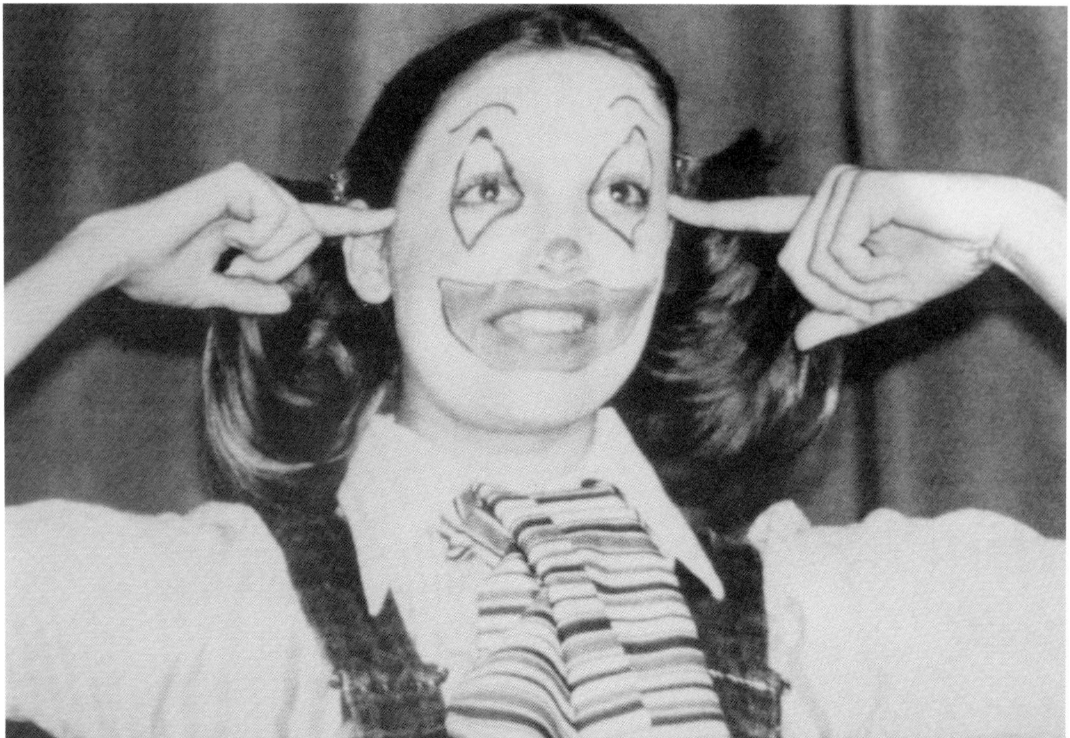

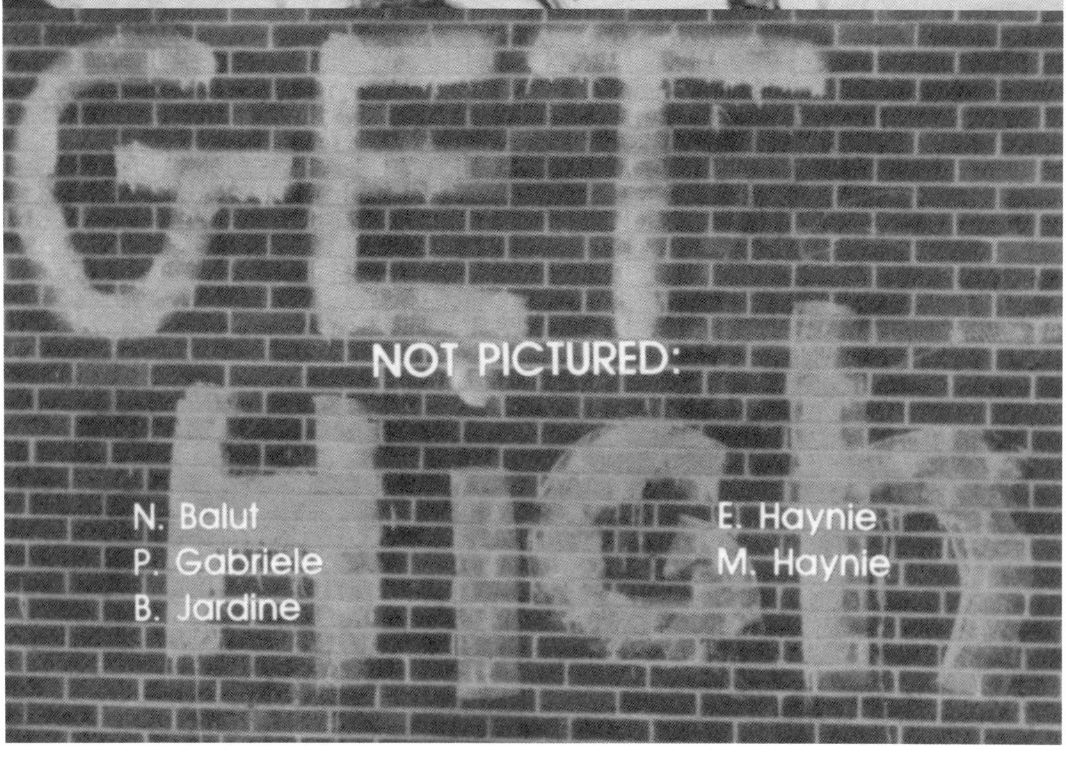

NOT PICTURED:

N. Balut
P. Gabriele
B. Jardine

E. Haynie
M. Haynie

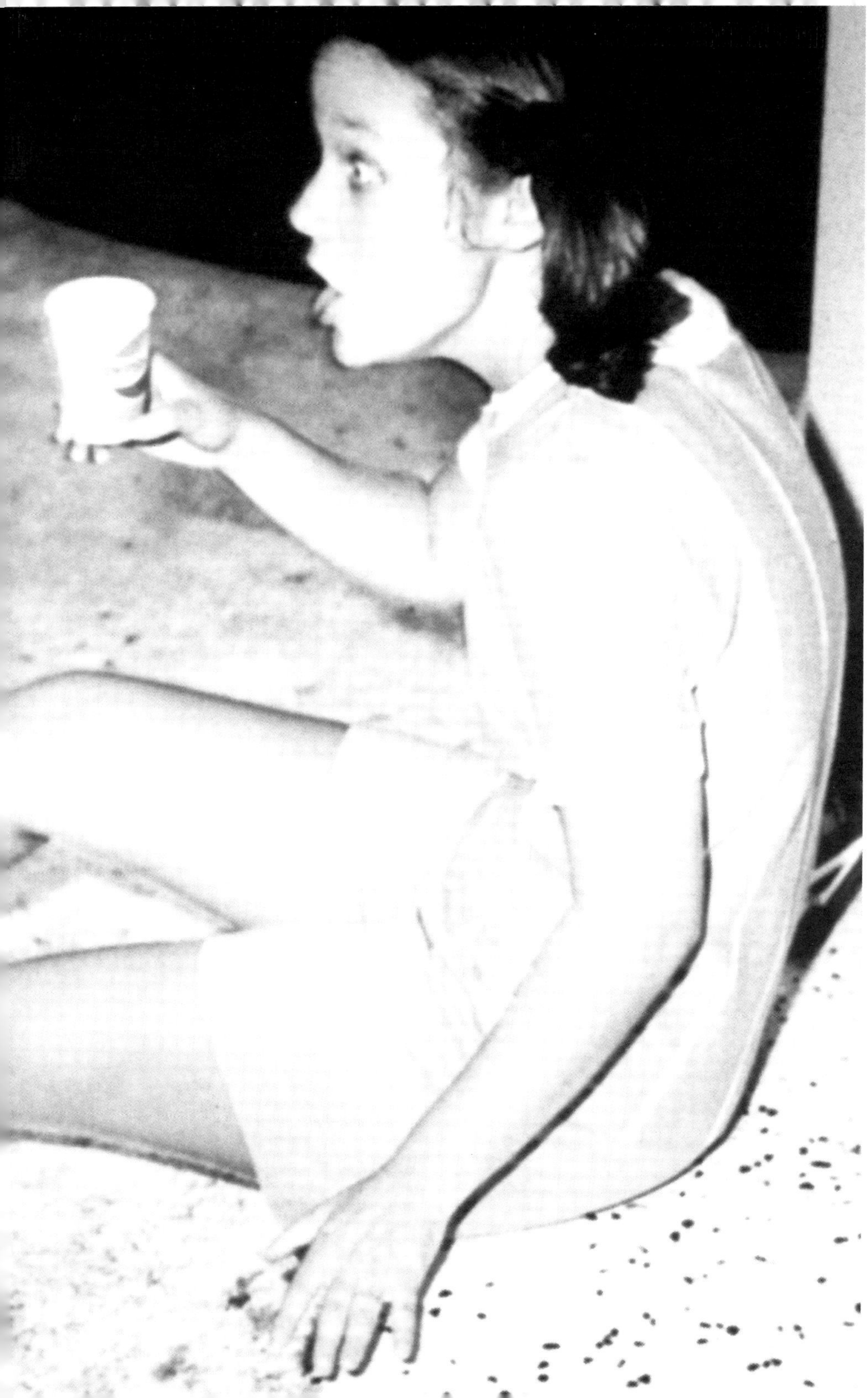

When I visit another high school, I always read the yearbooks stored in the administrative areas there. These yearbooks give me consolation and help me learn about the world I left behind. Yearbooks are actually the key to everything I'm supposed to be learning. Yearbooks offer clues, but never answers. They show the butterfly as a cocoon, but never the actual butterfly. High school students aren't real people. Not yet.

* * *

It must sound strange to hear that high school students aren't real people, but I mean it in the sense that when a person is young, you never see the finished person, only the work in progress. In high school you get to see what people yearn for, but you have to read the yearning between the lines. People in high school don't know who they are, let alone know what they want to be. They're larvae.

* * *

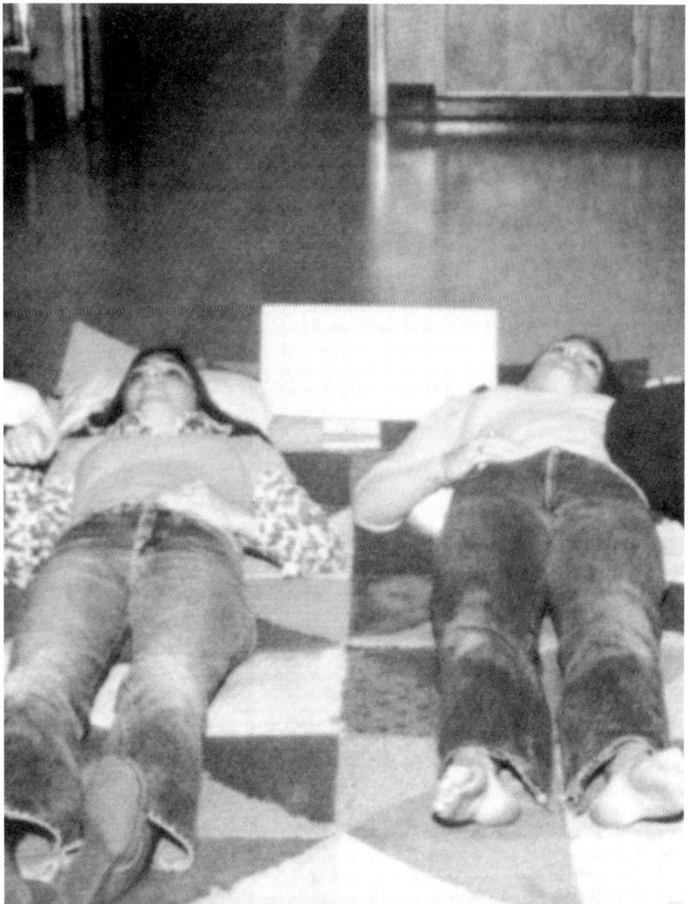

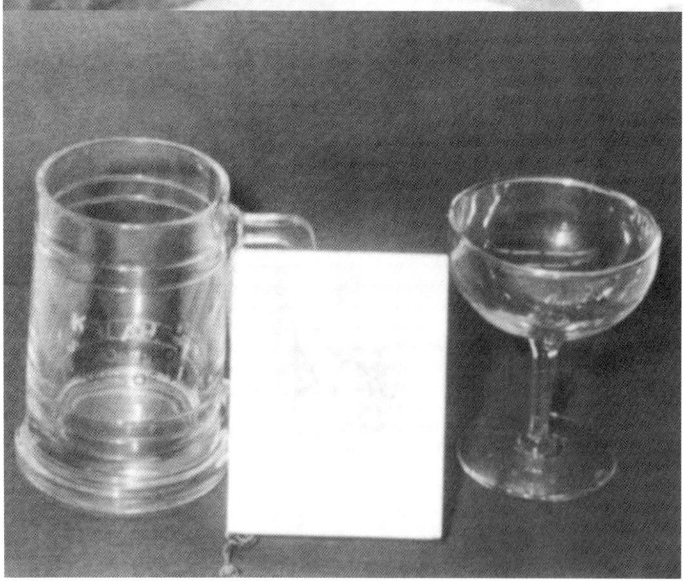

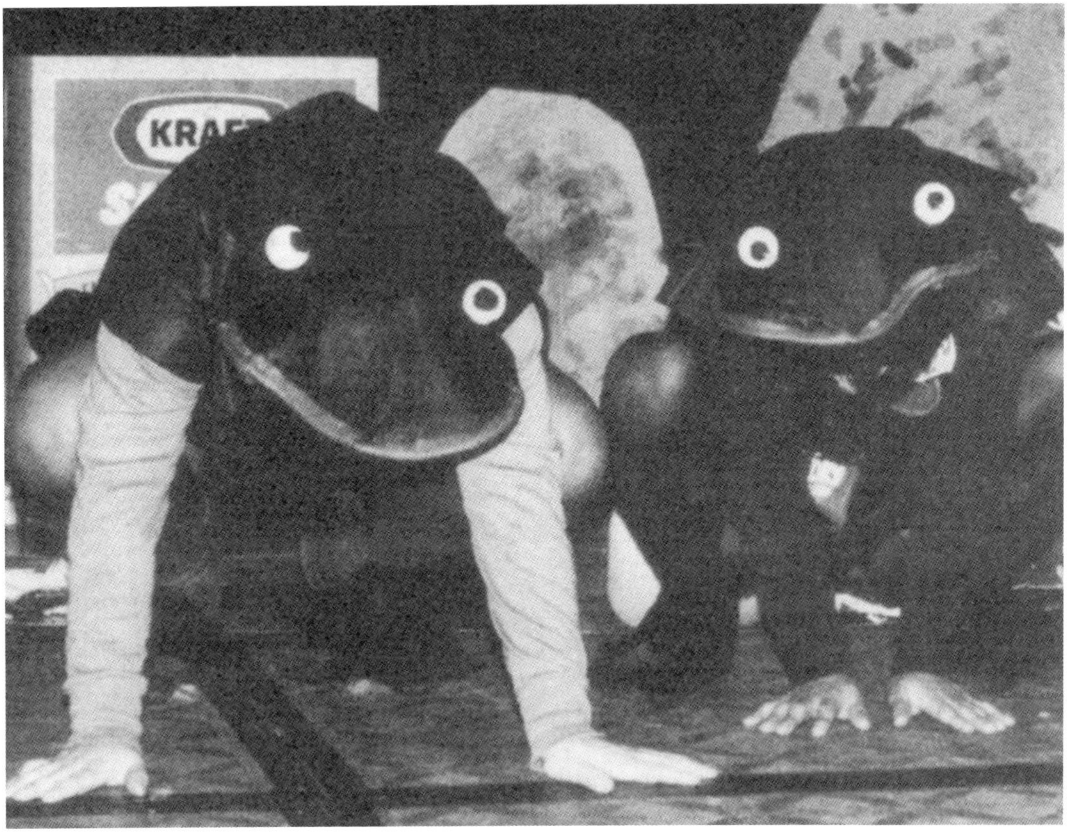

I, MICHAEL DAVIS, BEQUEATH NOTHING TO ANYBODY
BECAUSE I'M NOT GOING TO DIE.

MOON BEAM RAYS
MAGNETISM
DO I HAVE ANY MARKS
ON MY FACE?

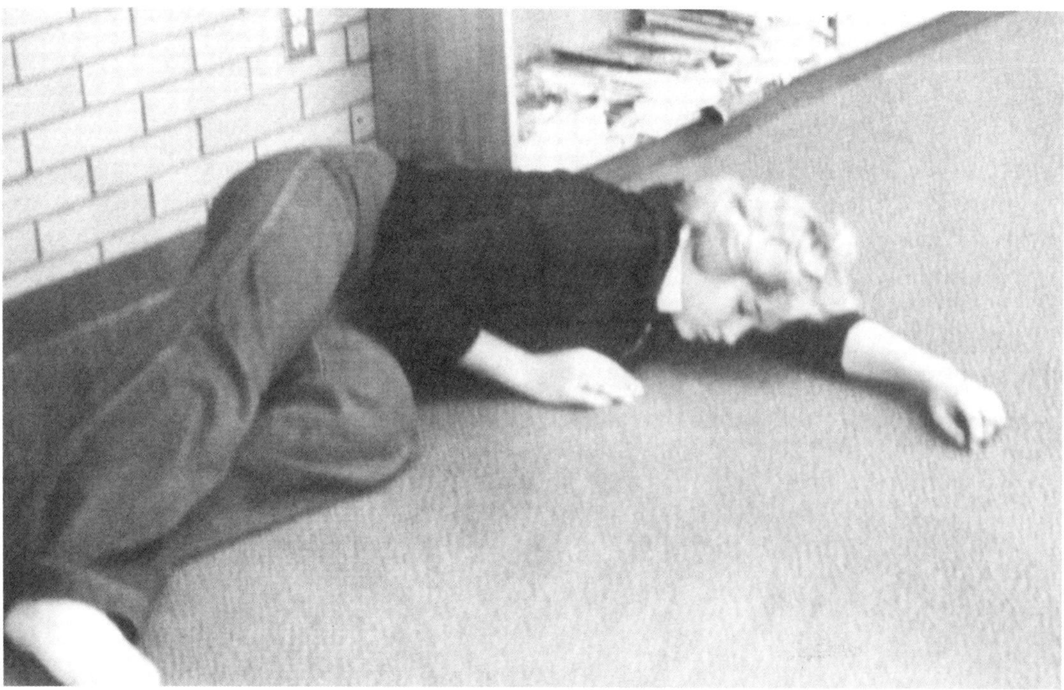

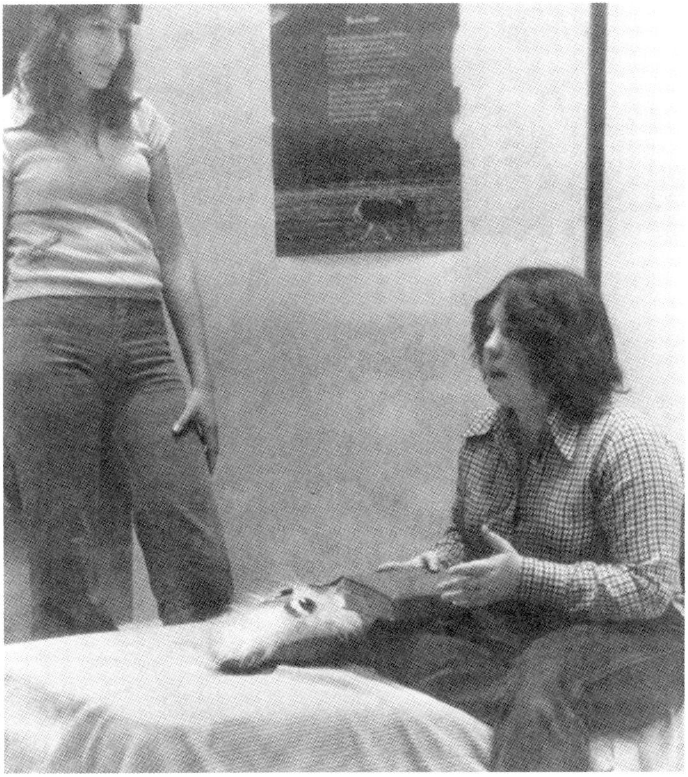

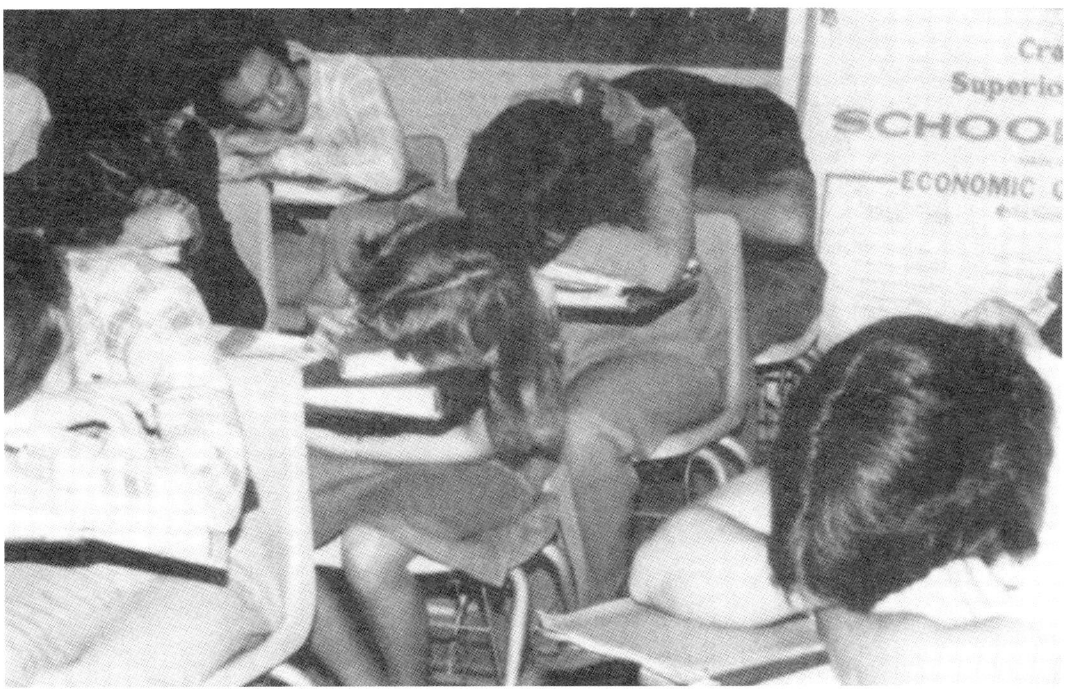
Cra
Superio
SCHOO
ECONOMIC

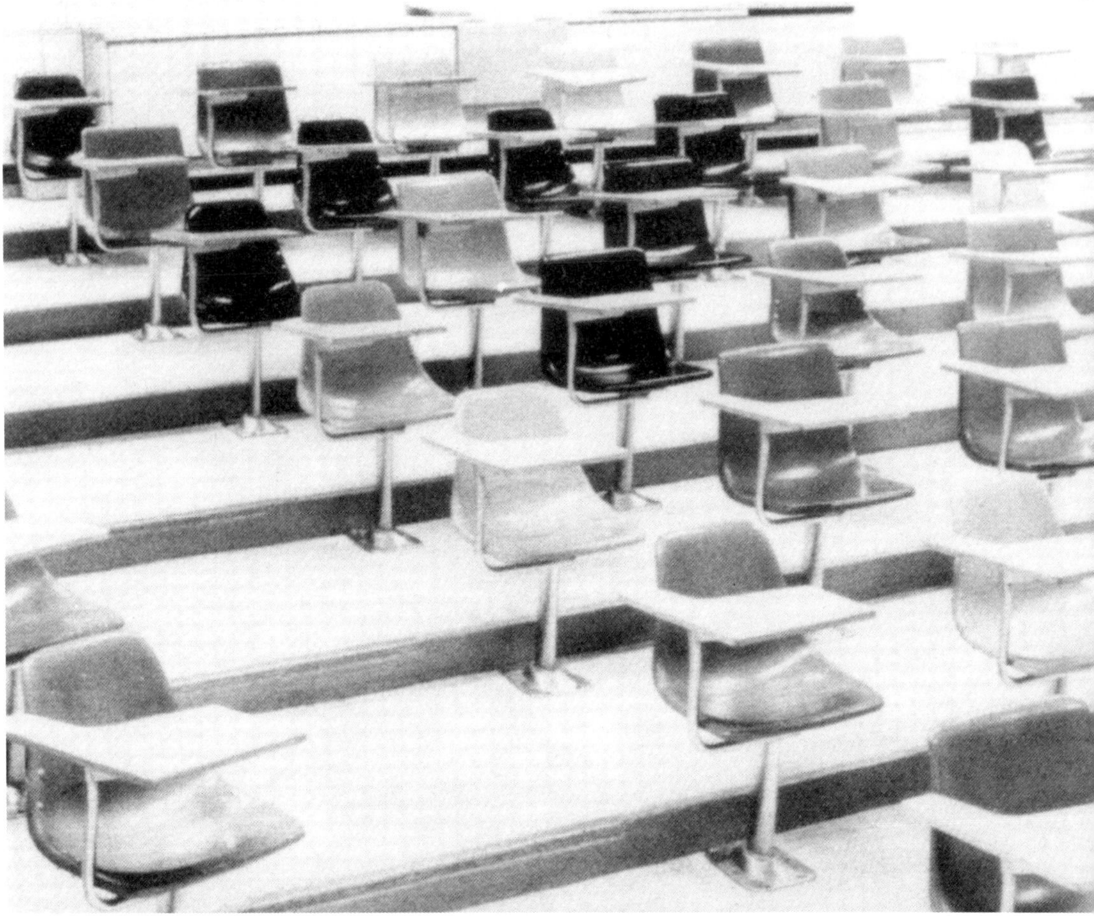

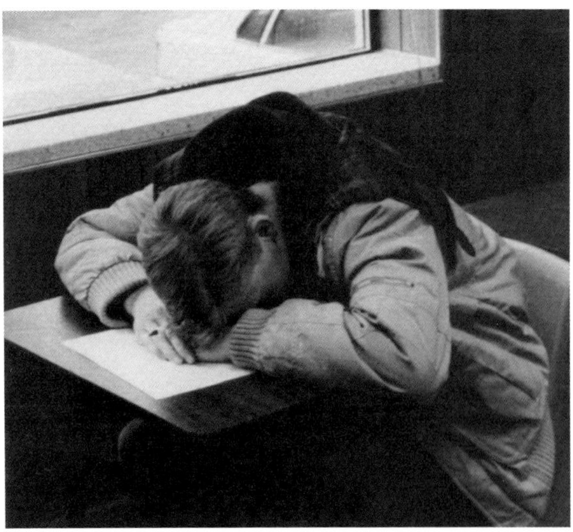

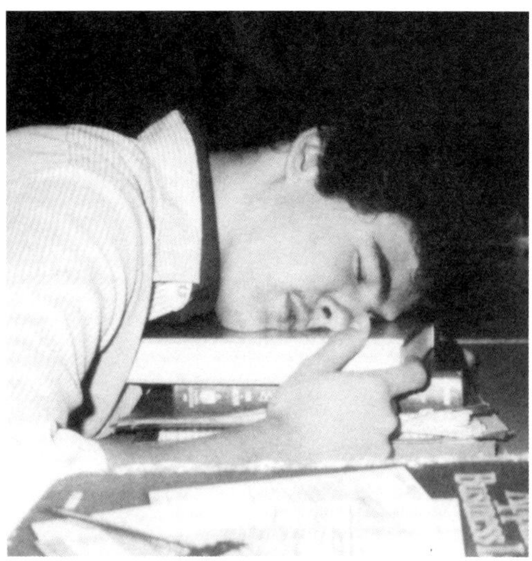

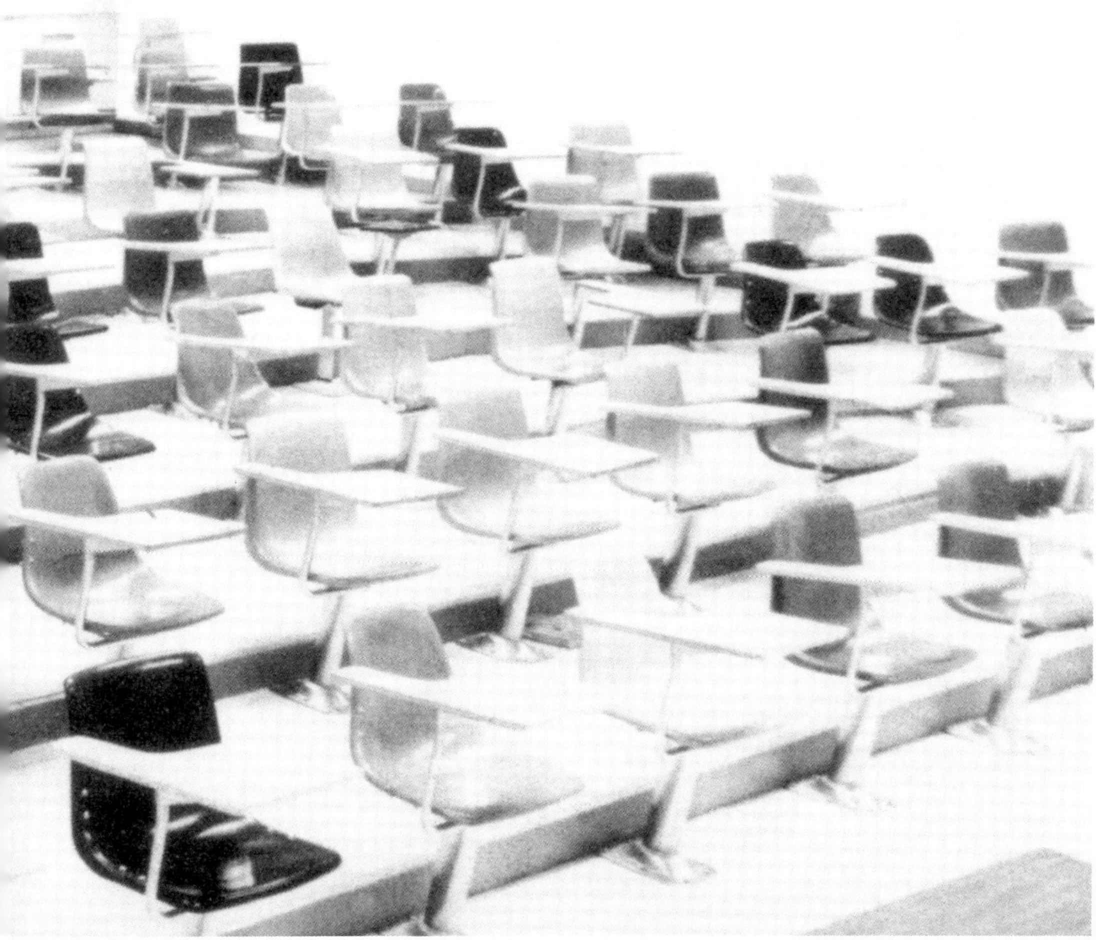

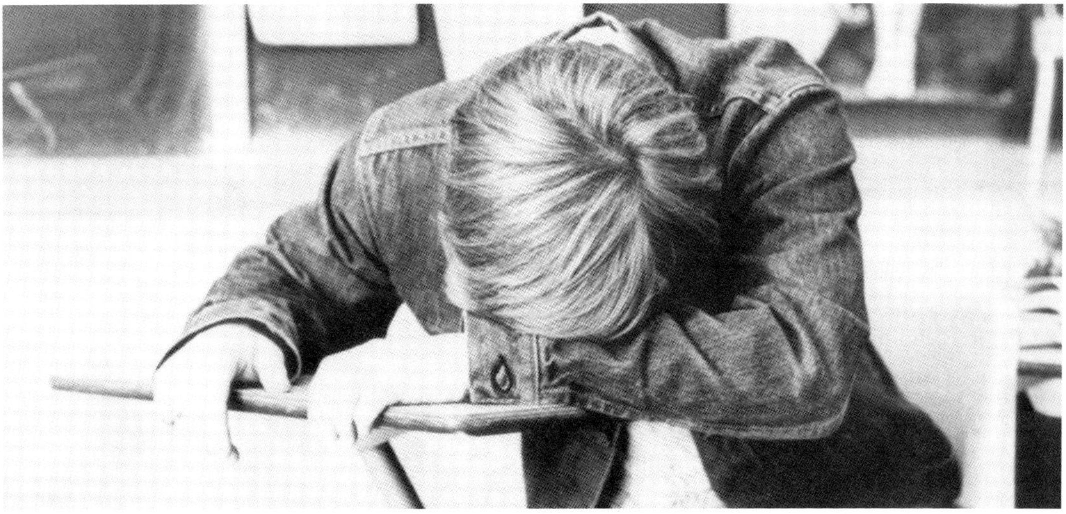

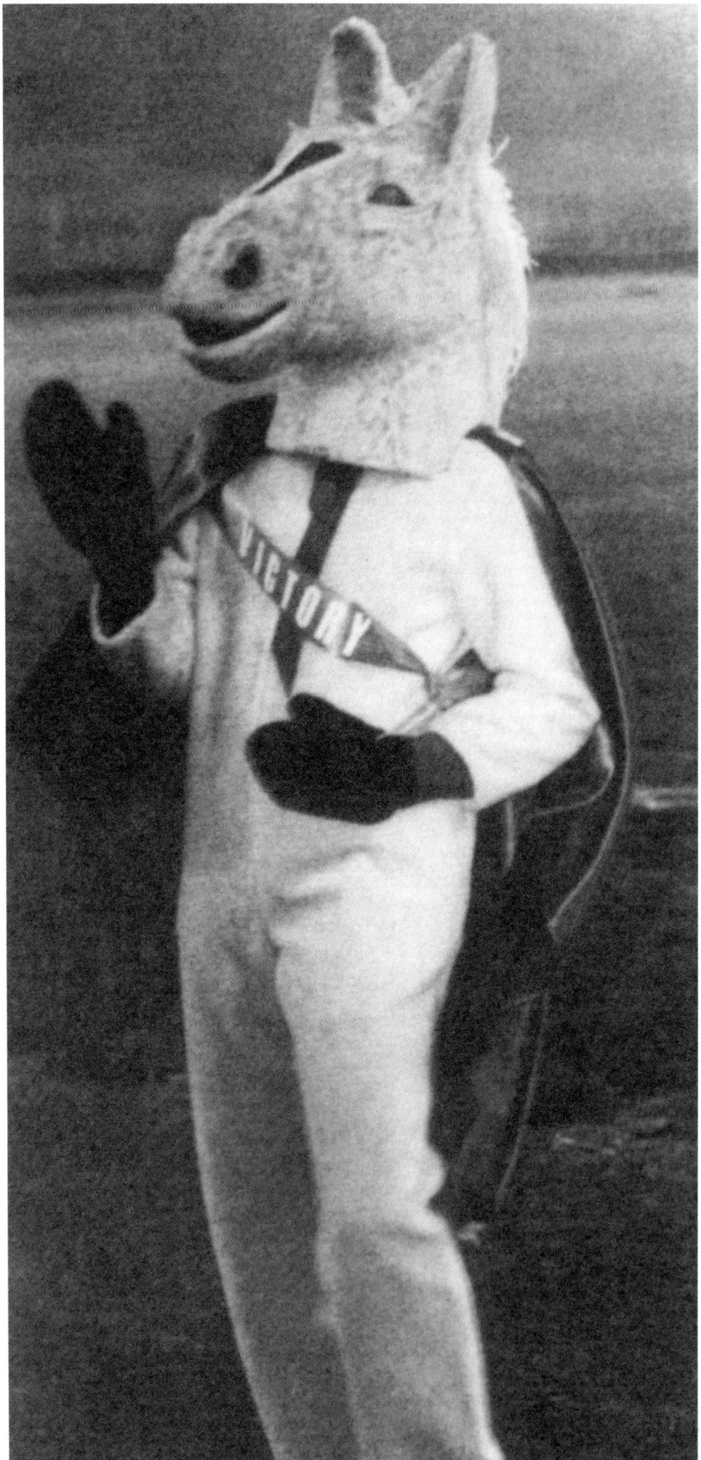
VICTORY

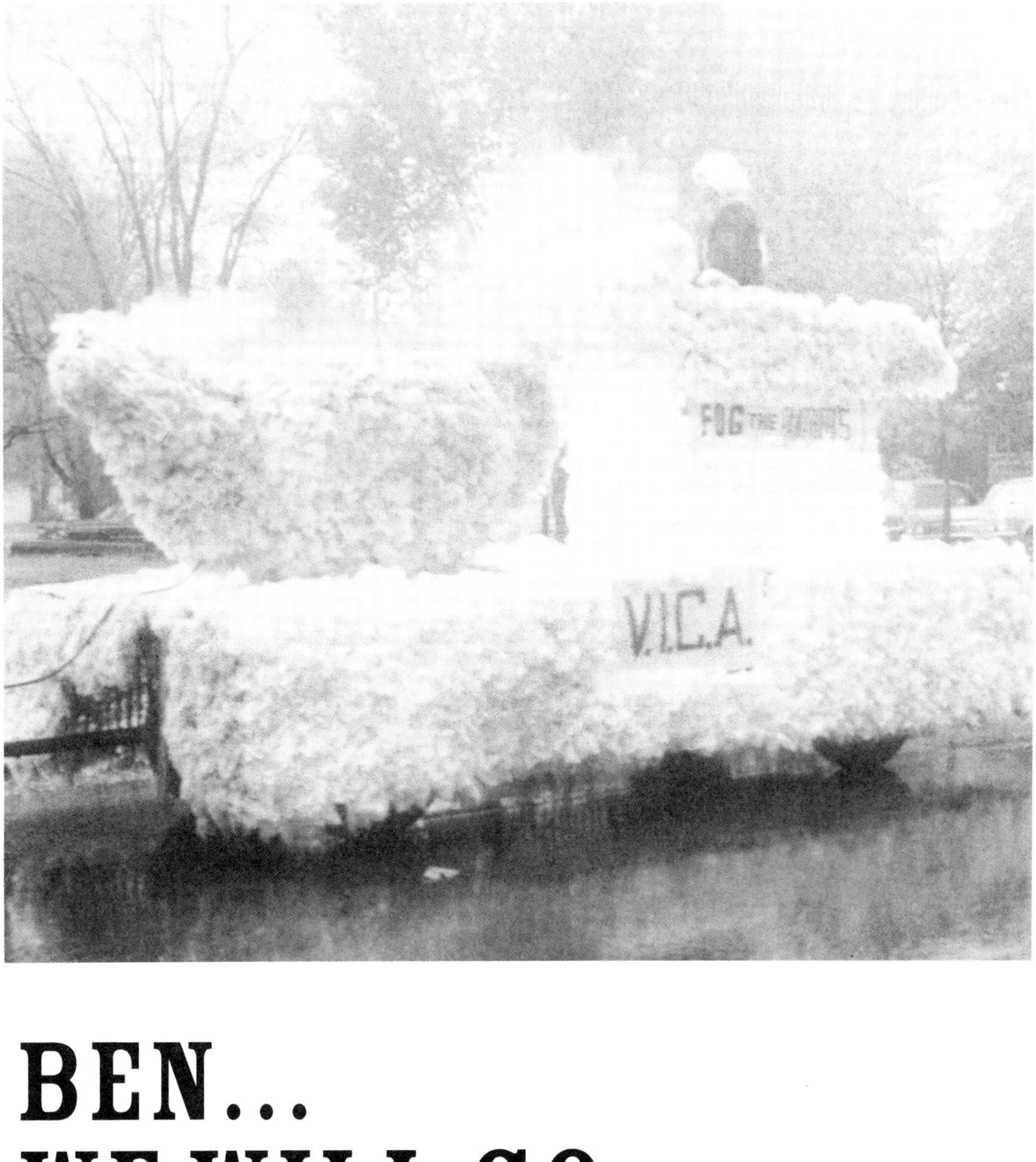

BEN...
WE WILL GO
SUPERNOVA.

WHAT DO YOU REALLY WANT TO DO IN LIFE?

HOW DO YOU THINK A FRIEND OR TEACHER WHO KNOWS YOU WELL MIGHT DESCRIBE YOU?

HOW DO YOU WORK UNDER PRESSURE?

WHAT HAVE YOU LEARNED FROM YOUR MISTAKES?

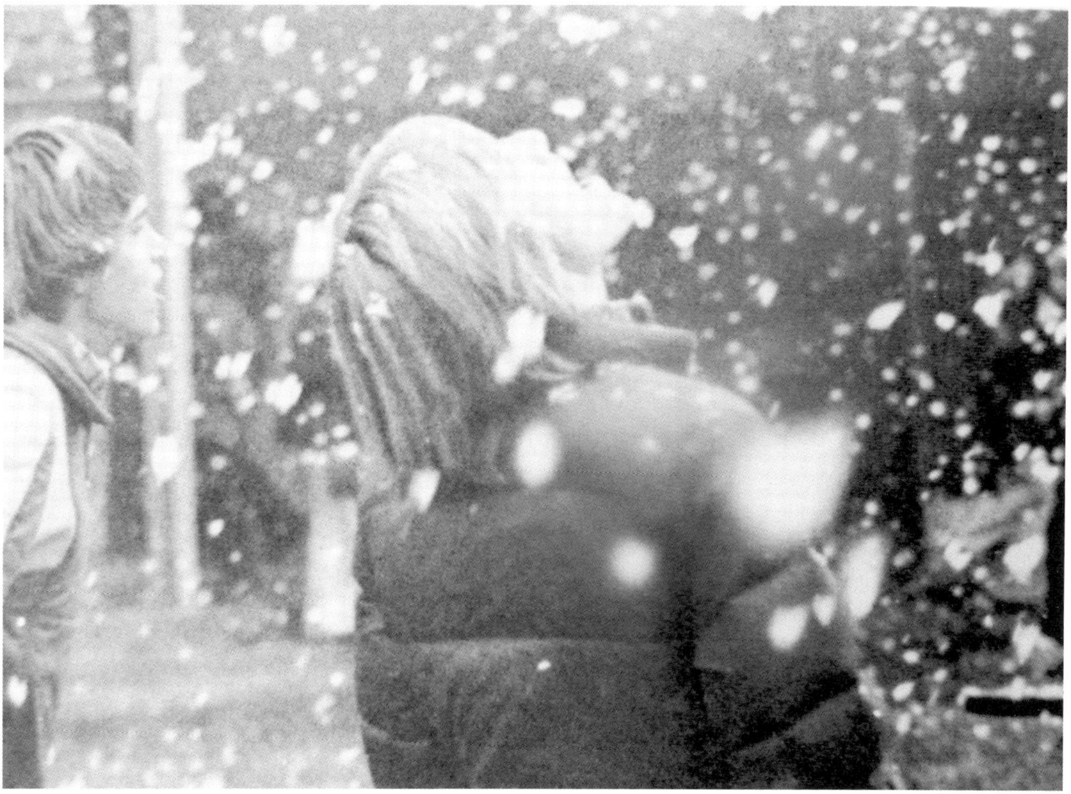

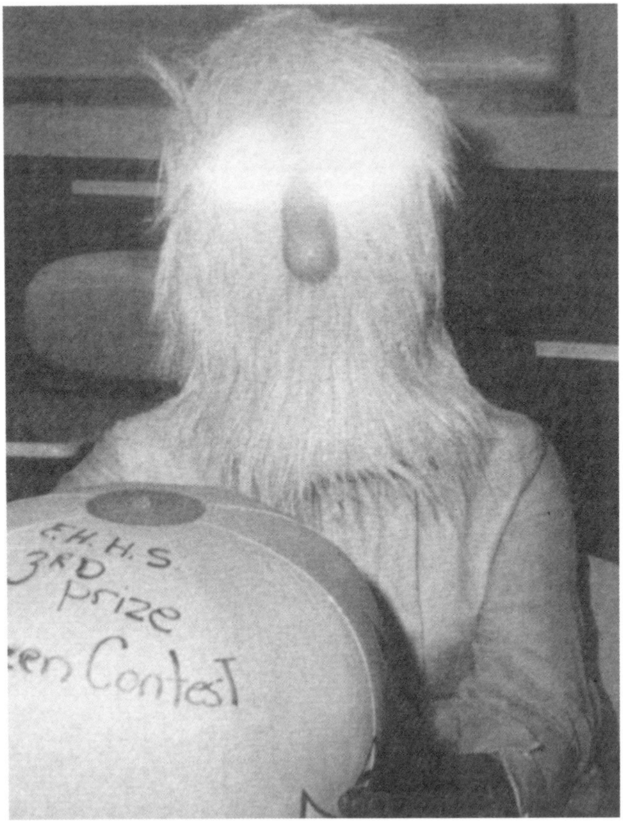
E.H. H.S
3RD
prize
Contest

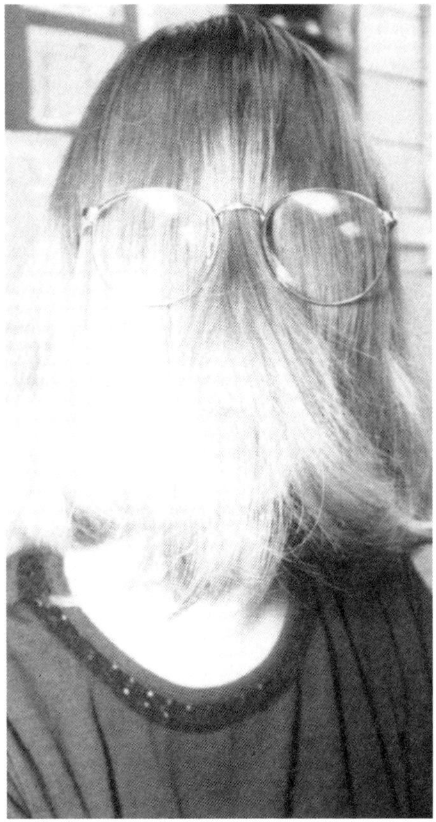

WHAT WILL
I REMEMBER ABOUT
YOU IN TWO WEEKS?

DO YOU HAVE A GIRLFRIEND/BOYFRIEND? IS IT SERIOUS?

WHAT KIND OF BOSS
DO YOU PREFER?
DO YOU LIKE
ROUTINE WORK?

DO YOU LIKE REGULAR HOURS?
WHAT IS YOUR MAJOR WEAKNESS?
CAN YOU TAKE INTSTRUCTIONS WITHOUT FEELING UPSET?
CAN YOU TAKE CRITICISM WITHOUT FEELING UPSET?

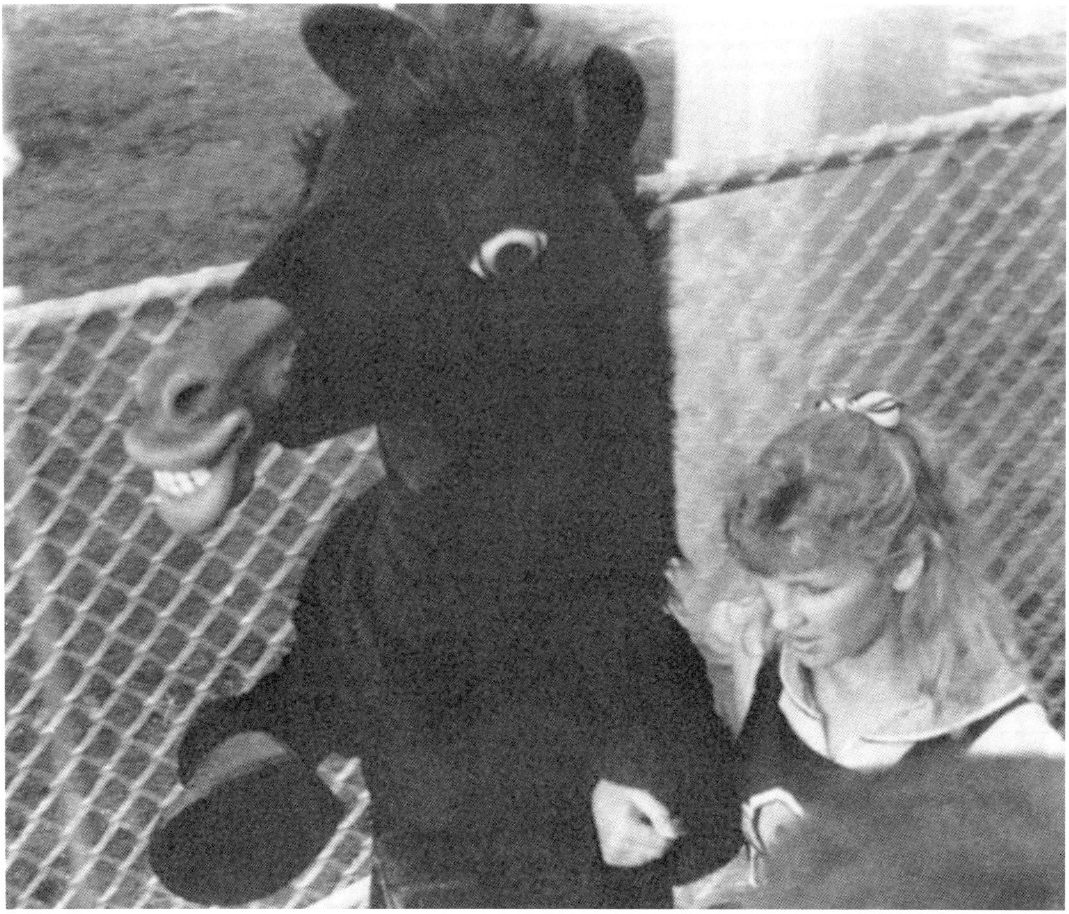

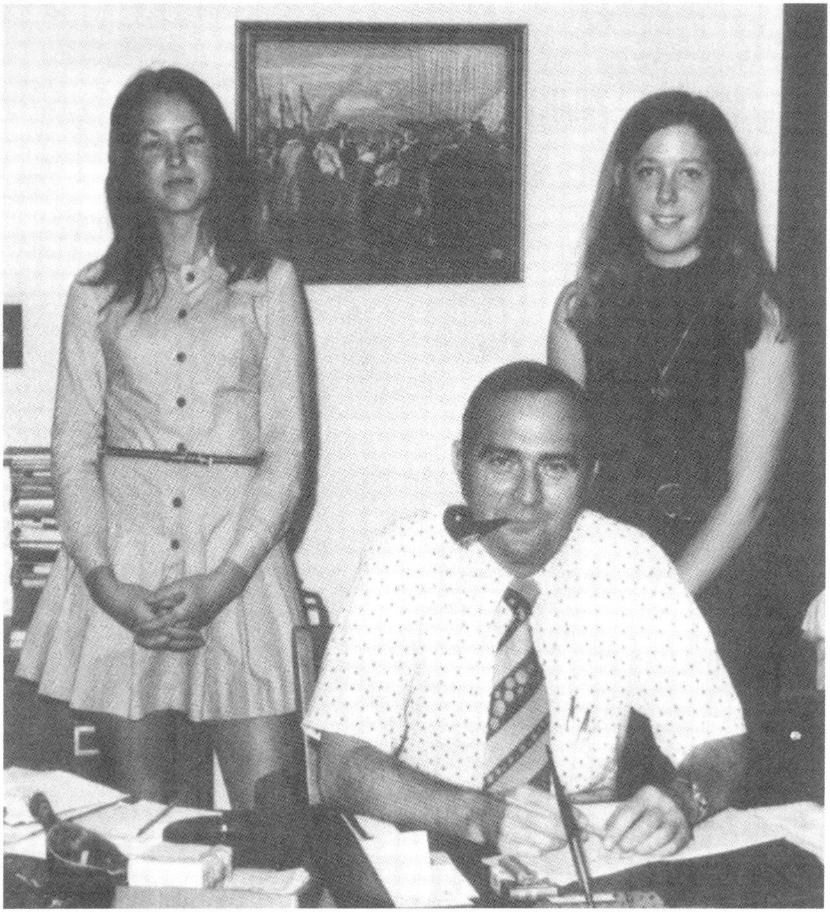

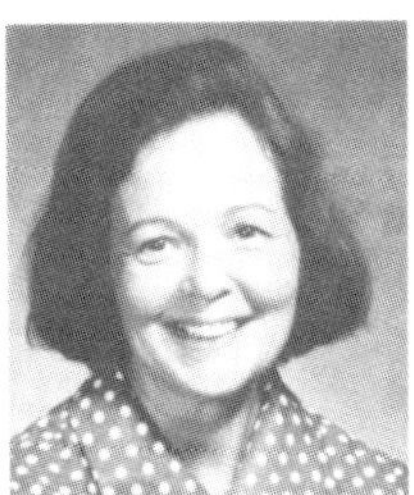

Jean Gehry

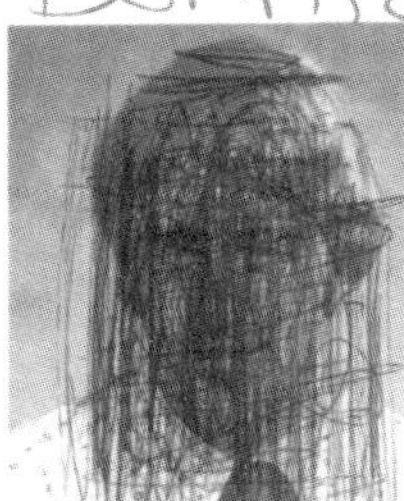

Richard Chocktaw

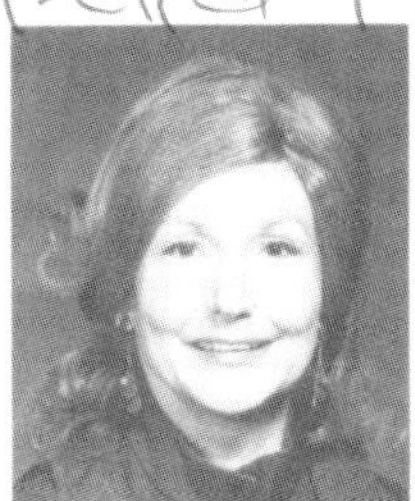

Carol Hunt

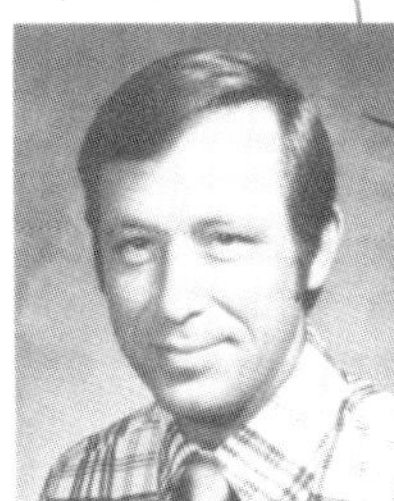

Harold Weiss

THOU SHALT BE INITIATED

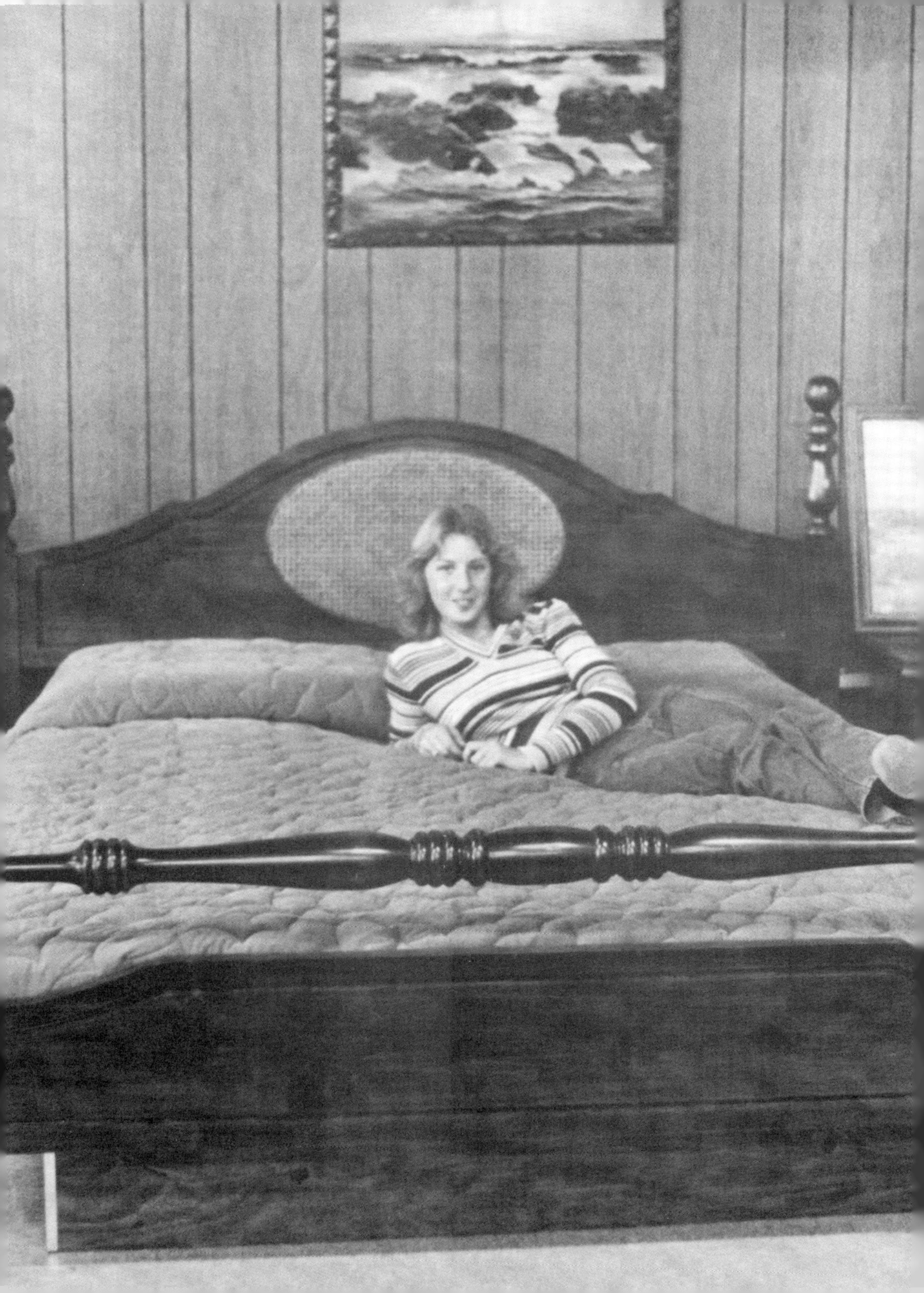

TAMMI,

WITHOUT U, THIS PAST YEAR WOULD HAVE BURNT ME TO A CRISP.

I KNOW THIS ISN'T THE END

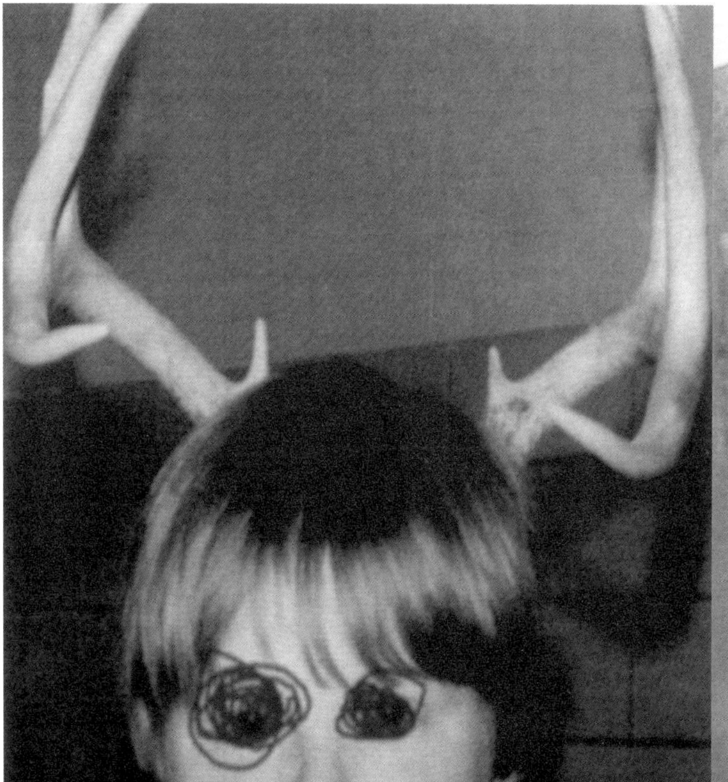

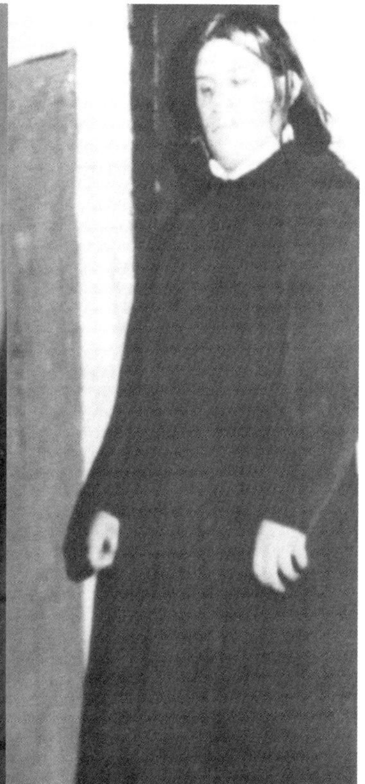

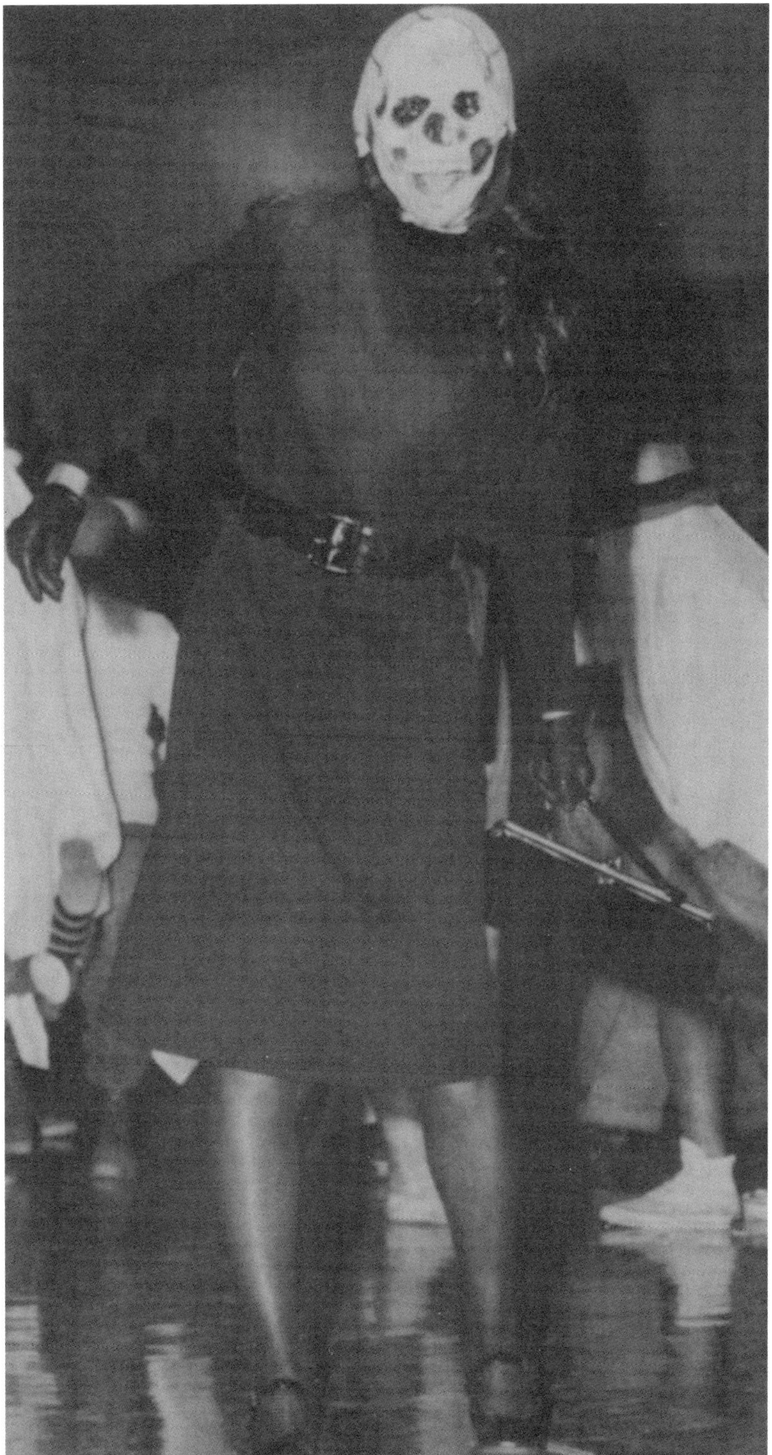

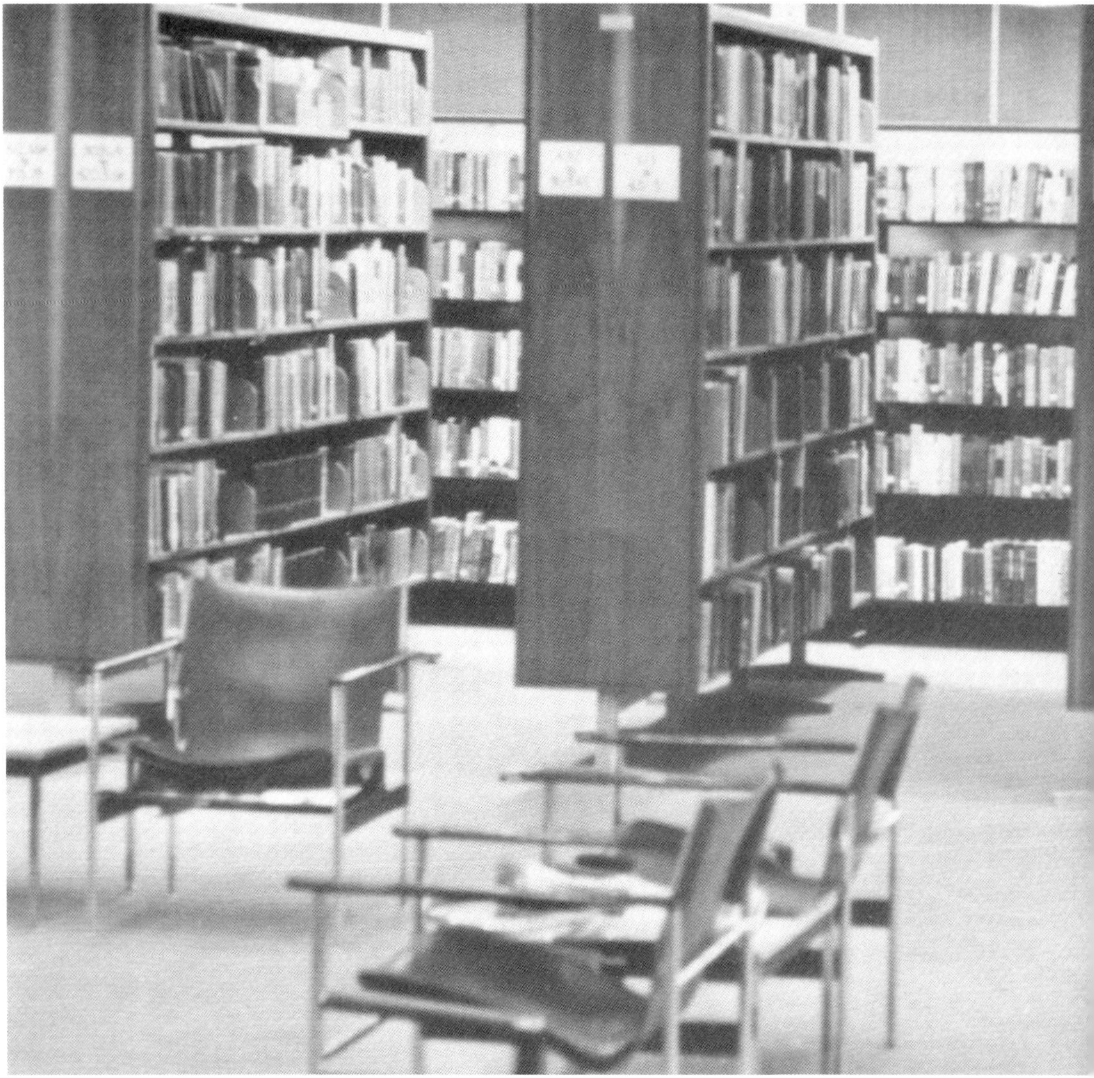

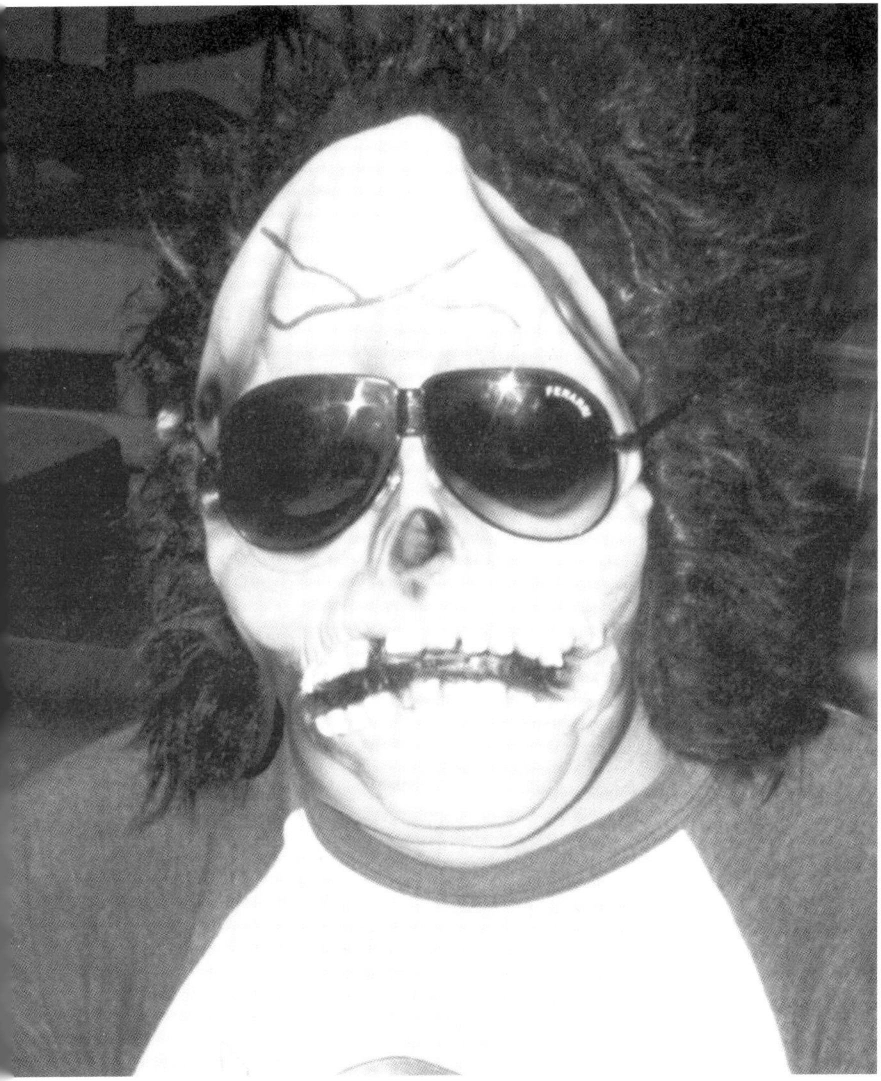

One of the biggest surprises to me in the past years has been the amount of sexual energy that fills high schools. I just realized recently that just about everyone my age was fucking like wild horses almost every week. How did I miss the signs? All of those clean faces and cereal box smiles, yet nearly all of them drenched in the scent of each other's insides and outsides – lunch hours and Friday nights and all of those car rides with no real destination. All of those bits of bodies growing and shrinking and struggling, expanding outward—in many cases not even being particular as to where they wanted to go.

* * *

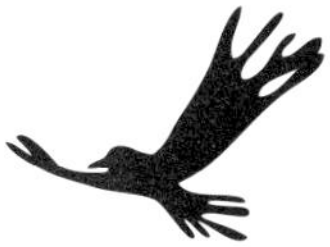

I always make a point of looking at art work in the schools I visit, both in the rooms and in the yearbooks, bad work, badly photographed in yearbooks, and also badly printed – a set of factors which actually loan the work honesty: murky souls generating murky images. Who am I? Why am I feeling these things that have no words or even images?

* * *

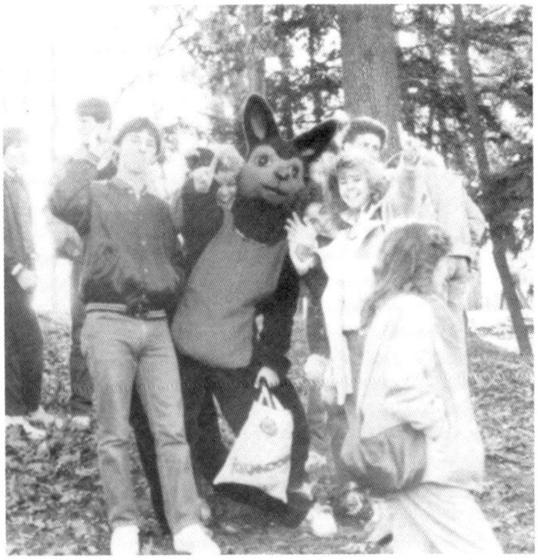

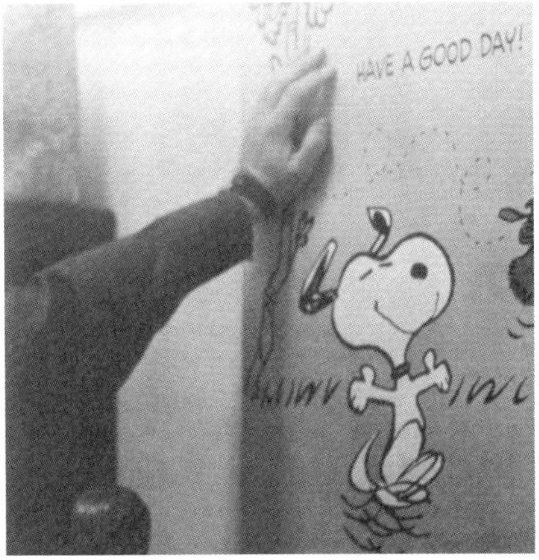
HAVE A GOOD DAY!

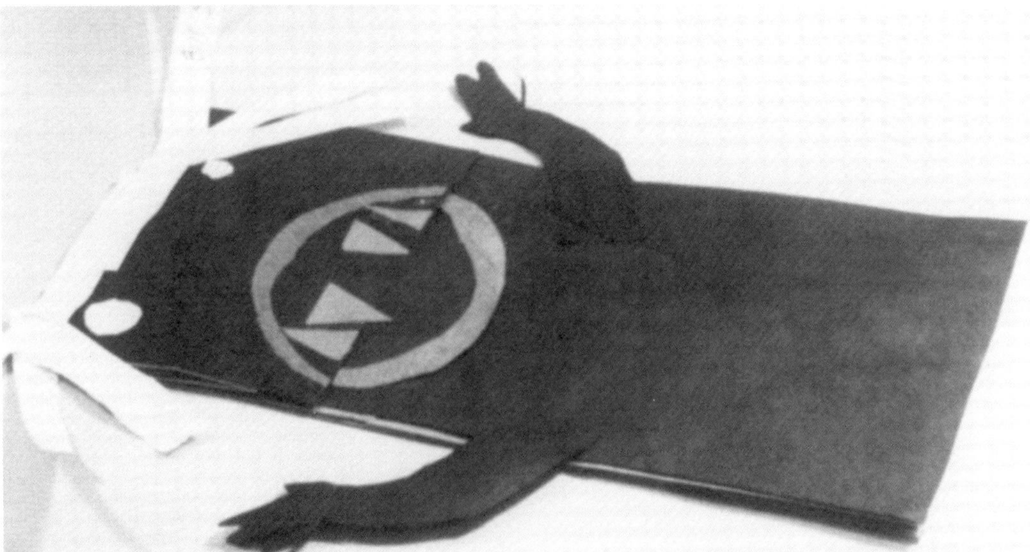

HEY MAN,
WHERE THE HELL WERE YOU ALL YEAR?
WE SHOULD HAVE BEEN DOING THINGS.
HAVE A GOOD SUMMER.
SCOTT

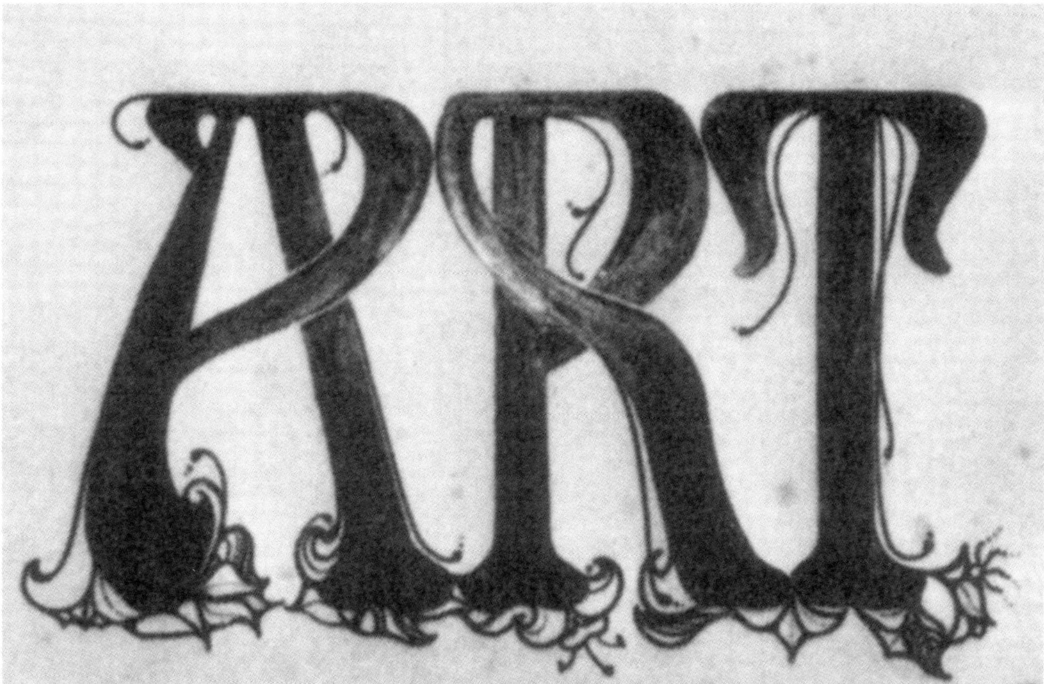

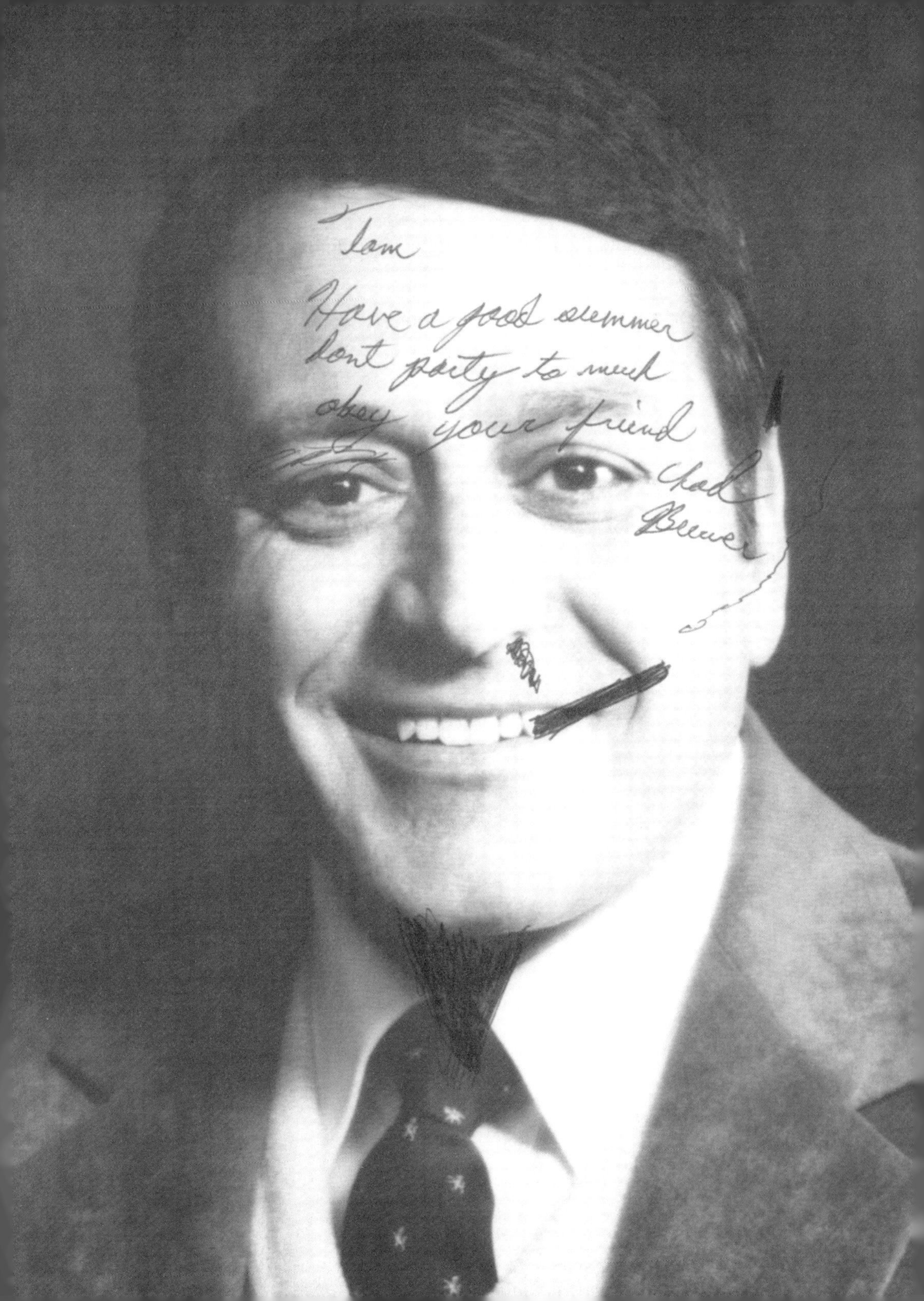
Tom
Have a good summer
dont party to much
obey your friend

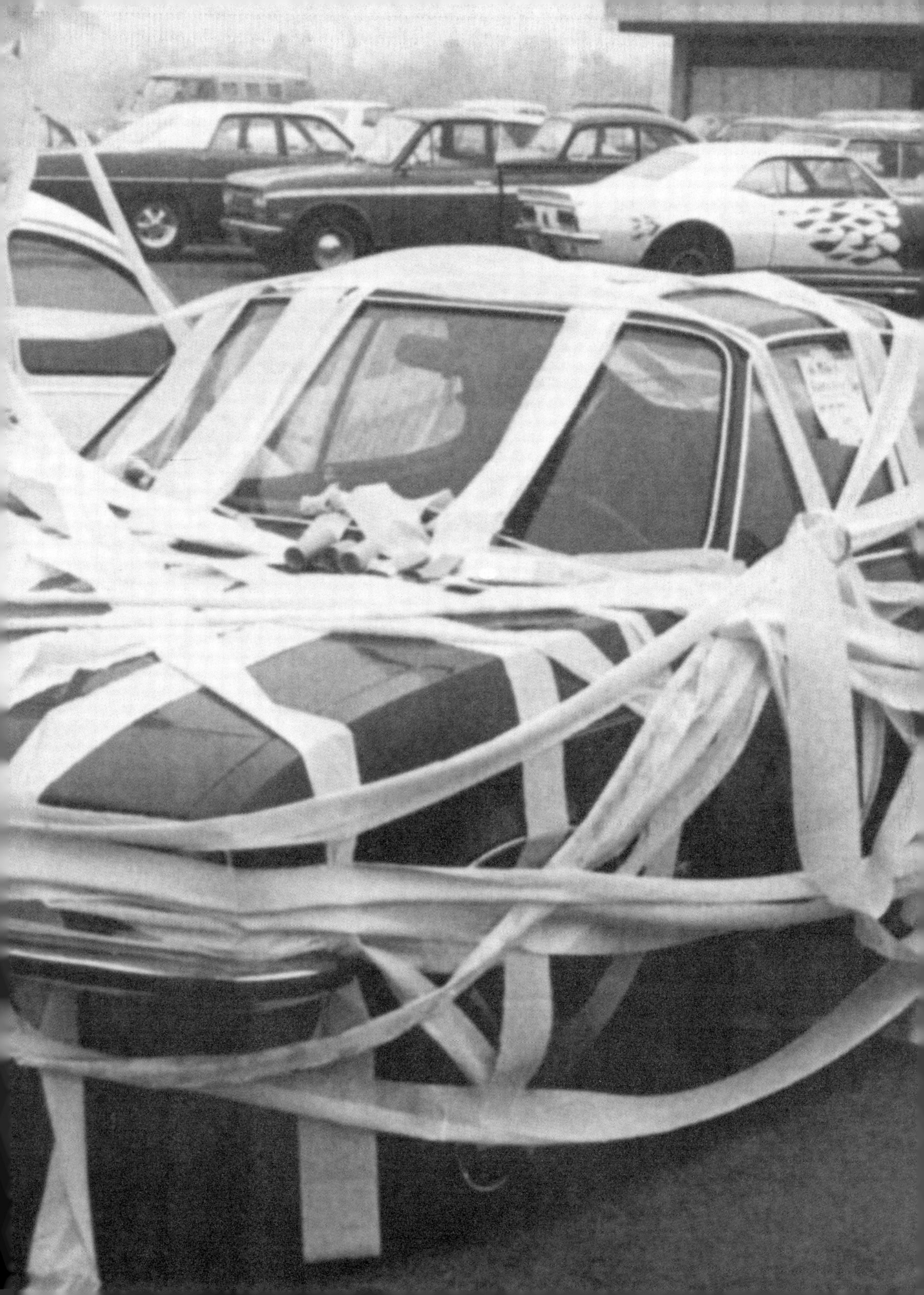

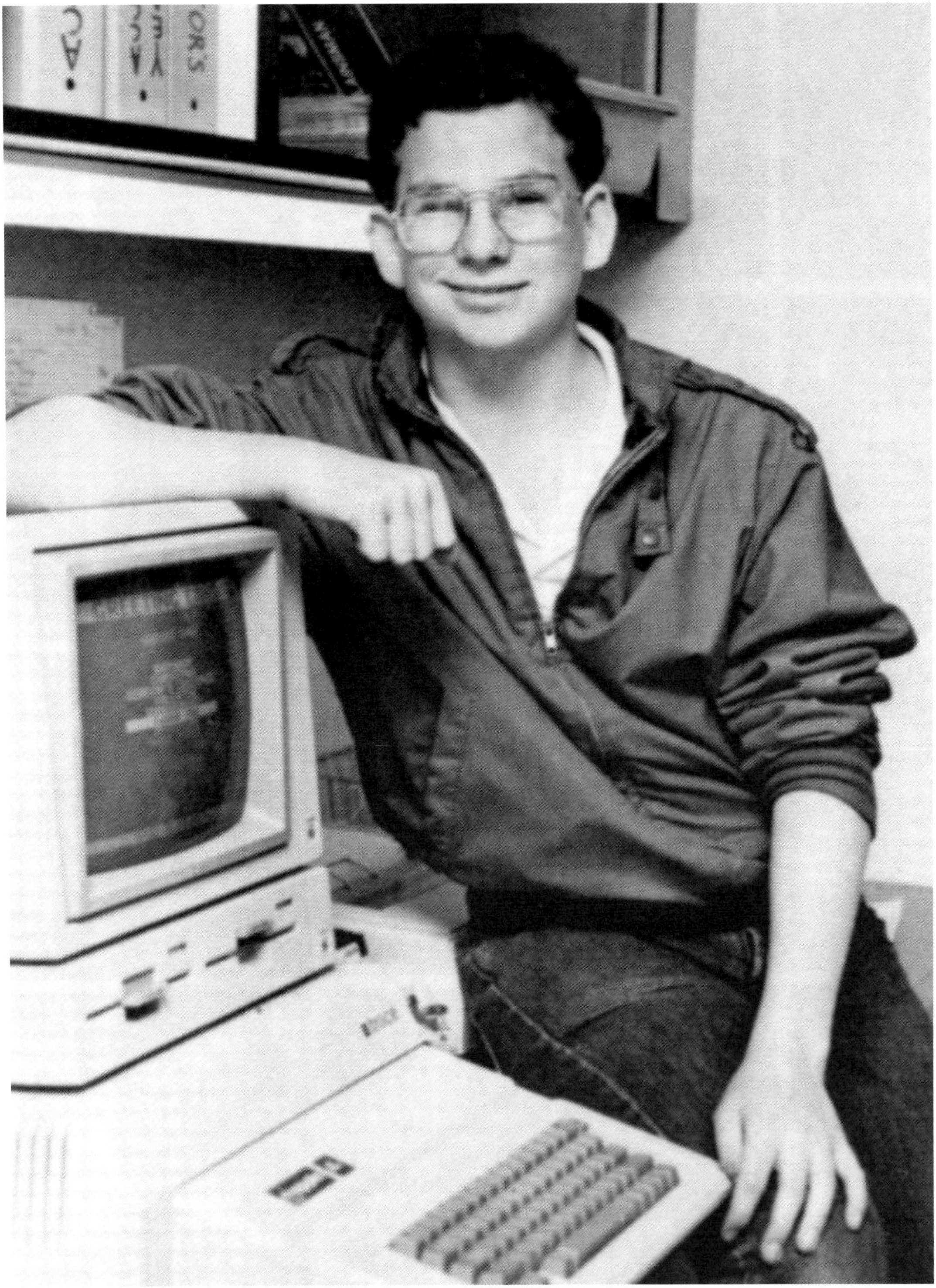

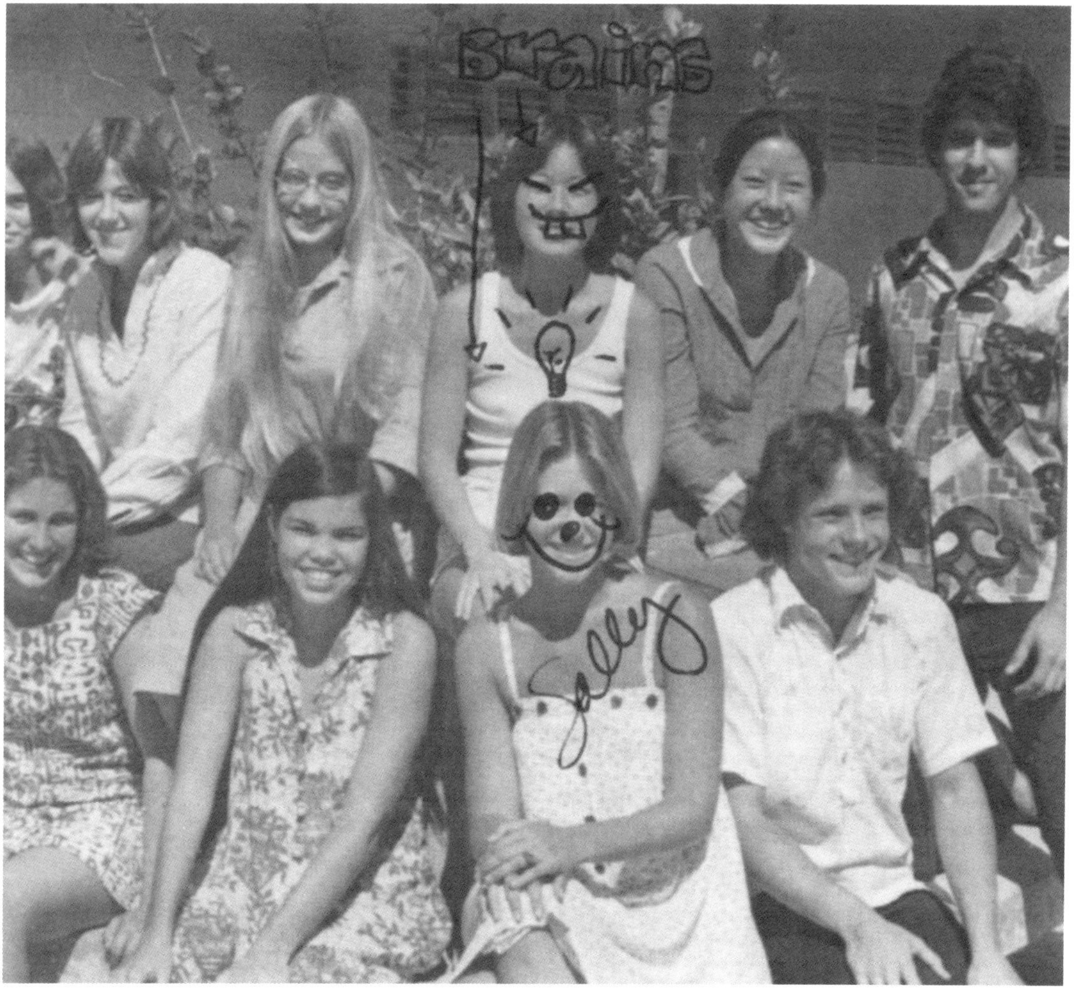

TIFFANY,

**I MISS NOT BEING YOUR PAL
THE WAY IT USED TO BE.
I ALWAYS LOOK UP AT THE STARS
AND REMEMBER THE OLD DAYS.**

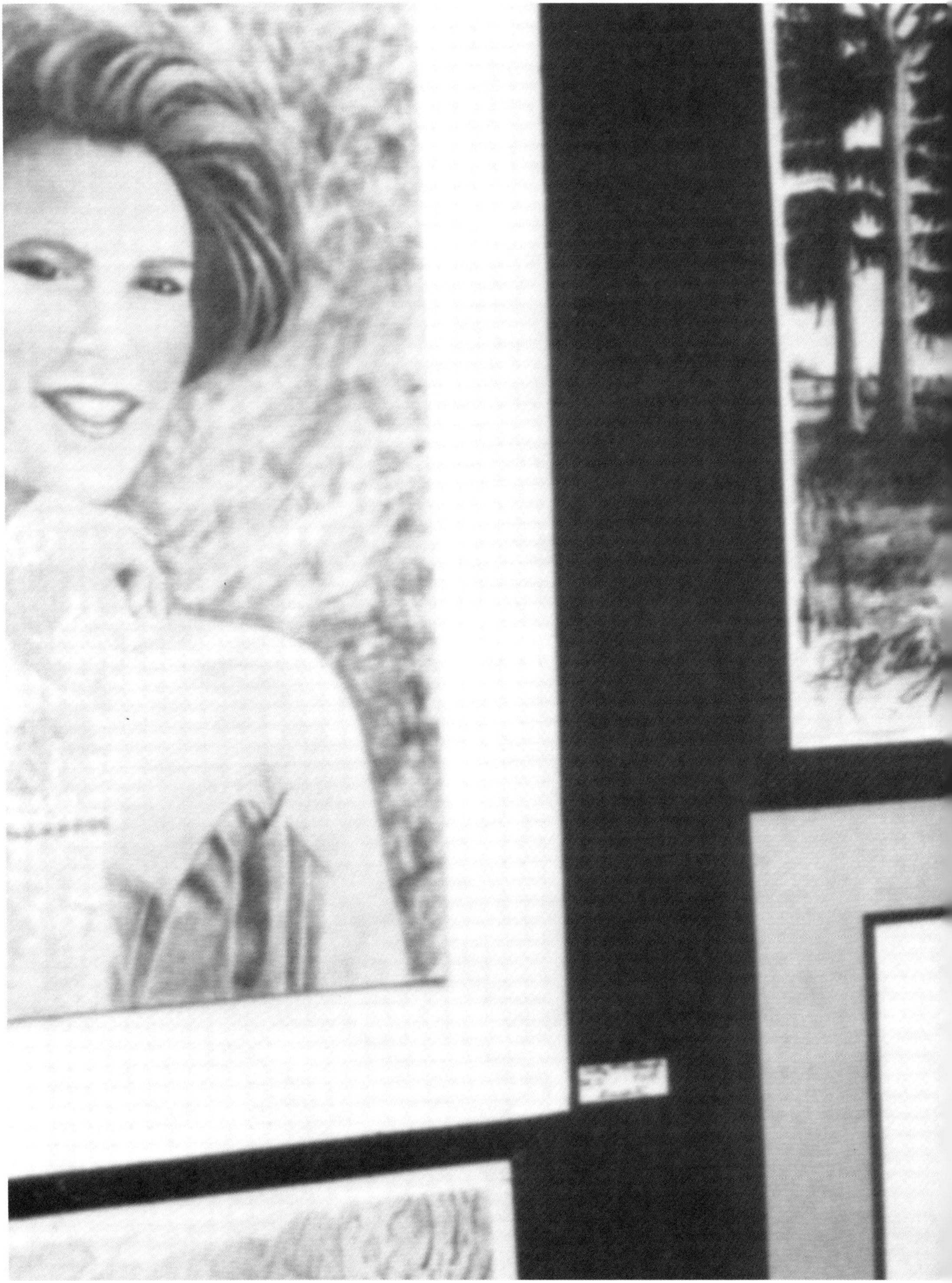

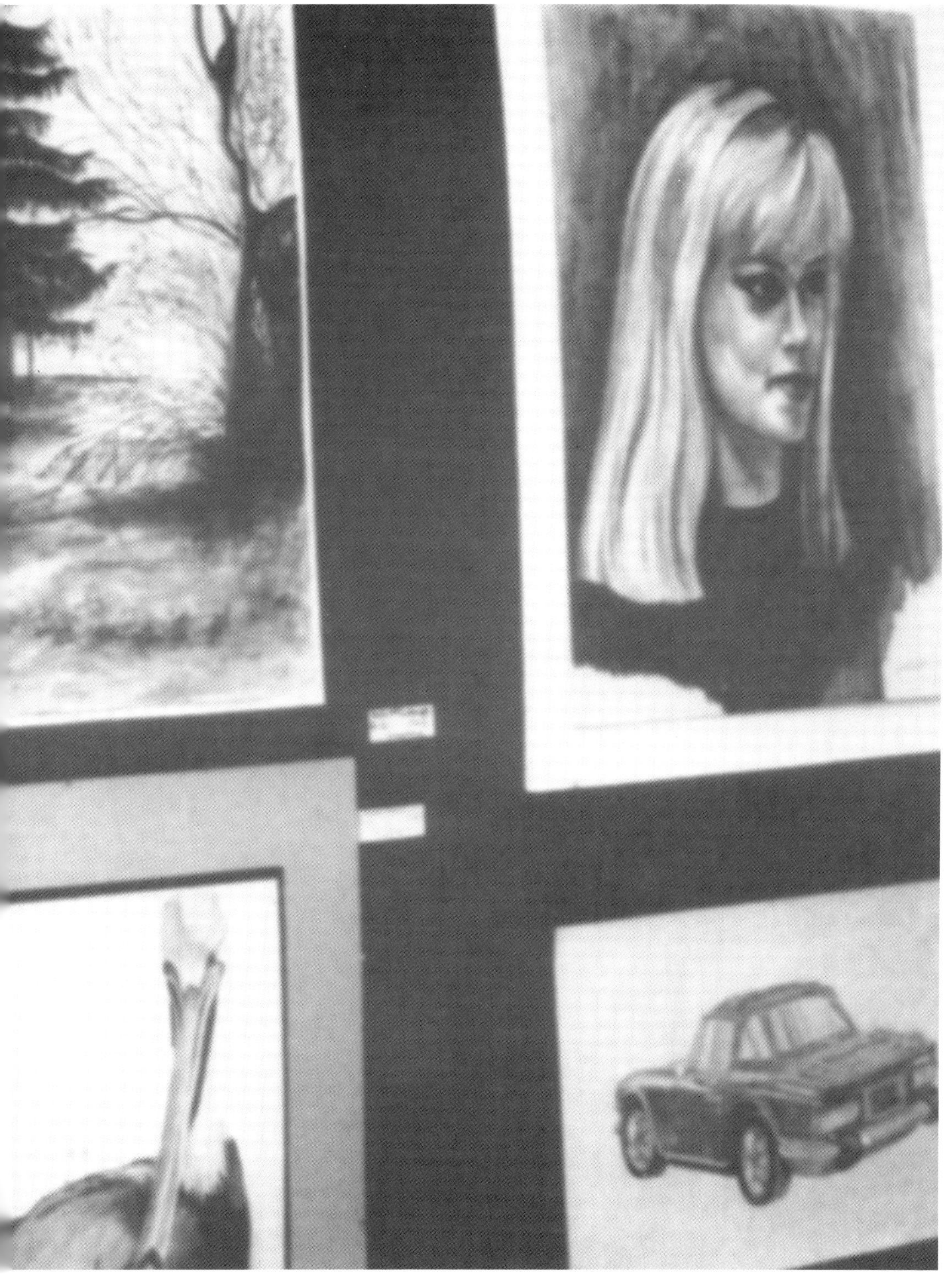

I think the saddest artworks are the collages where people simply create a catalogue of the products the either have or yearn to have. A red Camaro or sunglasses or... really useless crap, but it's almost poignant for me now to imagine that you can define yourself by your possessions.

* * *

I've noticed that schools have become more violent since my death. In 1984 I don't think a massacre would have been possible, but then who am I to say? Maybe dozens of massacres were almost about to happen but they got squelched before they occurred—somebody chickened out, or some parents found bullets and maps of the hallways in their kid's down jacket pockets, and called the cops.

* * *

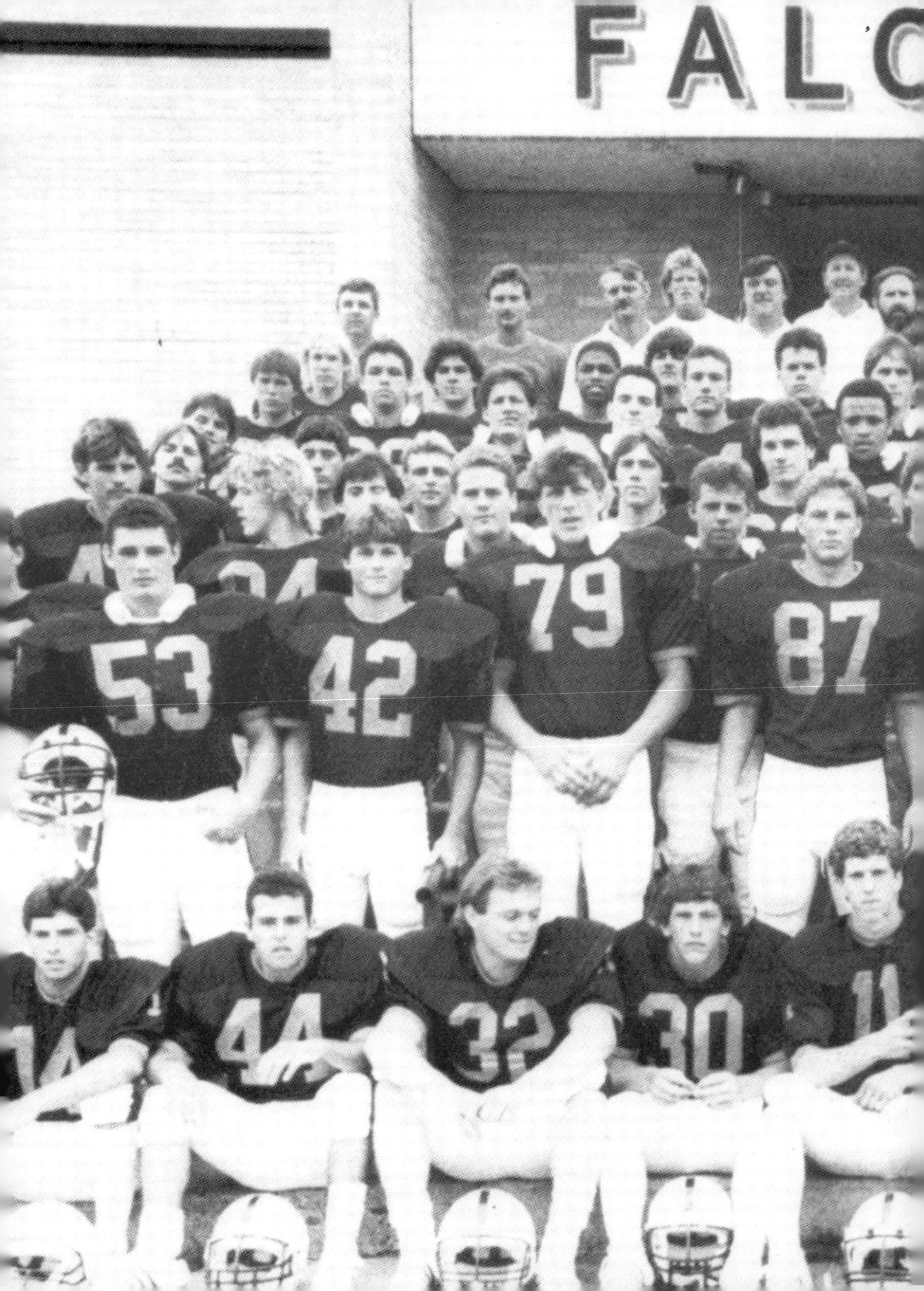
FALC

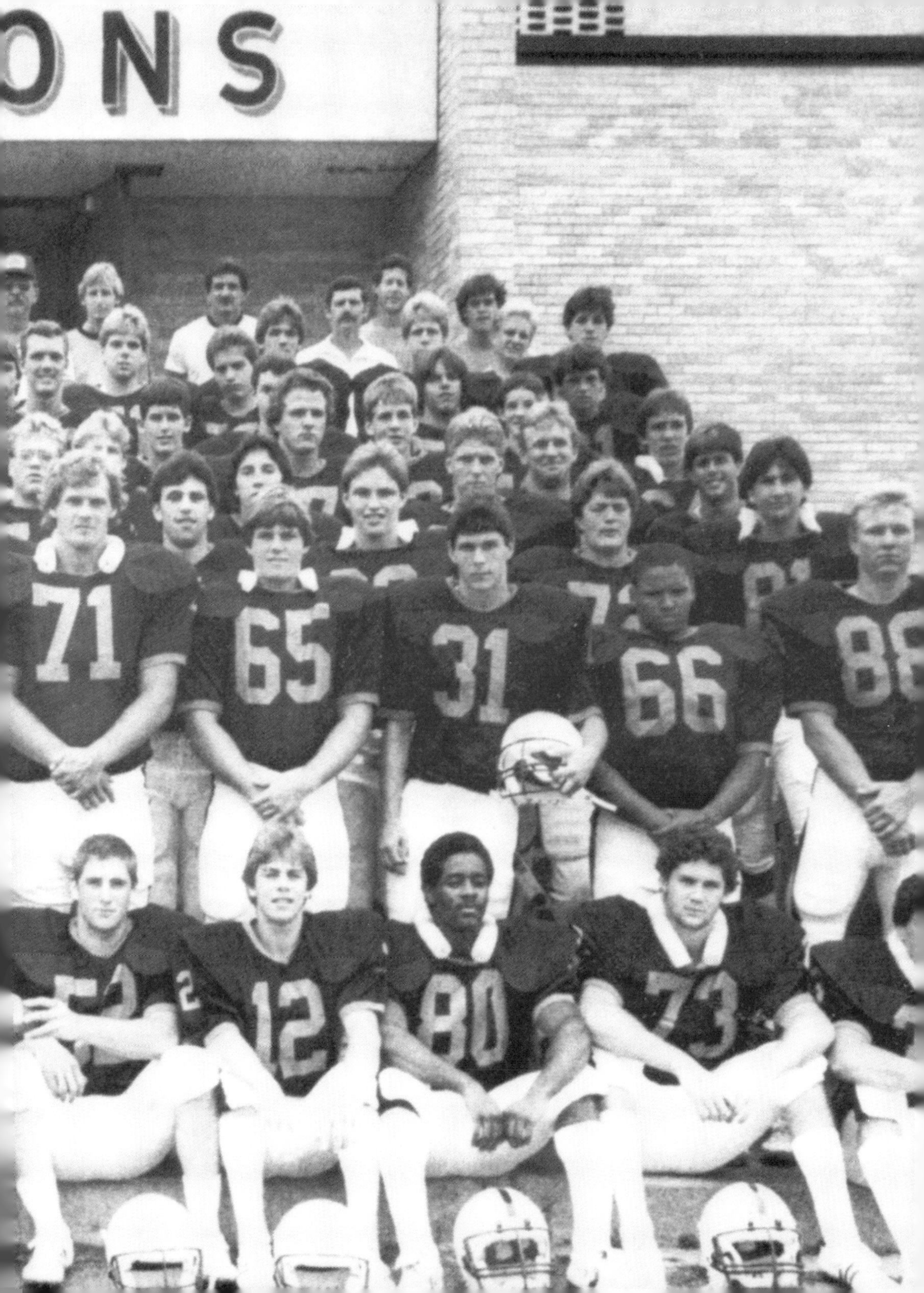
ONS

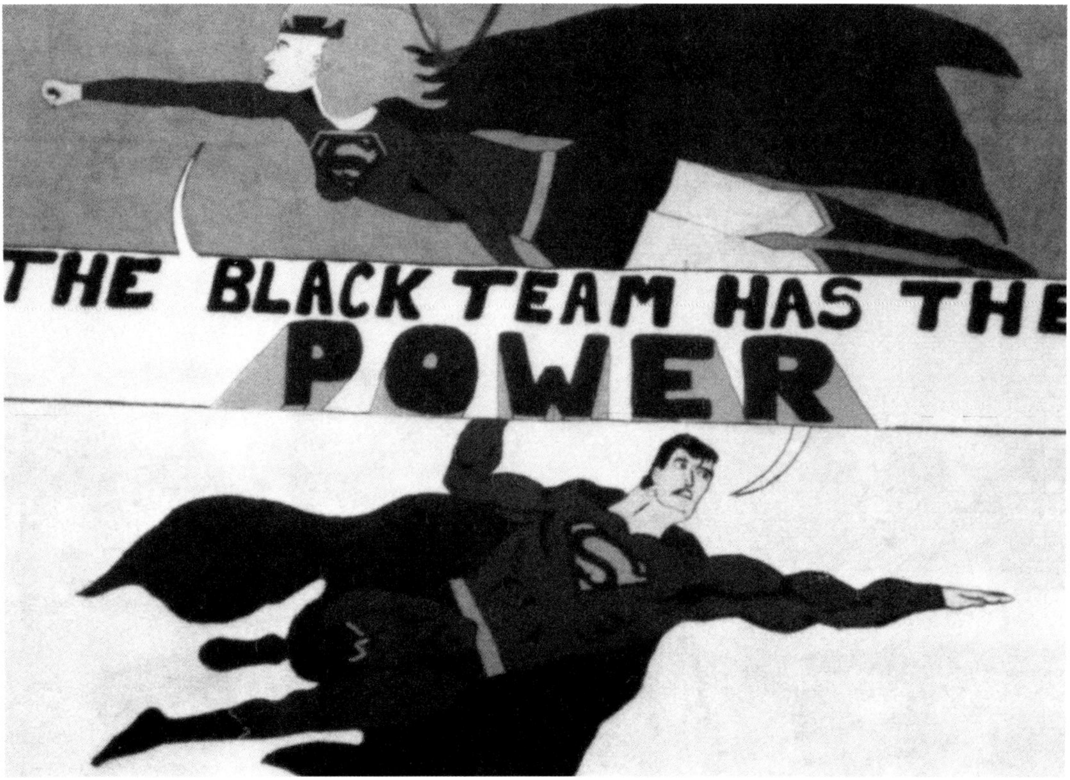

MIKE,
YOU'RE WELCOME FOR USING MY HOT TUB,
MY HOUSE, MY BEDROOM AND MY SKIM BOARD.
GOOFBALL.
DEVLIN.

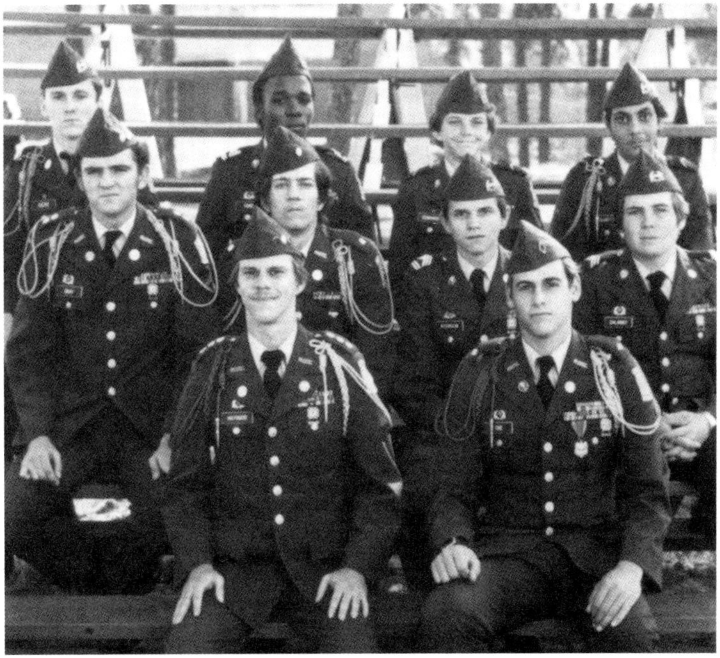

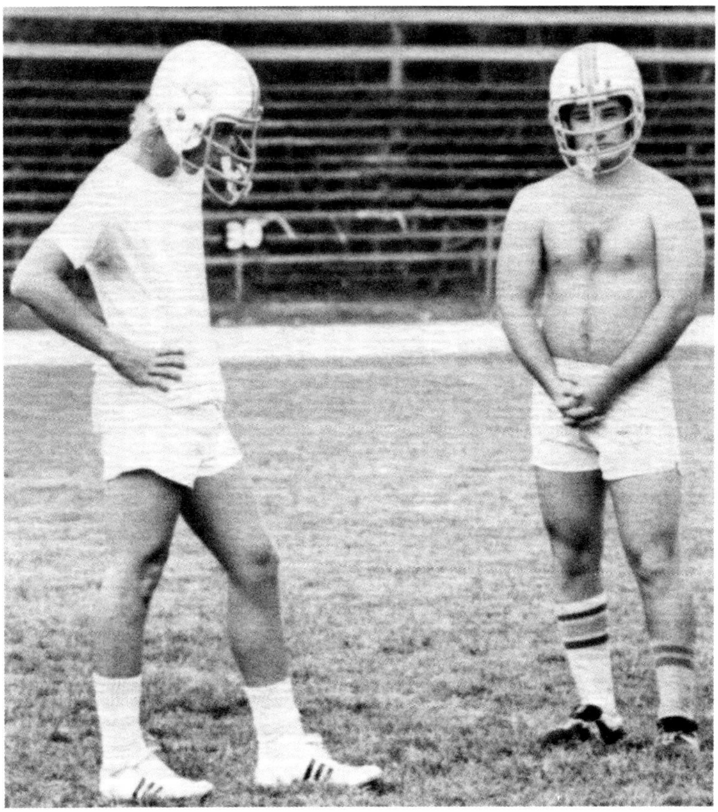

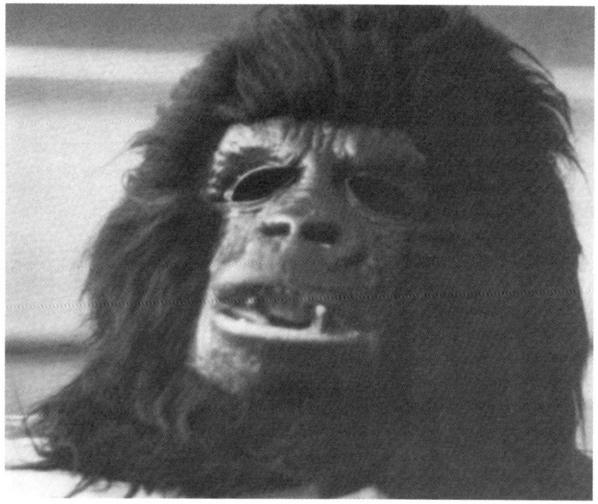

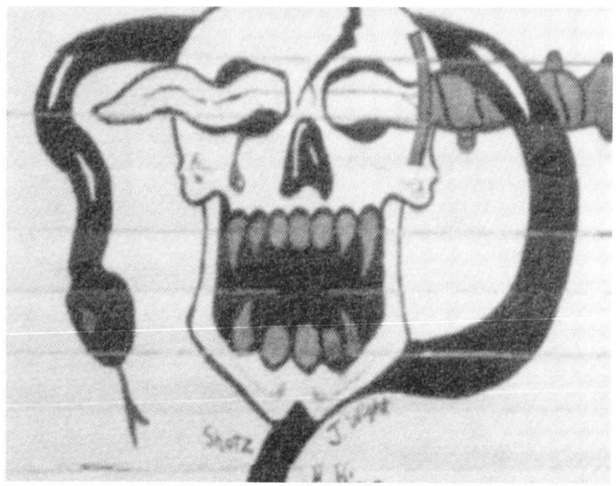

SHEP:
TO AN INCREDIBLY VACANT BODY OF LOW-COST PARTS,
I WISH I WAS HERE JUST ONE MORE YEAR,
AND I WISH I COULD GO THRU TRACK AGAIN.
I'M GOING TO MISS WRESTLING AND POLE VAULTING.
I WISH I COULD BEAT YOU UP AND POKE YOU
IN THE EYES WITH A SHARPENED STICK.
GOOD LUCK, AND I HOPE YOU MEET A VIRGIN WHO RAPES YOU.
RAMON

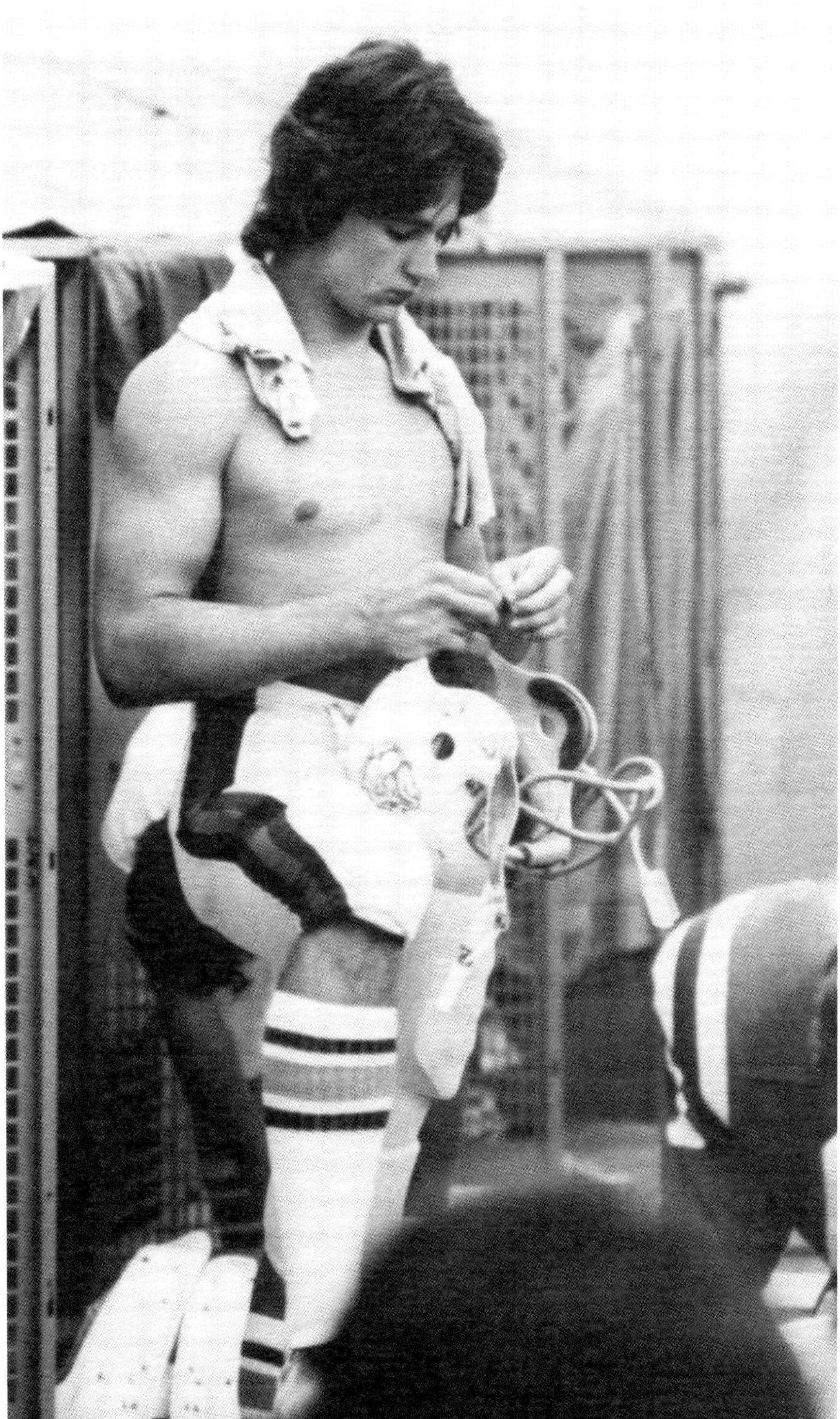

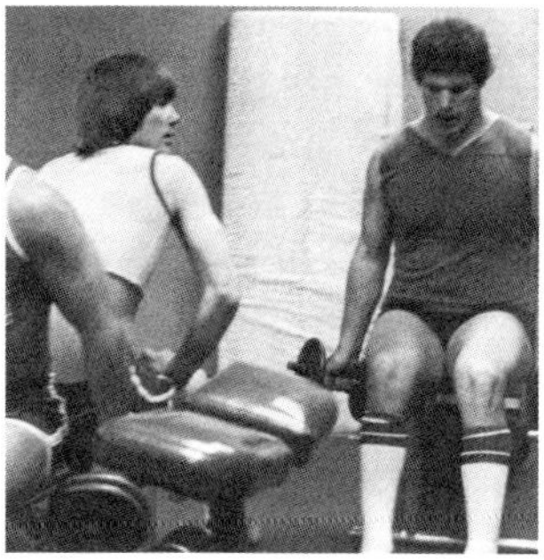

MIKE,

**WE BOTH SCREWED EACH OTHER OVER PRETTY BAD,
BUT WE KEPT A GREAT FRIENDSHIP DURING THE WORST OF TIMES.**

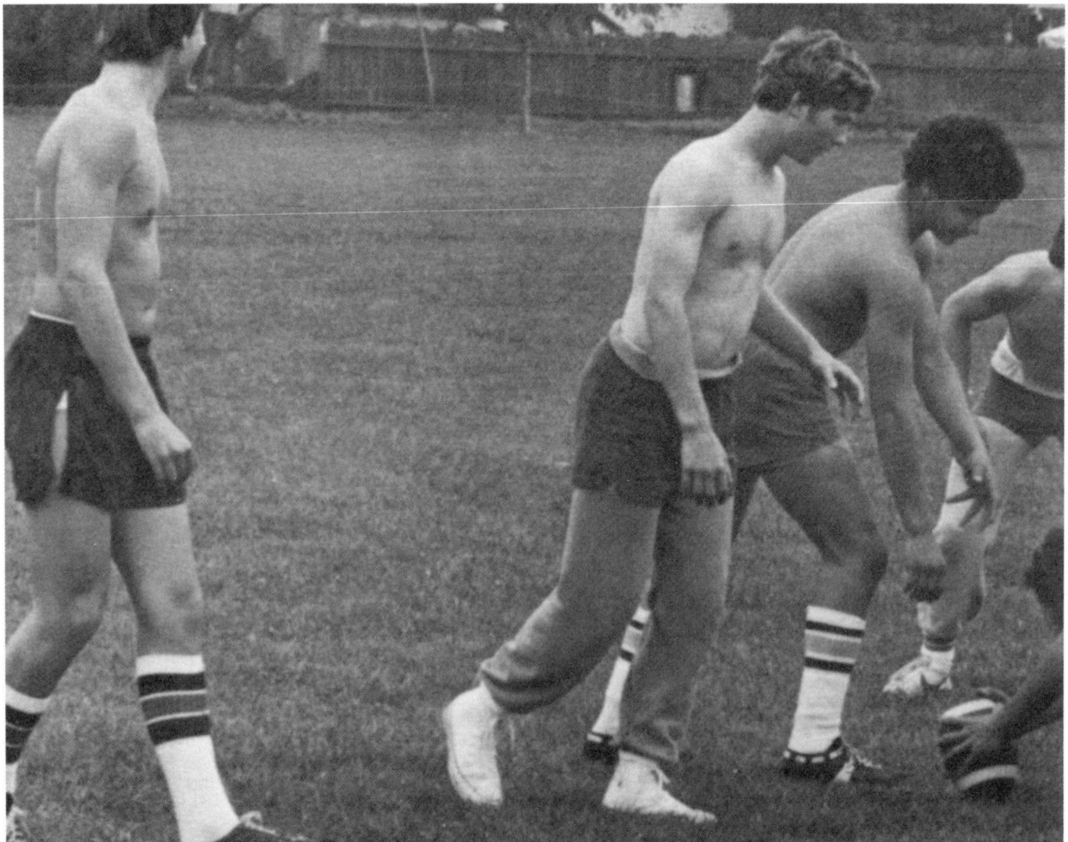

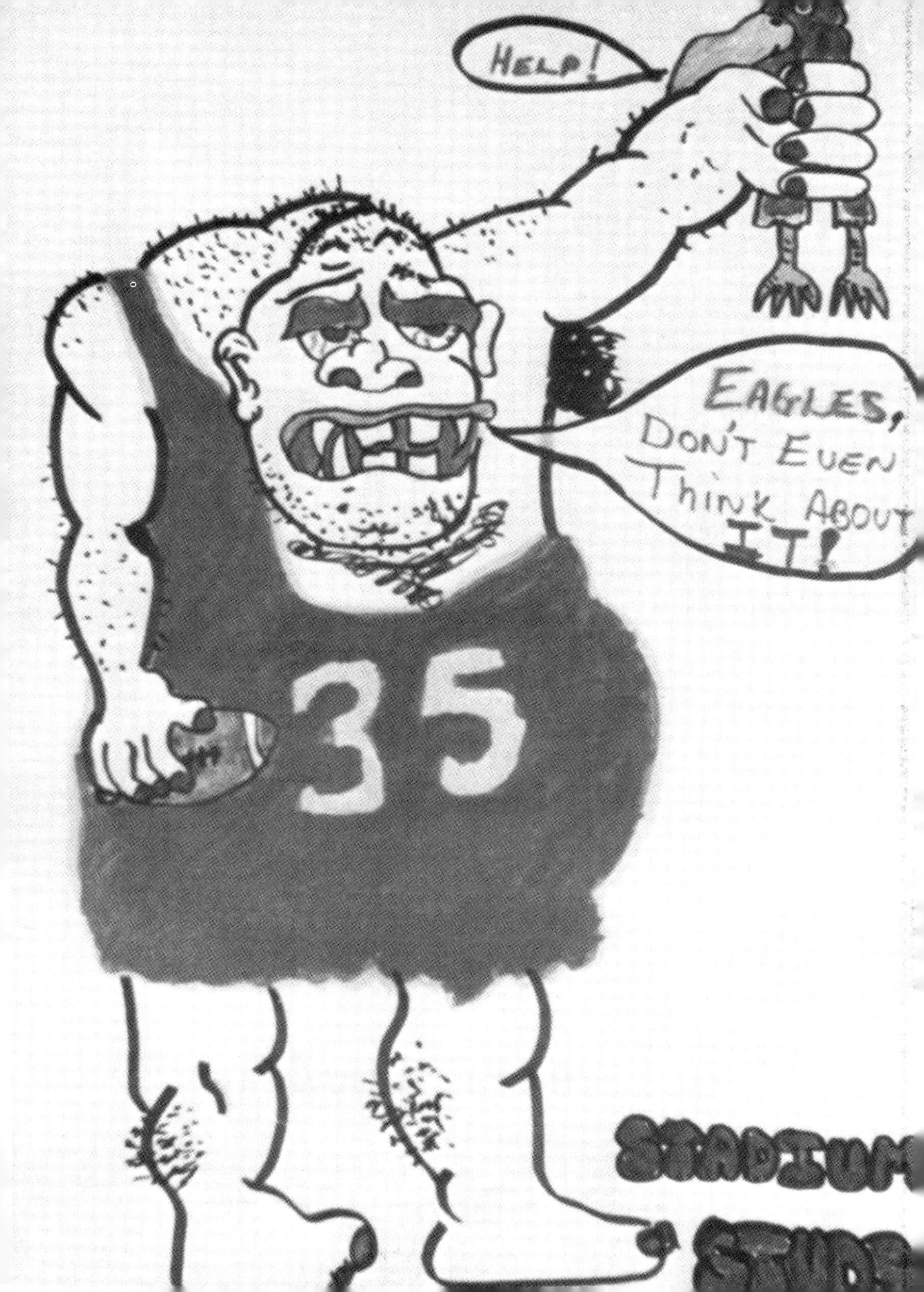

HELP!
EAGLES, DON'T EVEN THINK ABOUT IT!
STADIUM

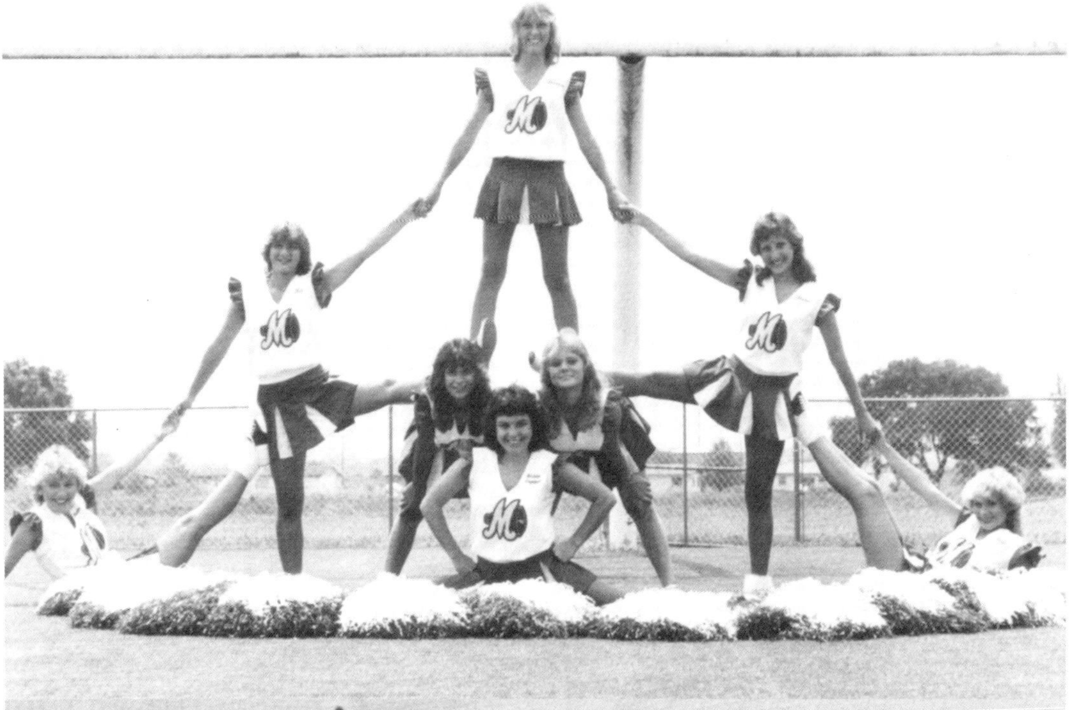

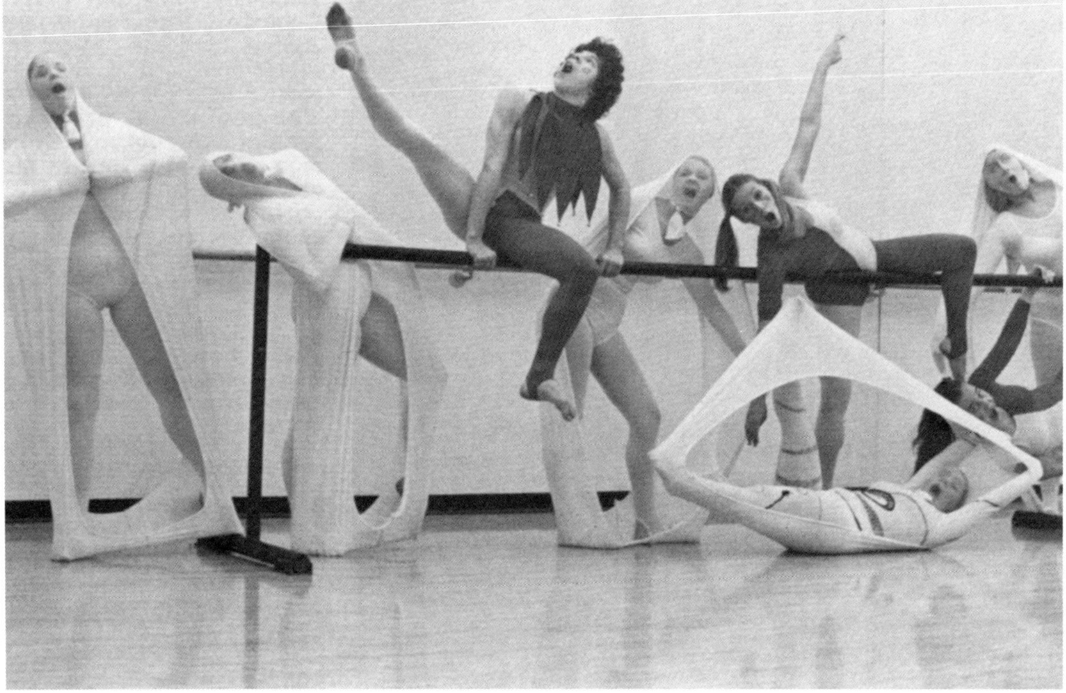

HEY GOOD LOOKIN!
IT WAS COOL 2 KNOW U.
CALL ME SOMETIME.
563-3668
MELANIE

ERICA,
THANKS FOR MAKING PROM NIGHT EVEN MORE MEMORABLE
(EVEN IF WE WERE A COUPLE OF CHICKENS.) I WISH YA LUCK
IN YOUR MARRIAGE. KEEP SMILING.
YOUR FIREND,
KORRINA.

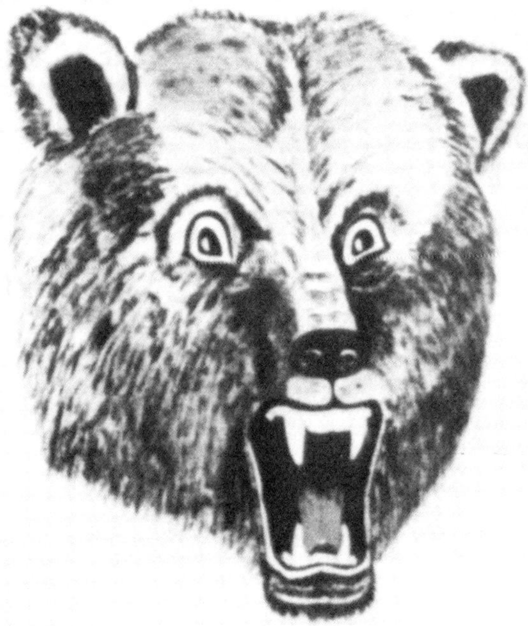

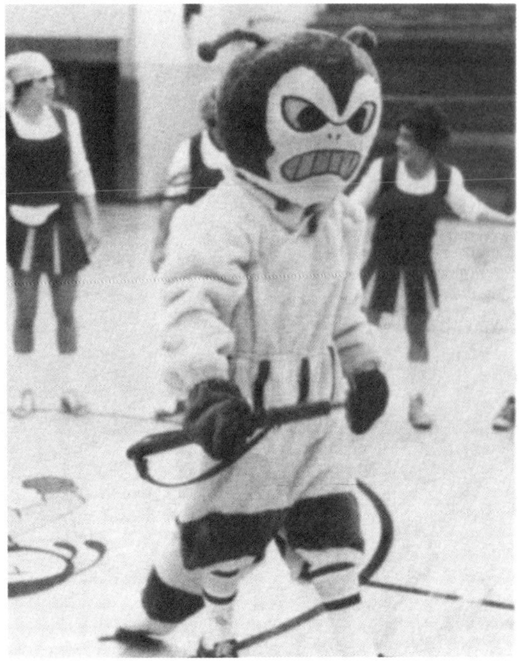

I AM THE LAST OF THE FAMOUS INTERNATIONAL PLAYBOYS

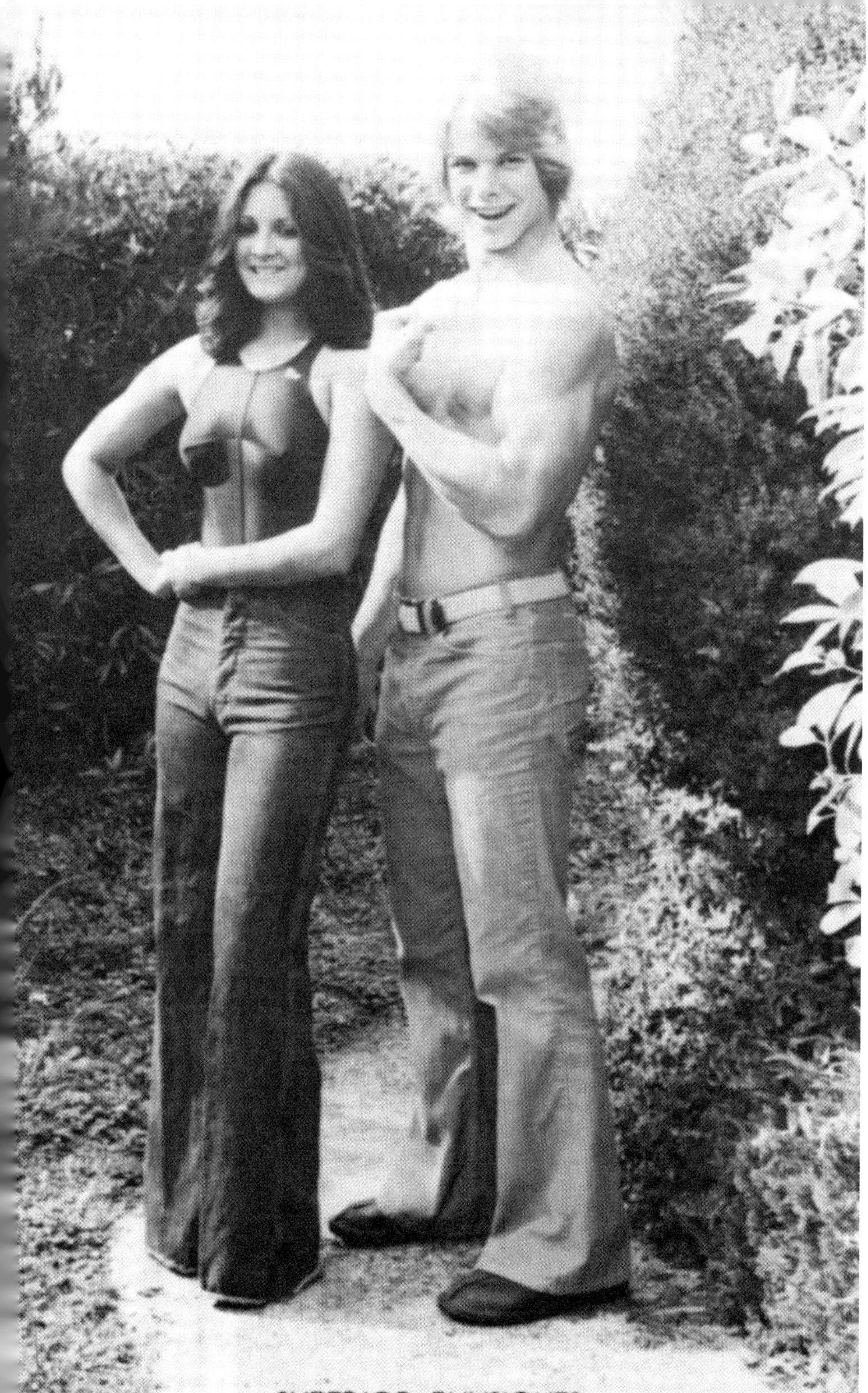

SUPERIOR PHYSIQUES

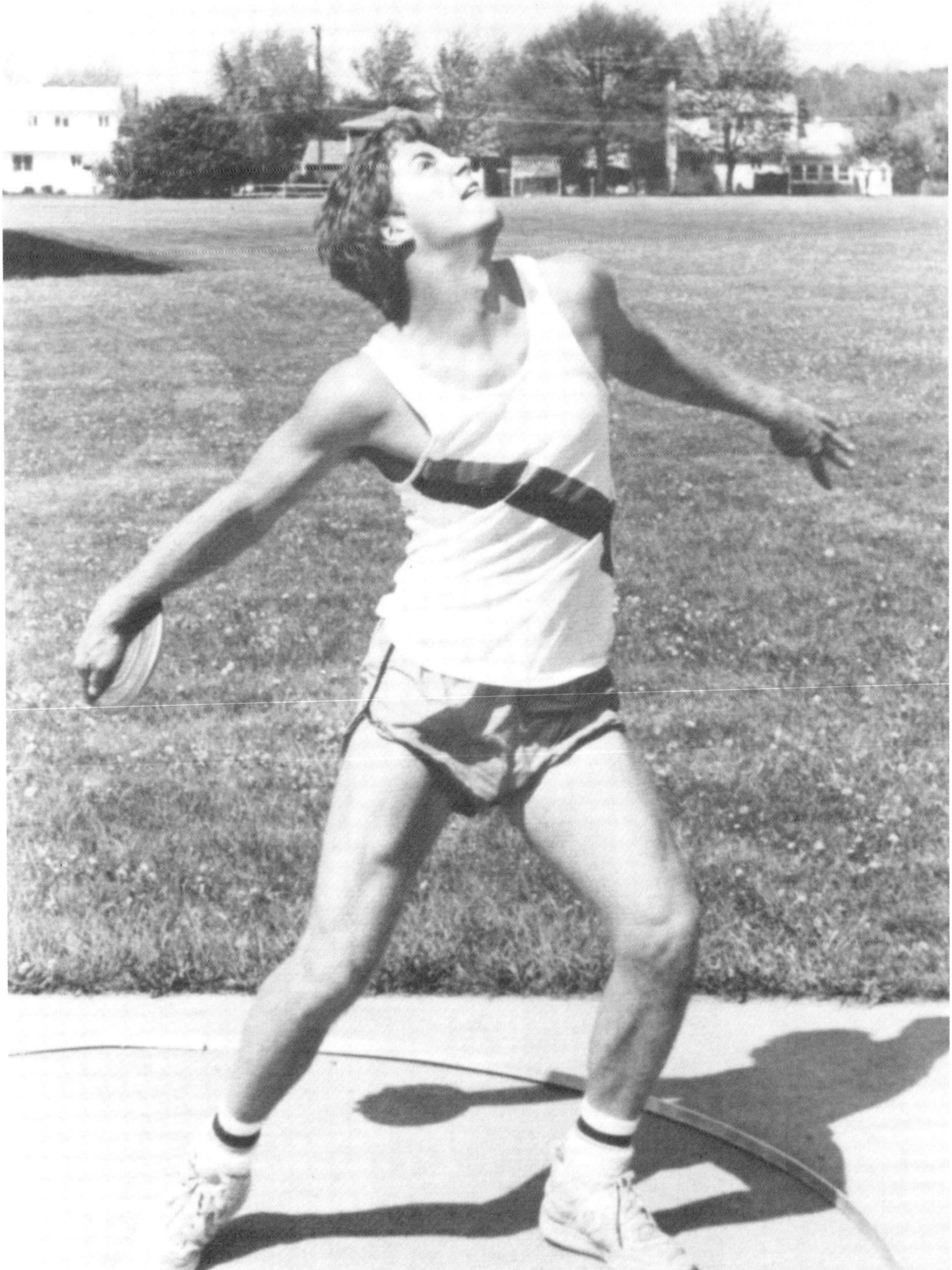

DAVE, YOU BIG STUD.

I HOPE YOU STILL LOVE YOUR CAR.
NEVER LOSE BABES.
WARREN.

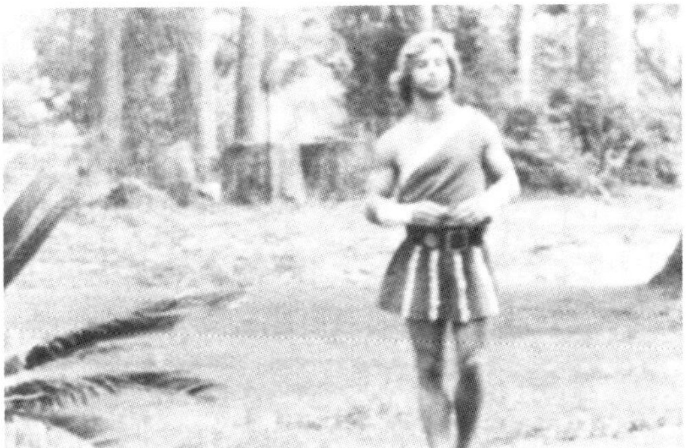

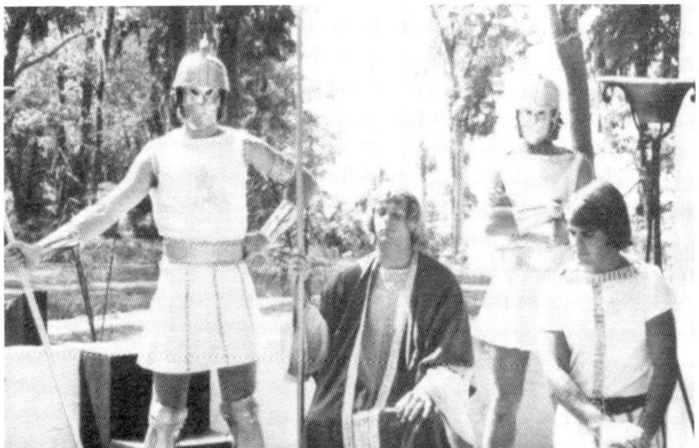

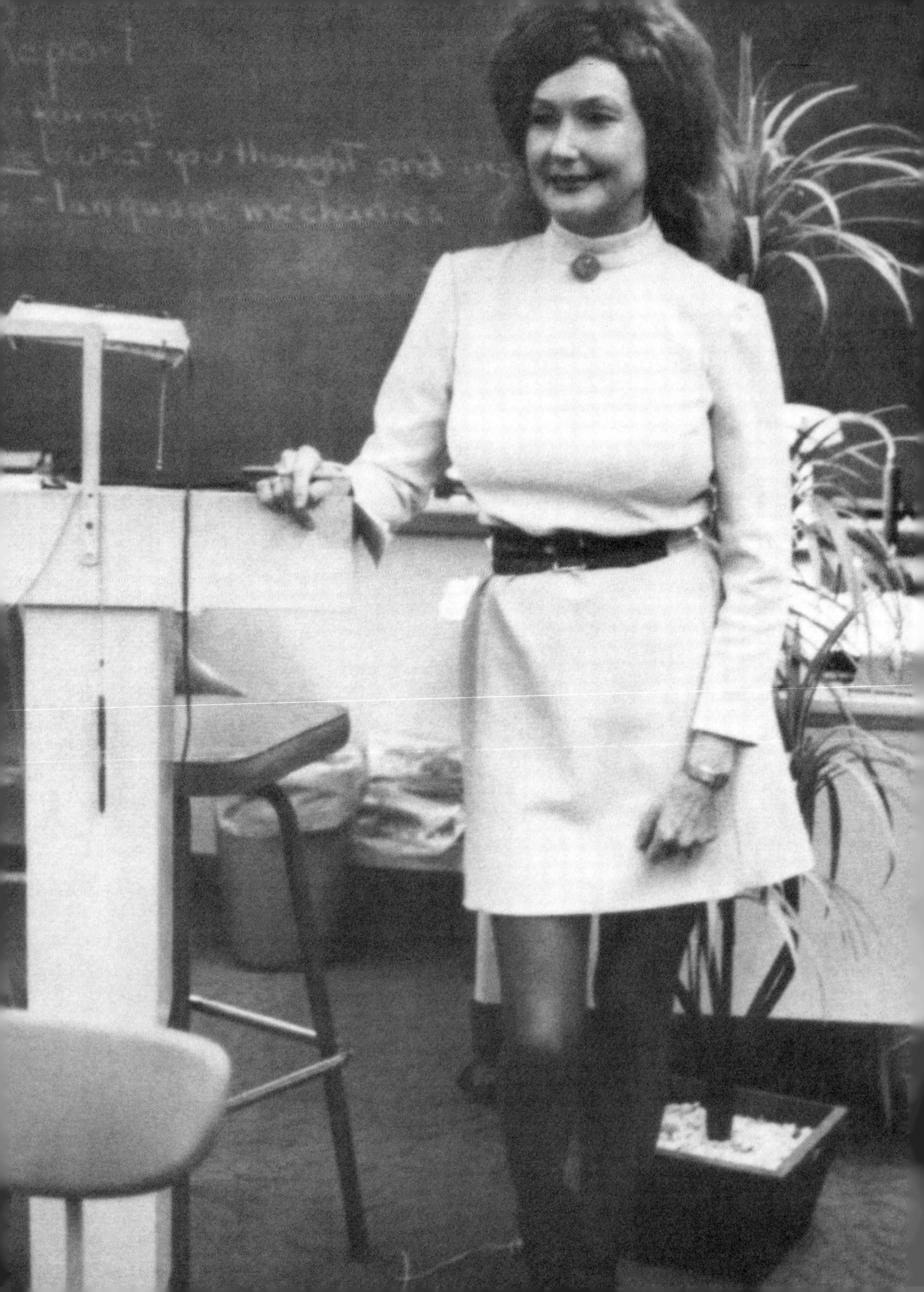

DAVE YOU STUDMUFFIN.
LET'S GO TO THE PRINCE CONCERT
THIS SUMMER.
E.

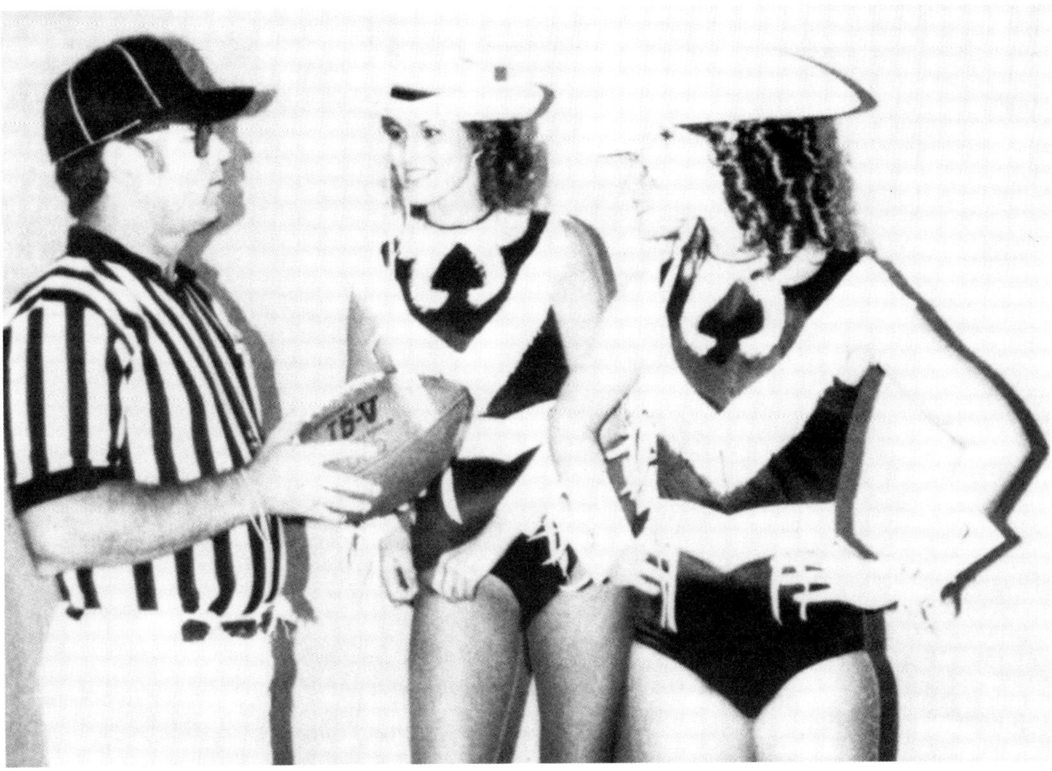

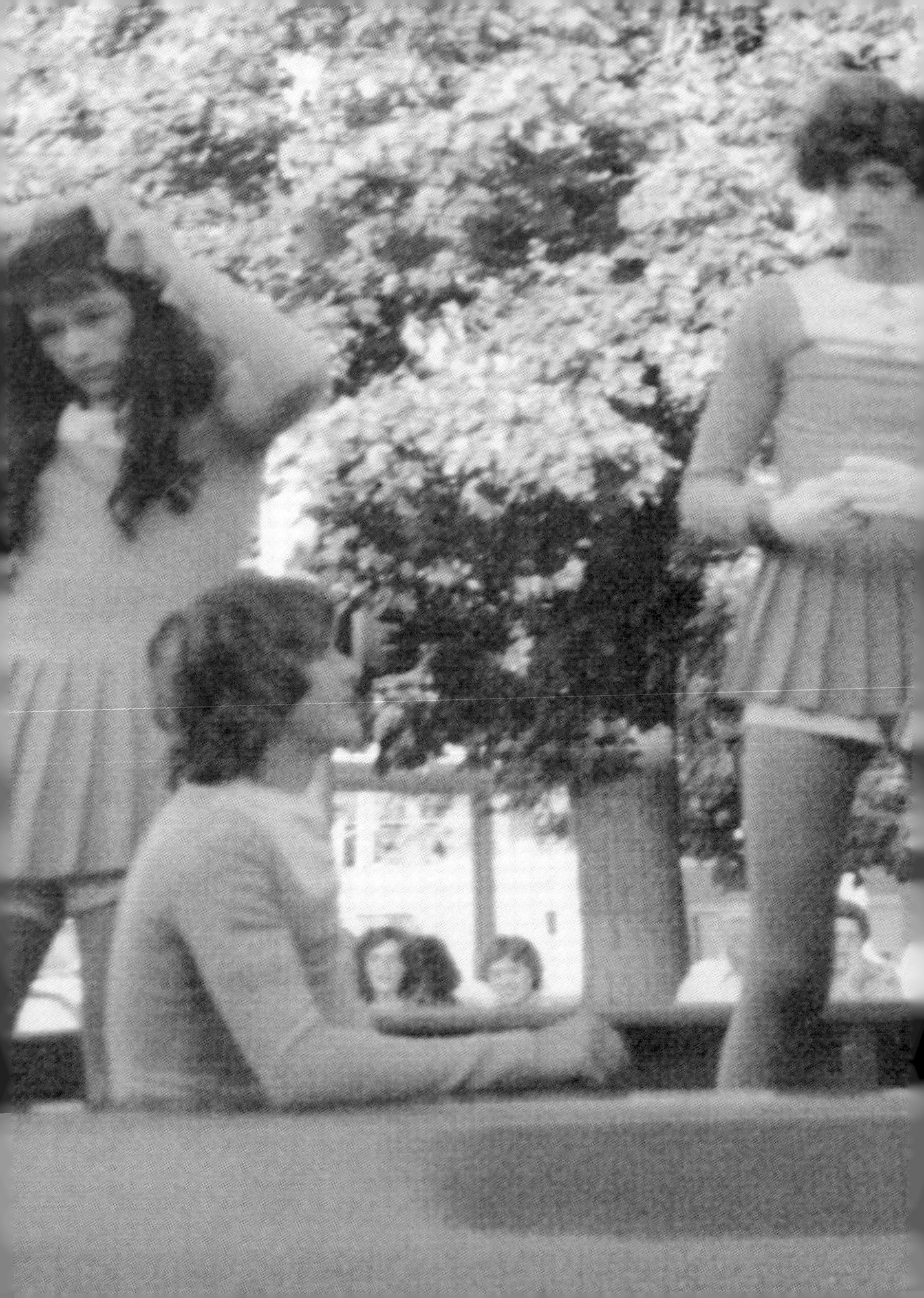

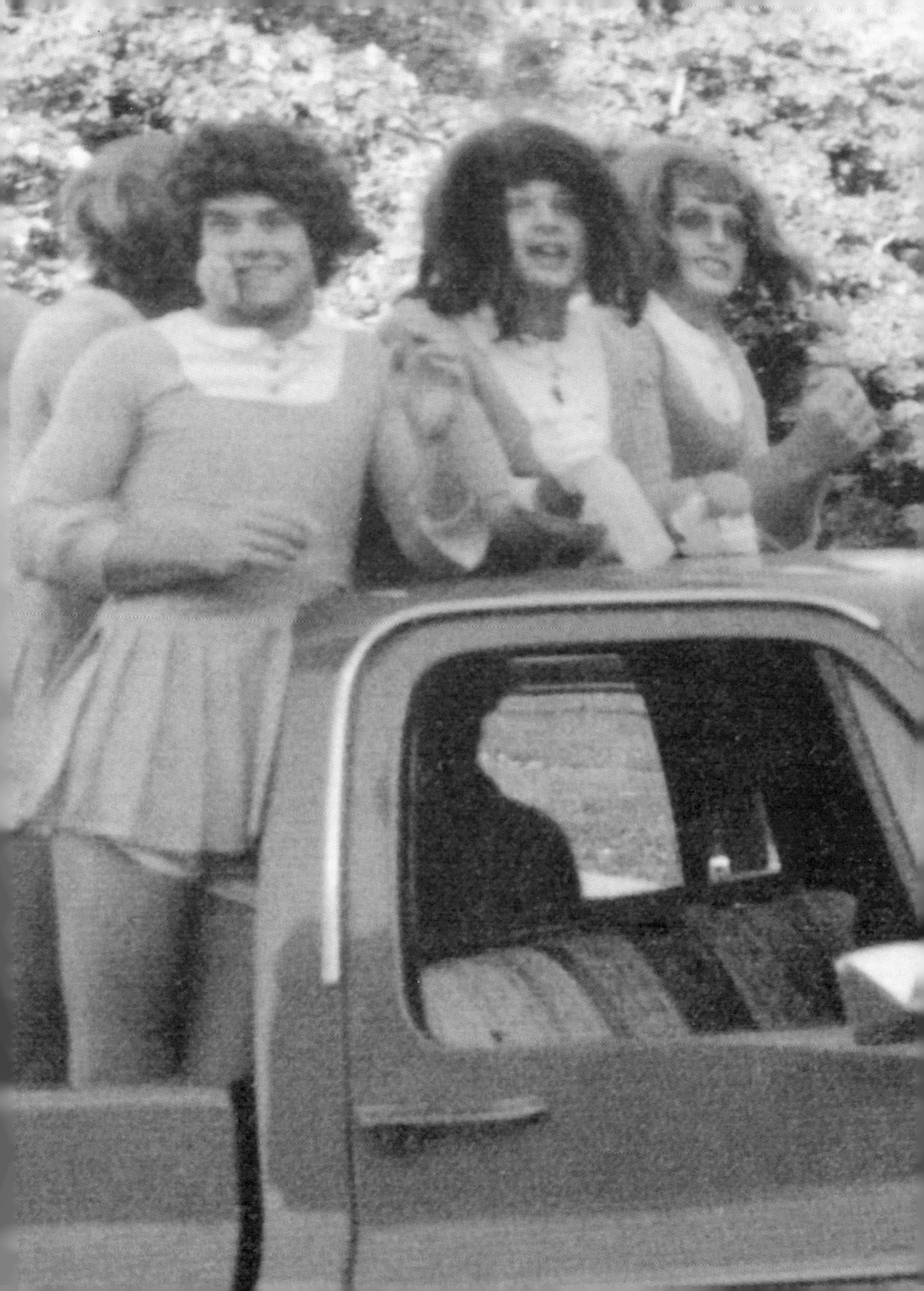

The only really interesting people at school are the losers and misfits, because once you leave school, everyone's a loser, so at least they're better prepared. That sounds callous. But even when you're thirty, you still end up eating lunch by yourself, and the phone still doesn't ring on Saturday night. Life is a lonely proposition. Even death is less lonely than life.

* * *

I think that young people are basically overwhelmed by everything that's inside them. They're frightened by whatever this alien being that's trying to explode from their insides. So they drink and do drugs and try and drop off the planet, simulating death.

* * *

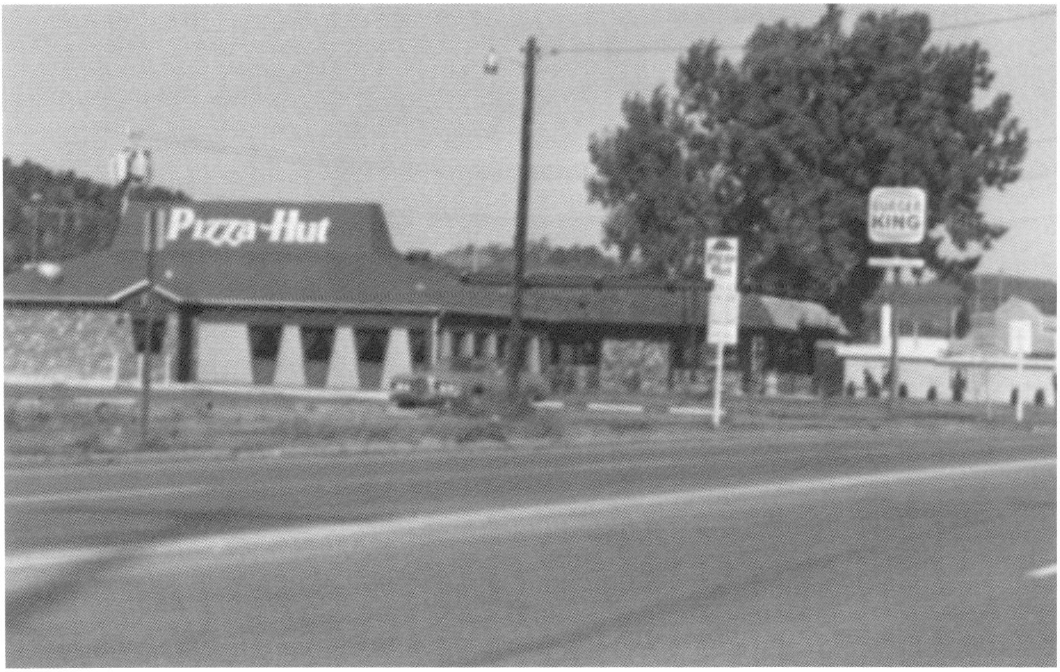

JEFF,
YOU DEAD BLIND GIMP,
I LOVE YOU.
EAT LOTS OF DONUTS AND
NEVER DRIVE OVER 72 MPH.

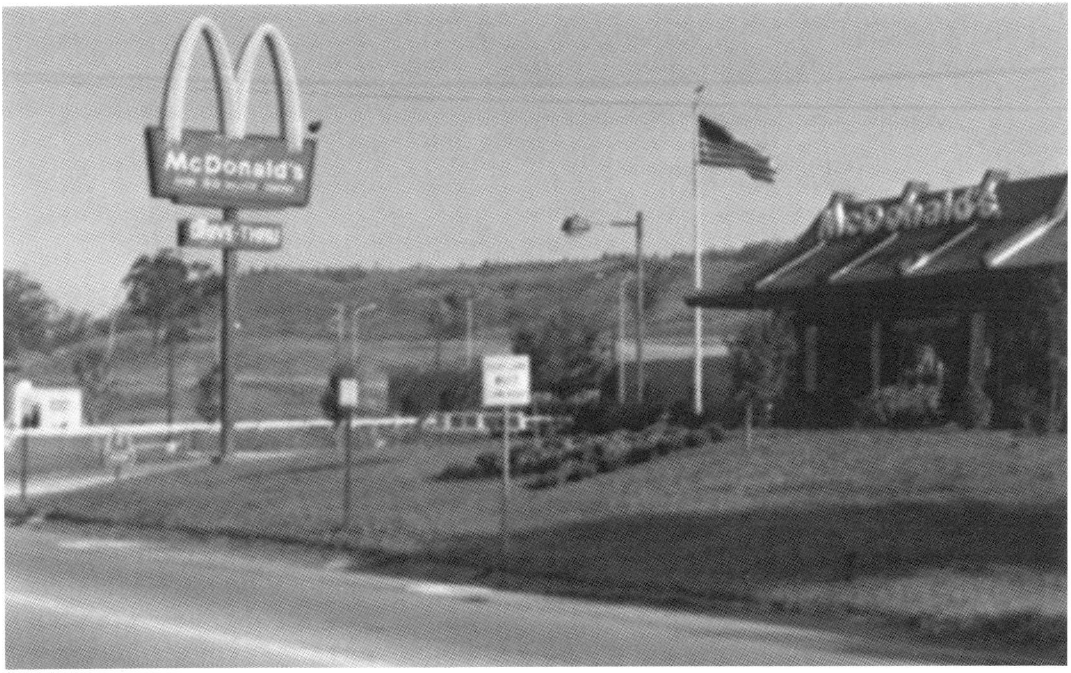
McDonald's
McDonald's

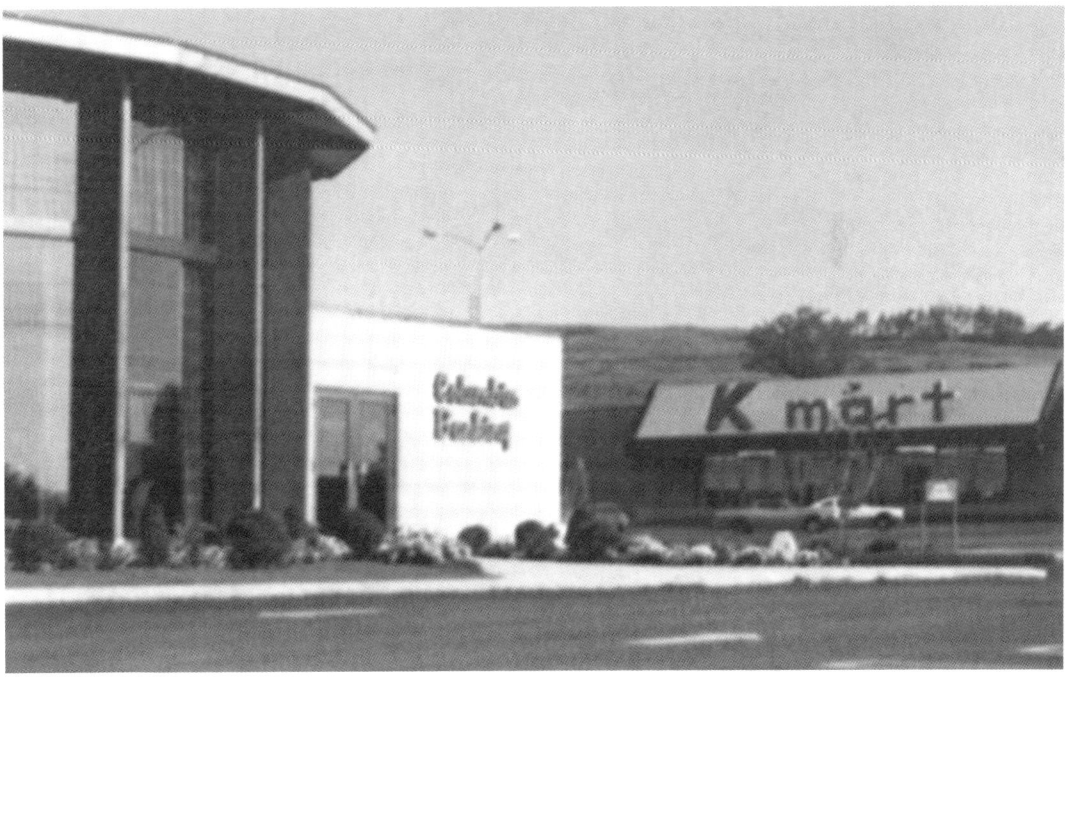
K mart

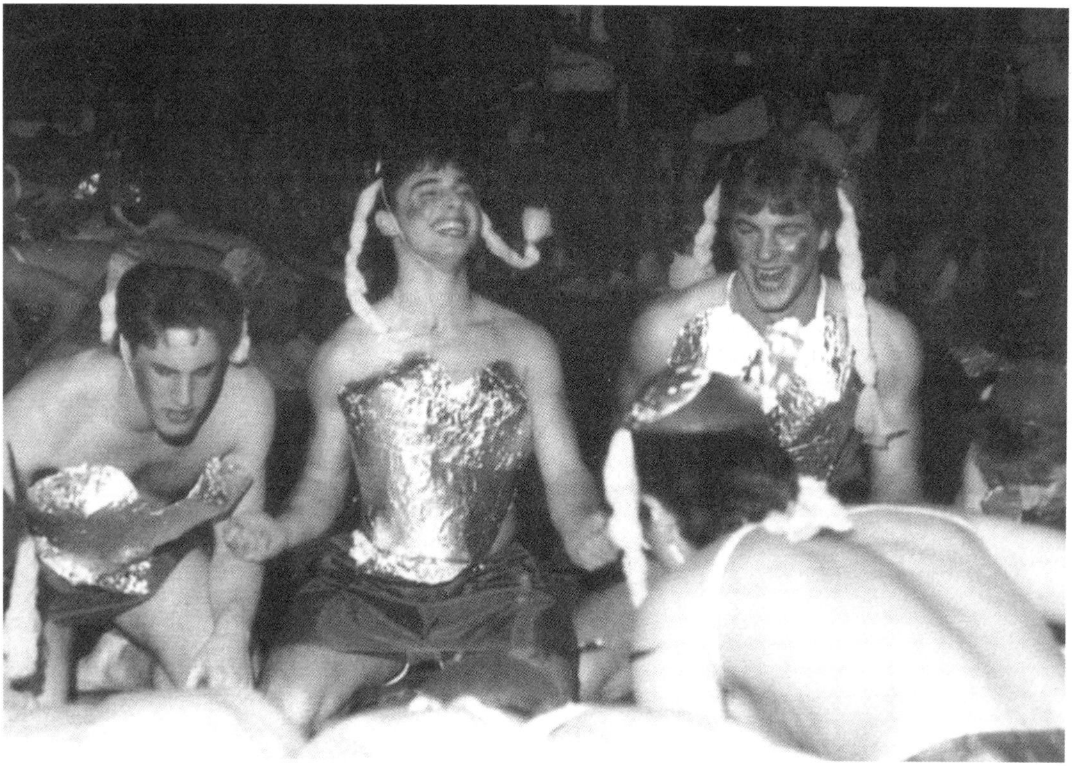

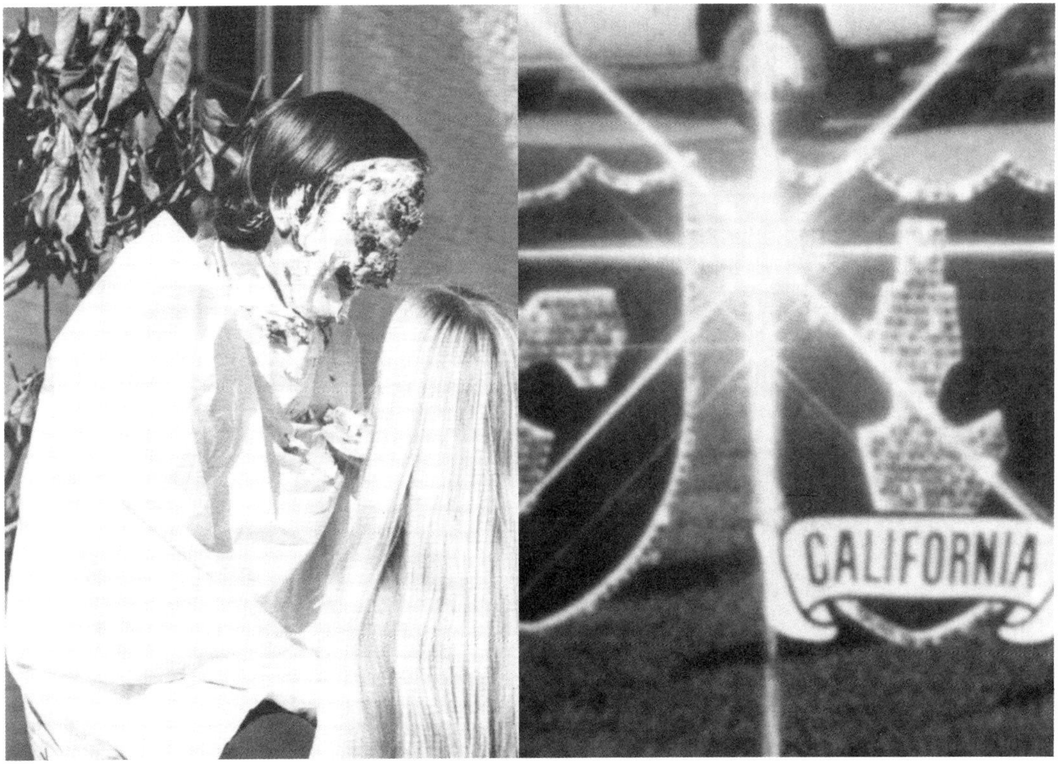

WHIPPED CREAM
BIG BEAR
OVERDUE VIDEOS
FOUR-COLOR PENS

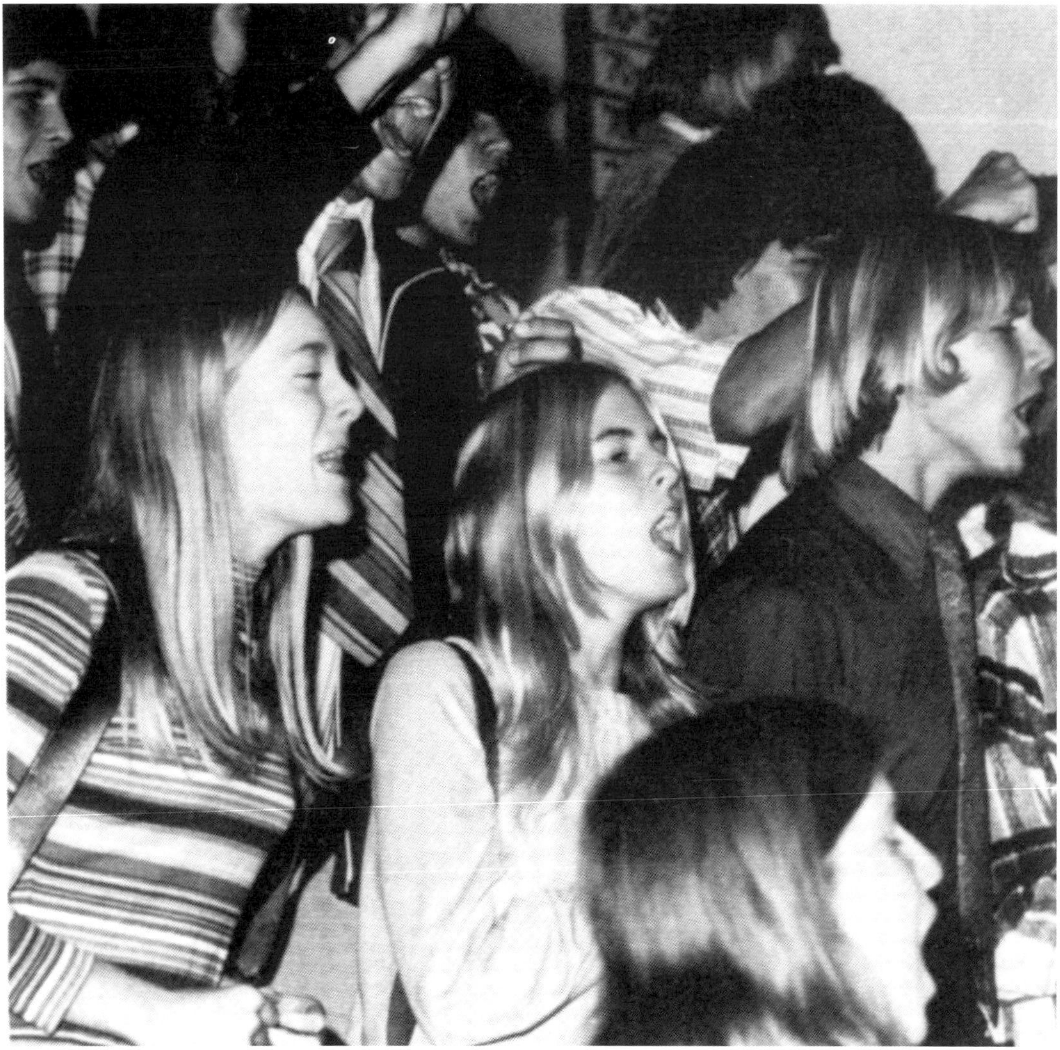

DALE,
HAVE A NICE SUMMER AND
DON'T GET TOO STUCK UP.
SEE YOU IN 20 YEARS,
LAURA

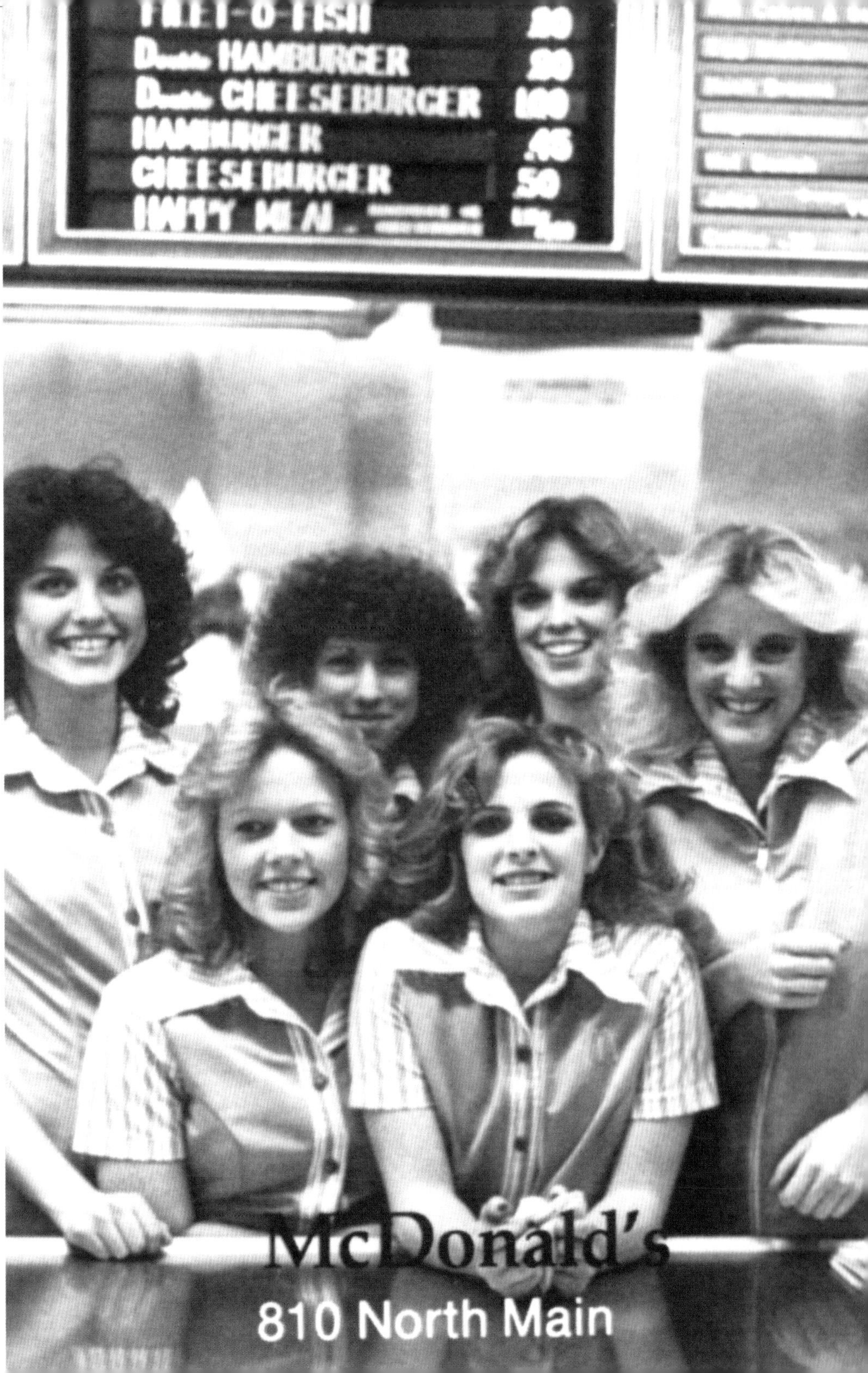

McDonald's

810 North Main

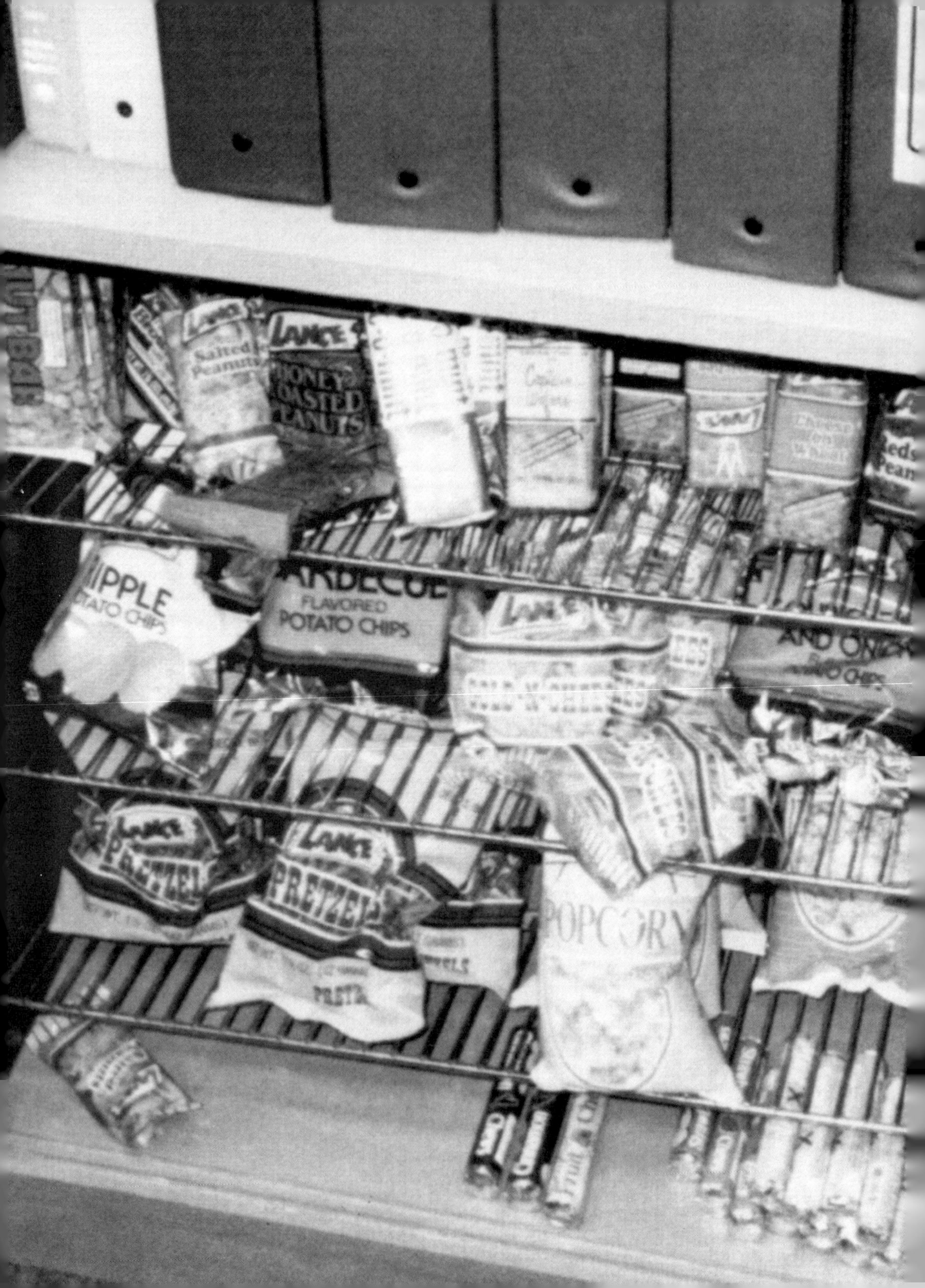
Lance
Salted Peanuts
Lance
FLAVORED
POTATO CHIPS
AND ONION
Lance
PRETZELS

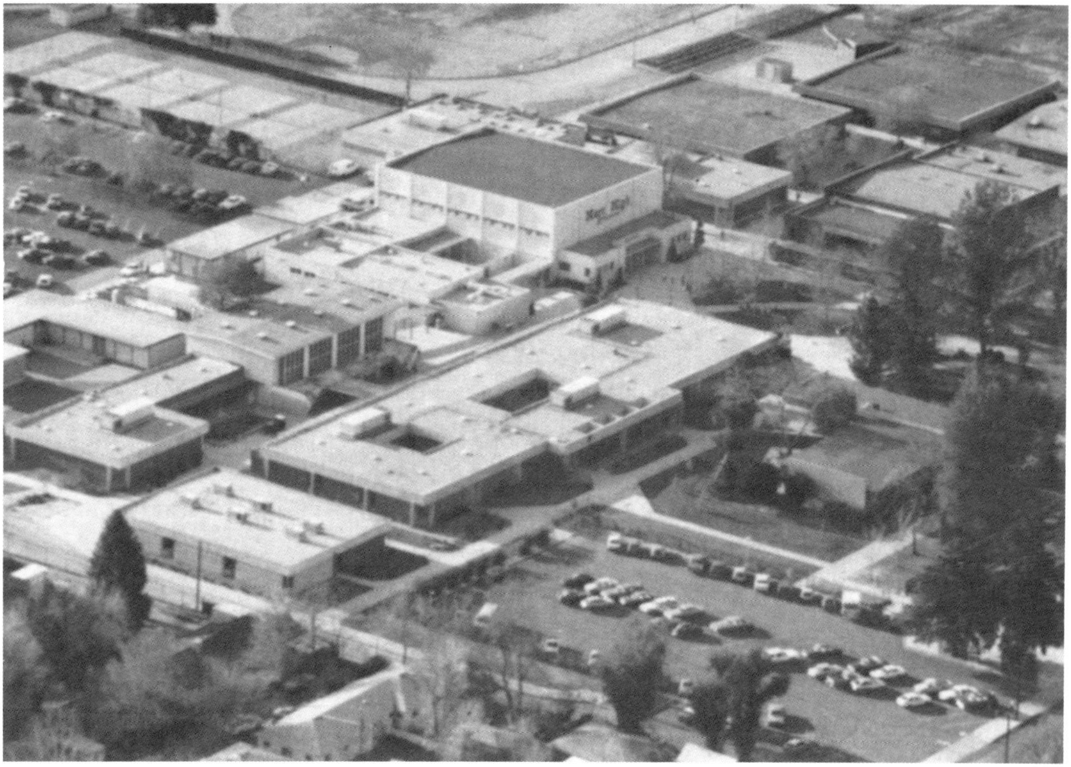

**I, DEBBIE WATT GIVE AND BEQUEATH
TO MY LITTLE SISTER MY KILLER PARKING SPOT
NEAR THE SOUTH EXIT.**

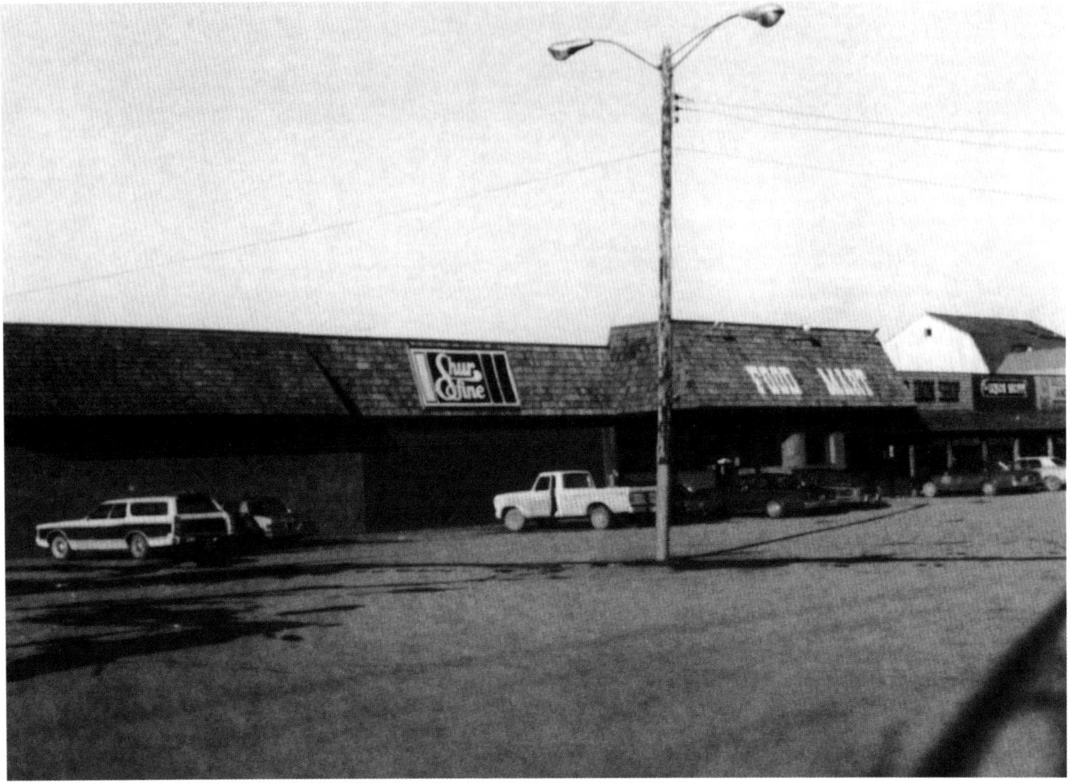

AEROSMITH
GUNS 'N' ROSES
THE LASER SHOW
LOBSTERS
WEEKEND IN PHOENIX...

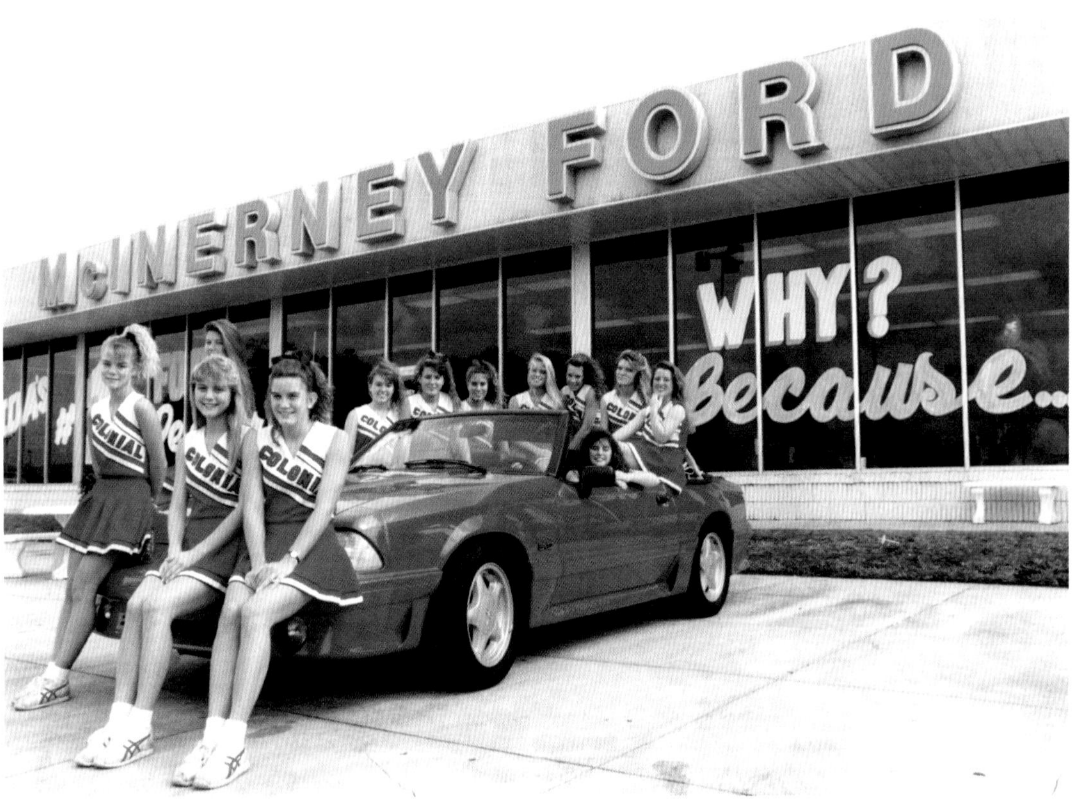

...RIDING SHOTGUN
THE DENT IN
THE MUSTANG'S FENDER
CAUGHT SMOKING
SUPER FLY

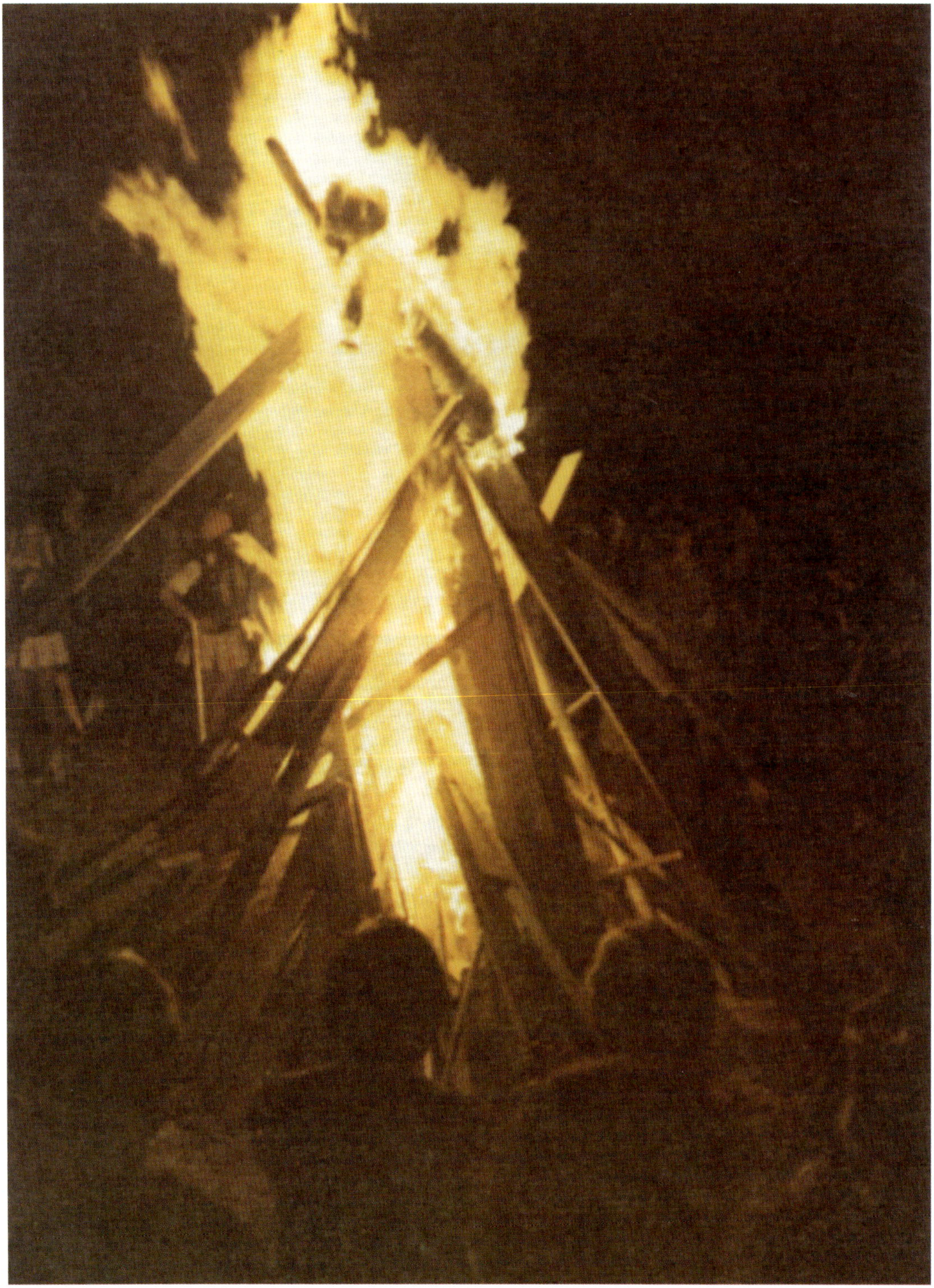

WELL BOB, WE FINALLY MADE IT.

HAVE AN AMAZING REST OF YOUR LIFE.

DARRIN.

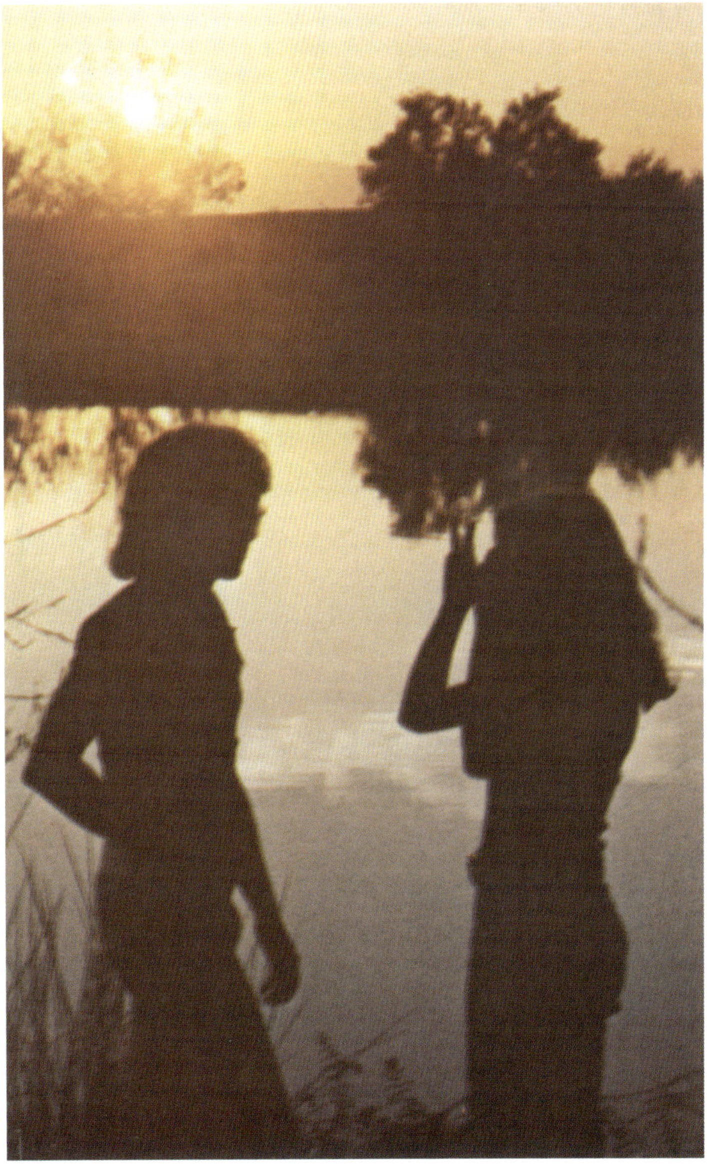

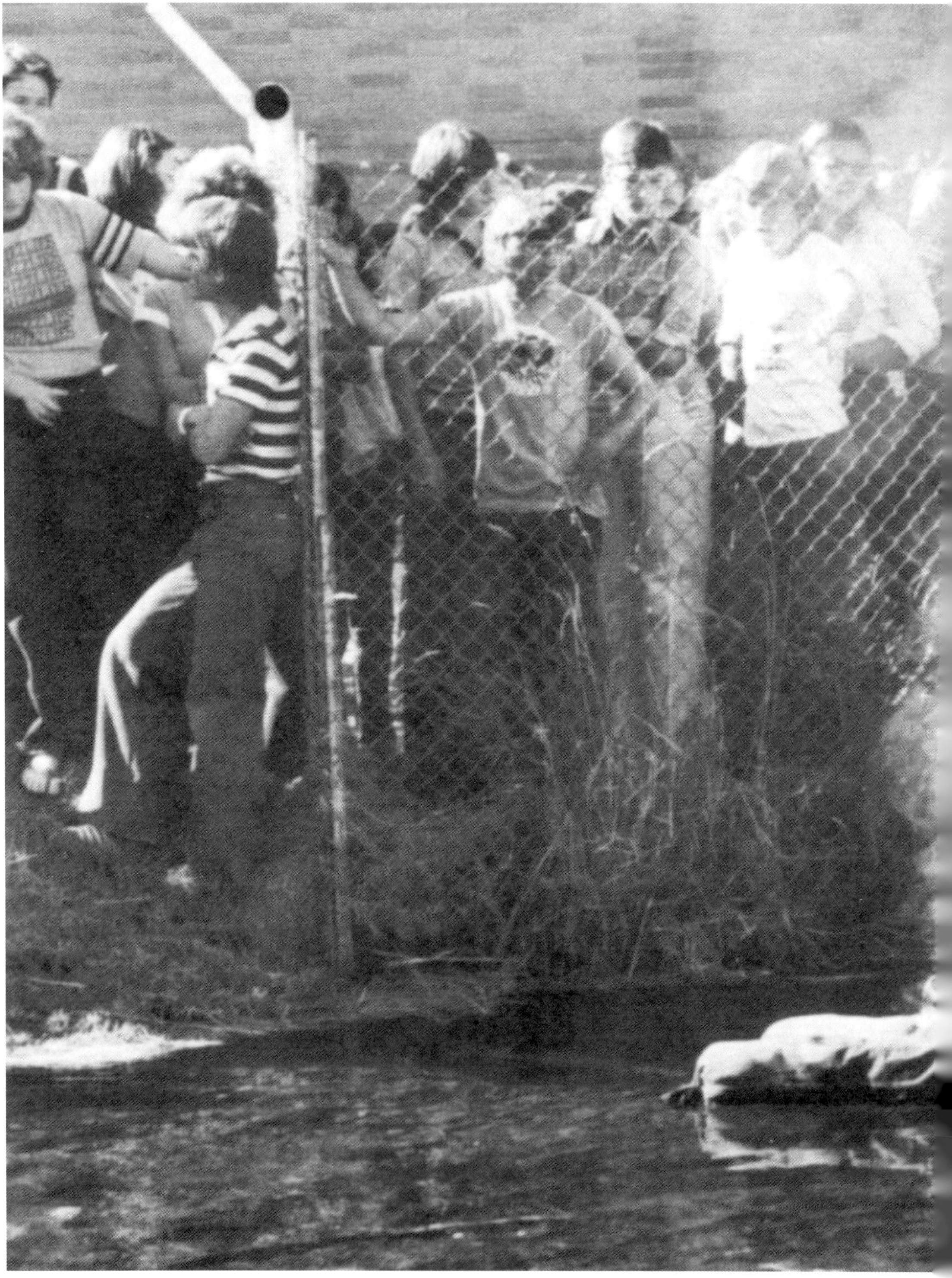

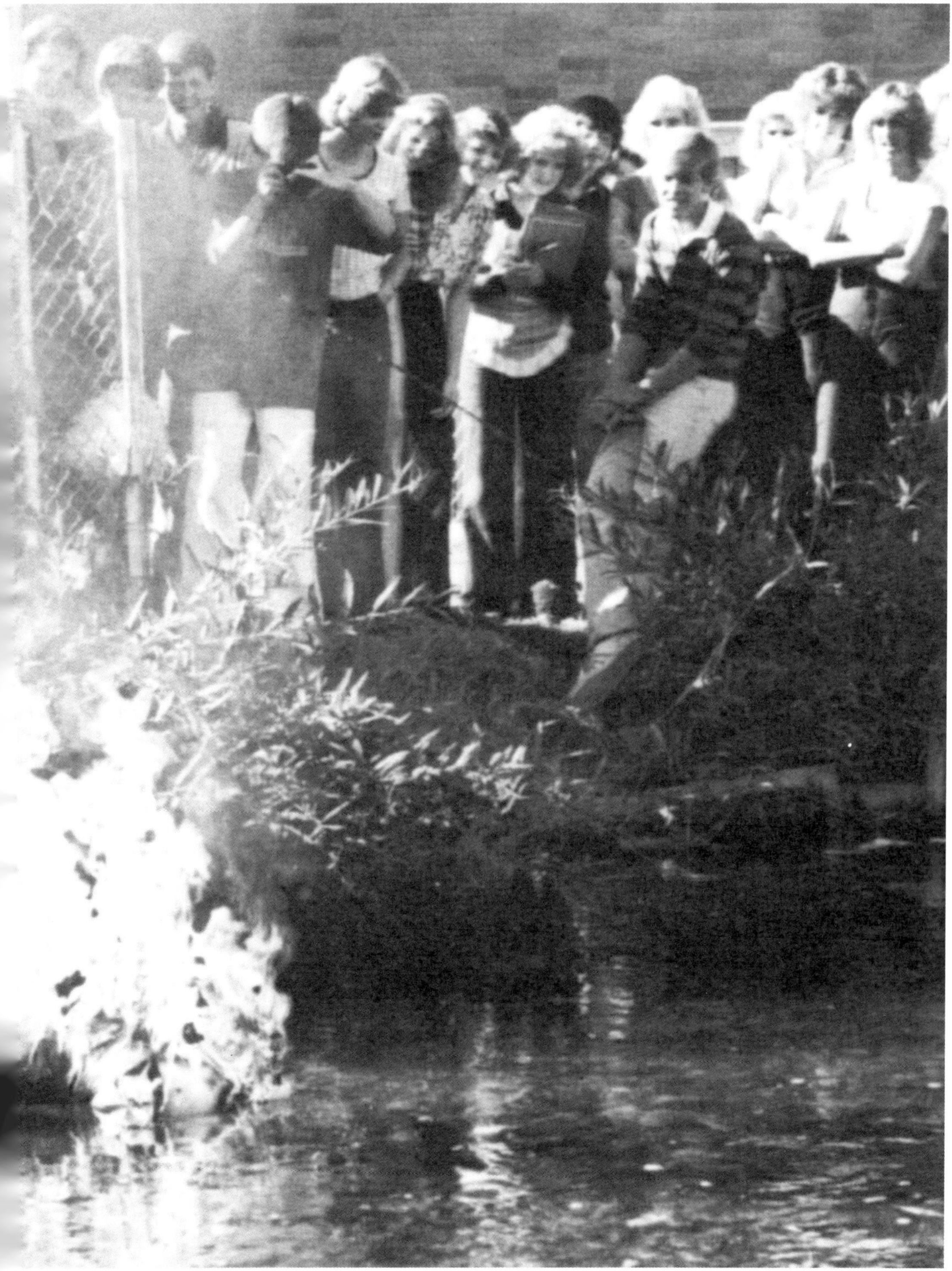

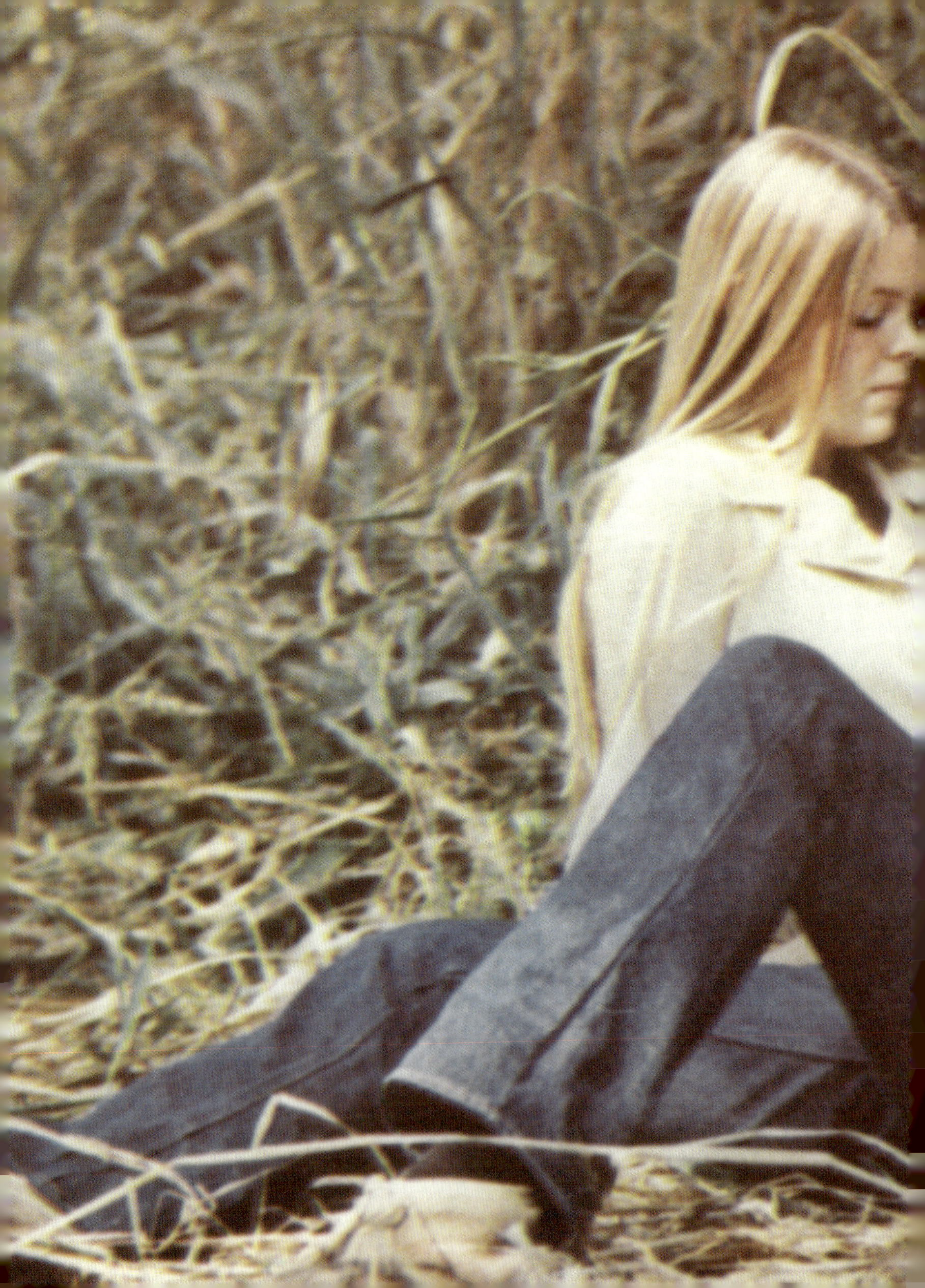

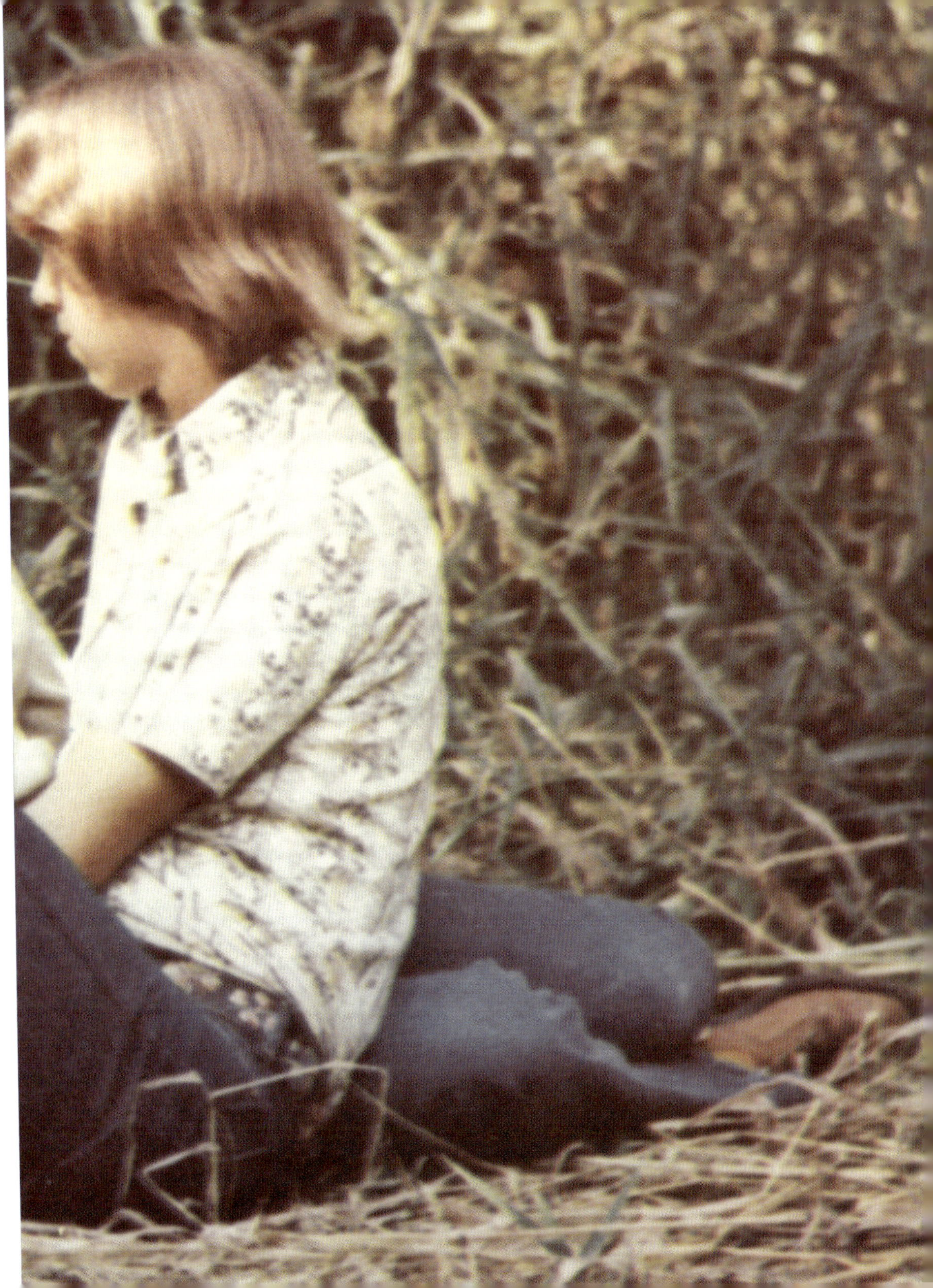

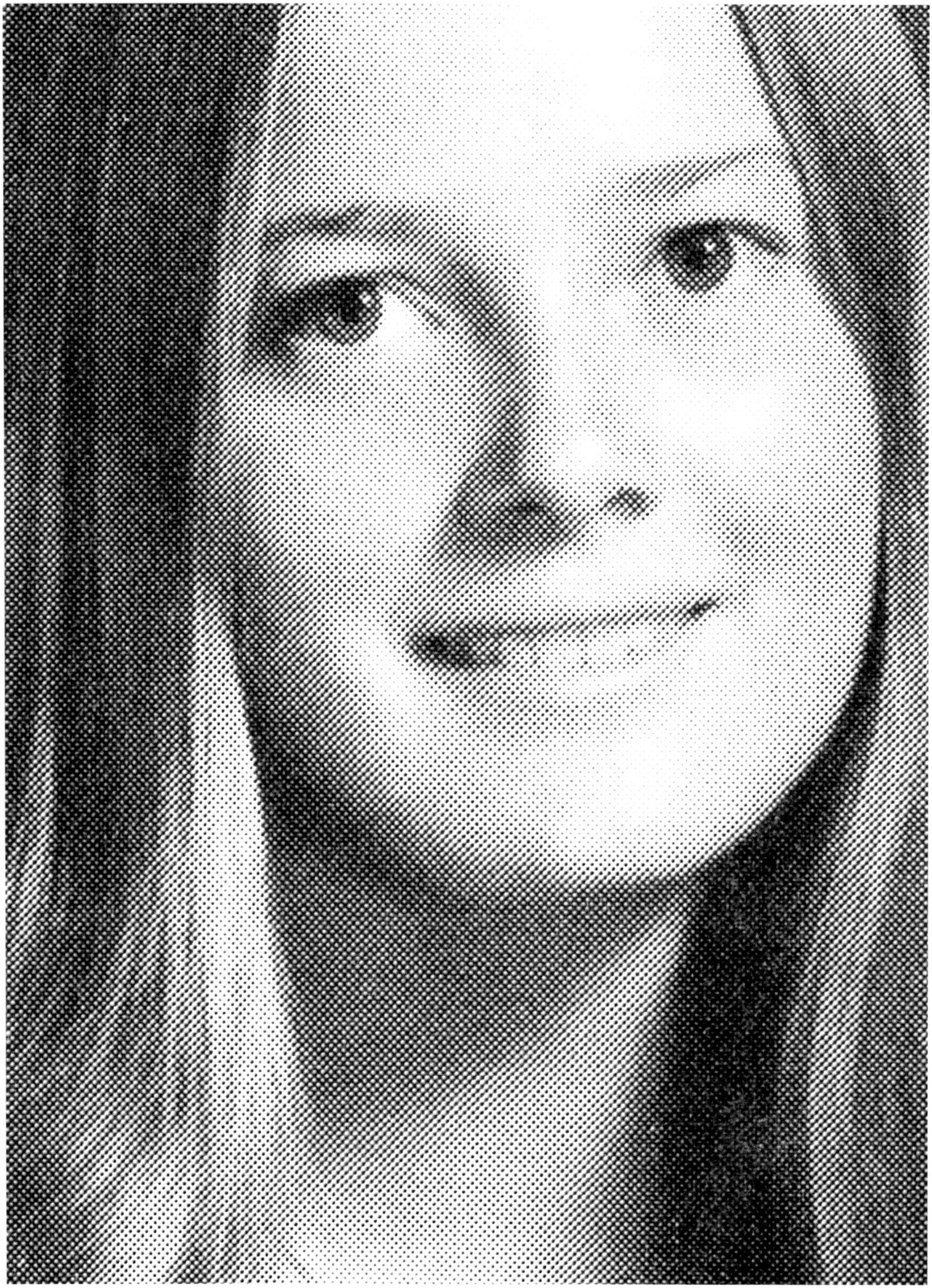

SHARLYN...

CAN I BORROW YOUR SWEATER FOREVER?

I, LAWRENCE ANTHONY GIRELLI LEAVE
TO MY YOUNGER BROTHER MY AWESOME ABILITY
TO PICK UP WOMEN AT ANY GIVEN TIME AND PLACE.

I, KEVIN HEARNE, GIVE AND BEQUEATH
MY "ICEMAN" ABILITIES TO ANYONE WHO CAN LIVE UP TO THE NAME

I, SANDRA REED GIVE AND BEQUEATH
TO THE WORLD MY ABILITY TO WORSHIP PHILLIP HUNT FROM AFAR

I, ROB STRATTON GIVE AND BEQUEATH
TO ANY STUDENT WHO FOLLOWS ME,
THE ONE SINGLE 'A' I EVER GOT IN ALL MY SCHOOL YEARS.

I JODI GIVE AND BEQUEATH
POSTERITY MY LEGACY OF CLEAVAGE
AND NOTEPADS FULL OF NOTHING BUT DOODLES.

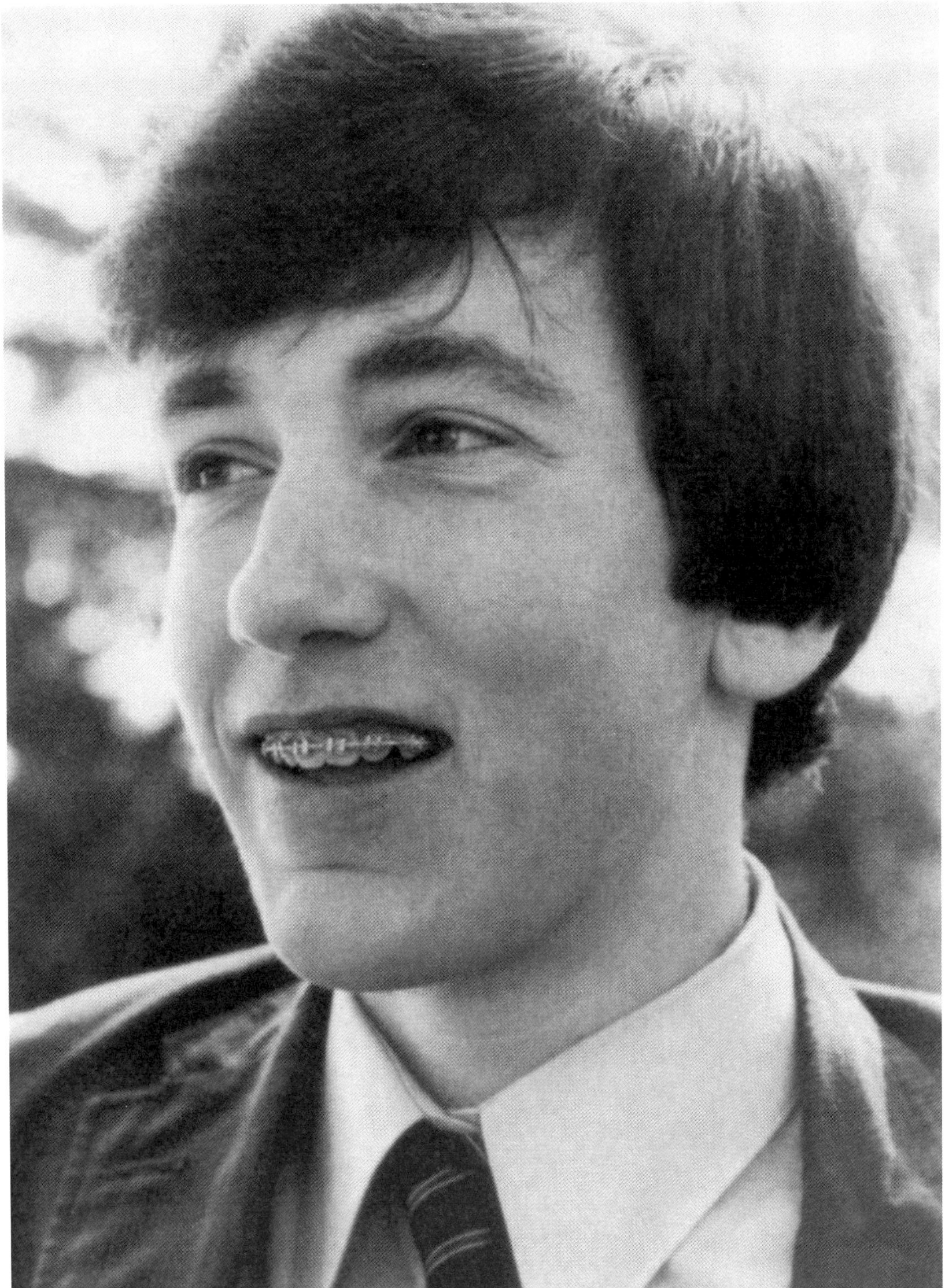

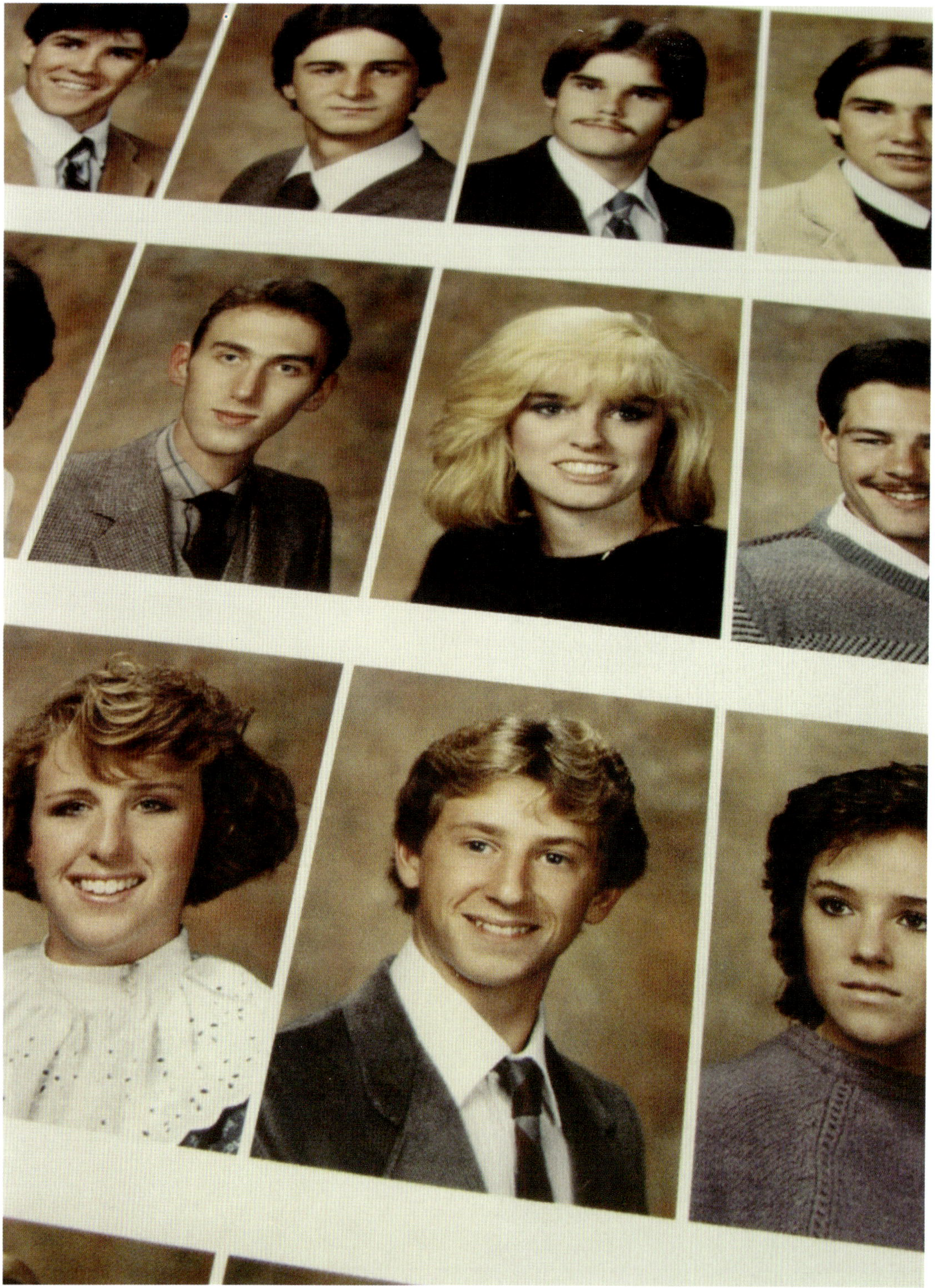

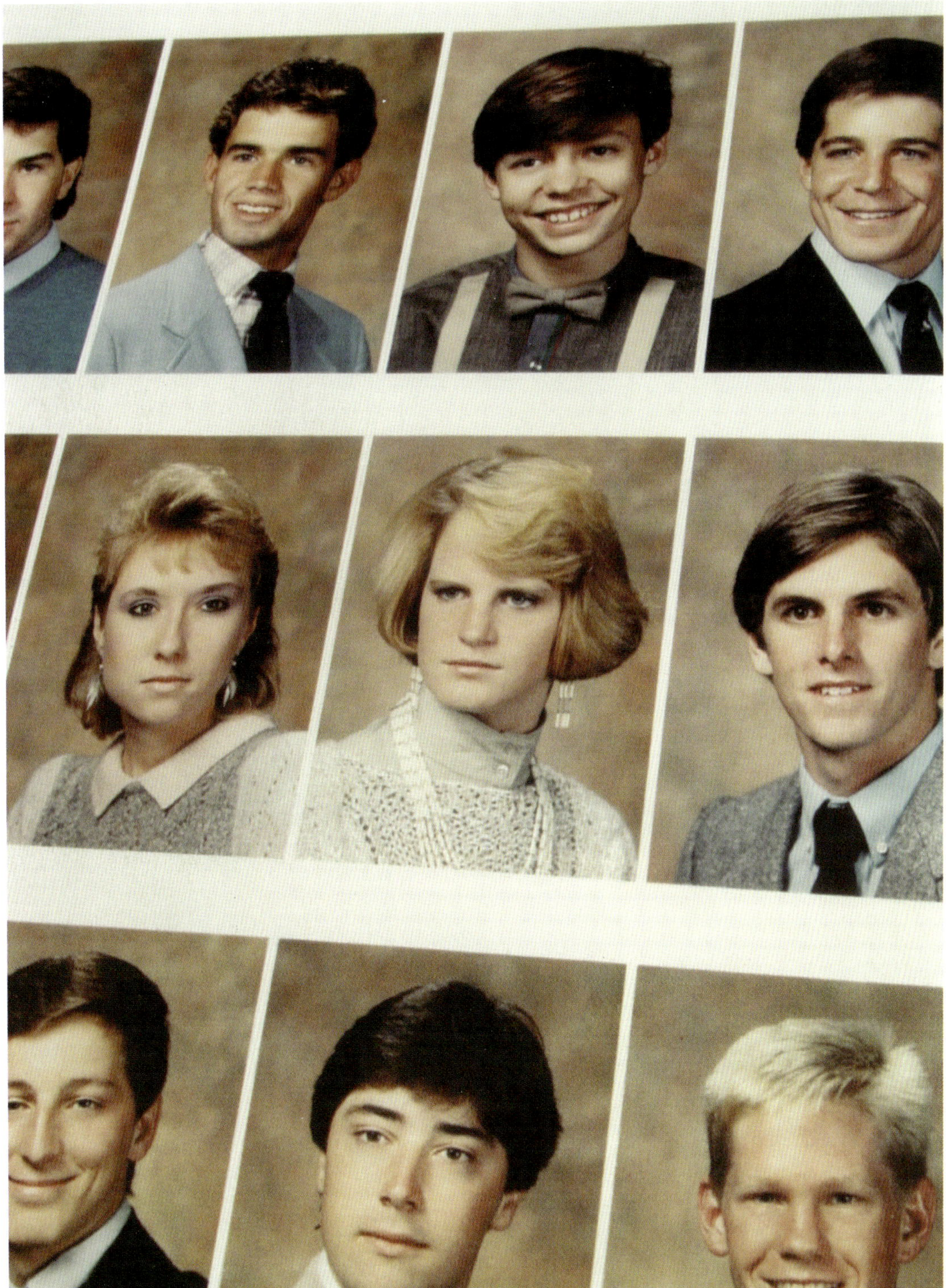

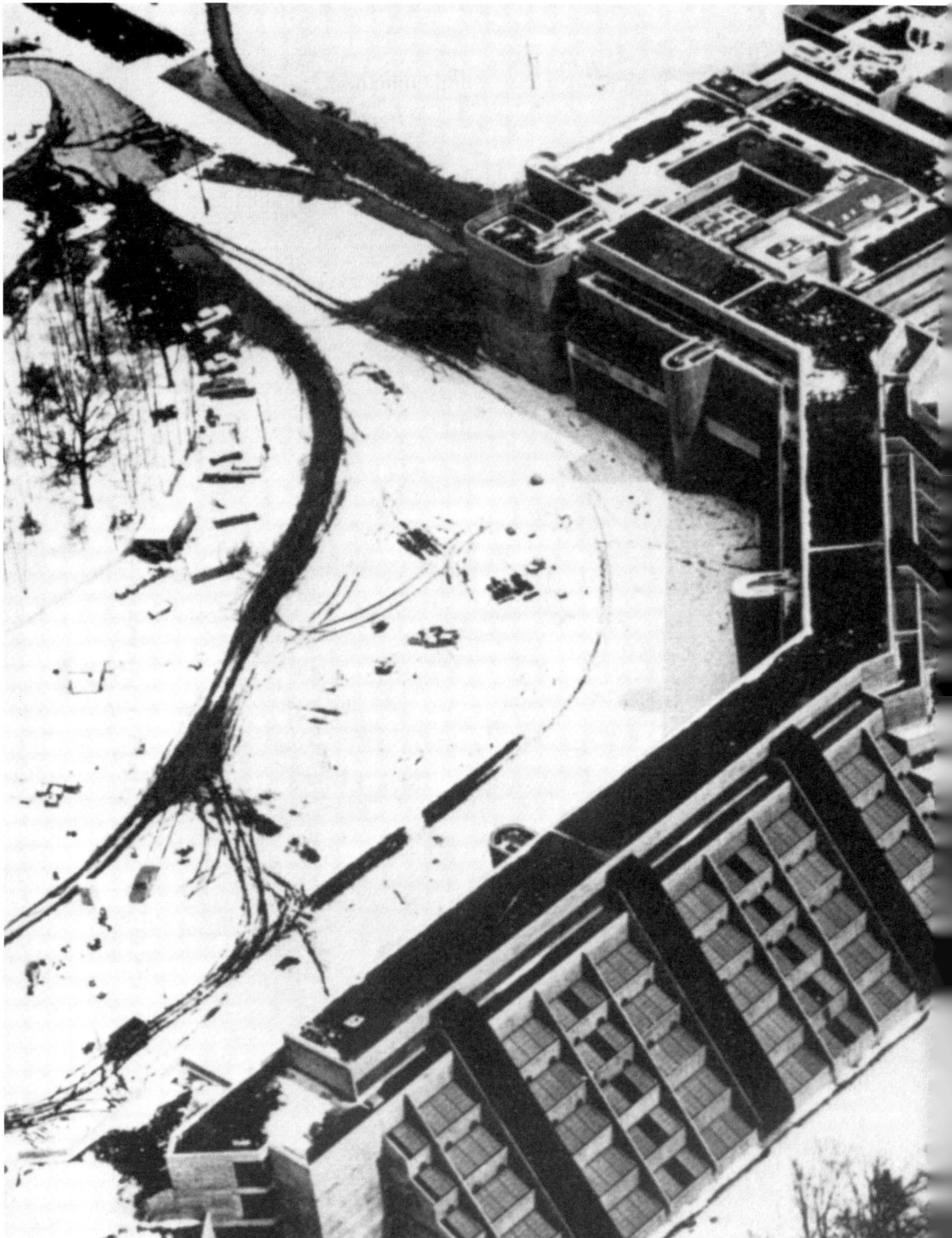

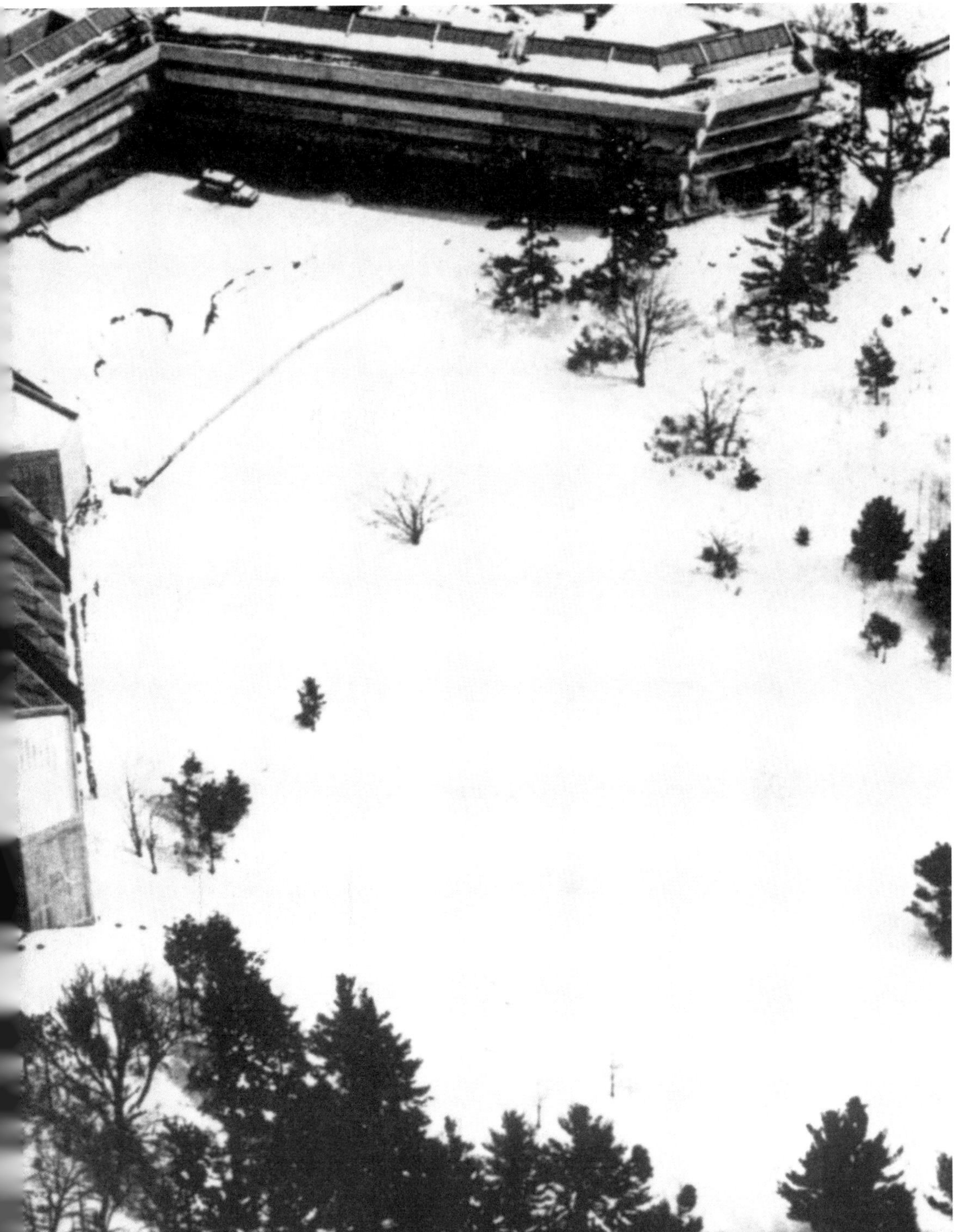

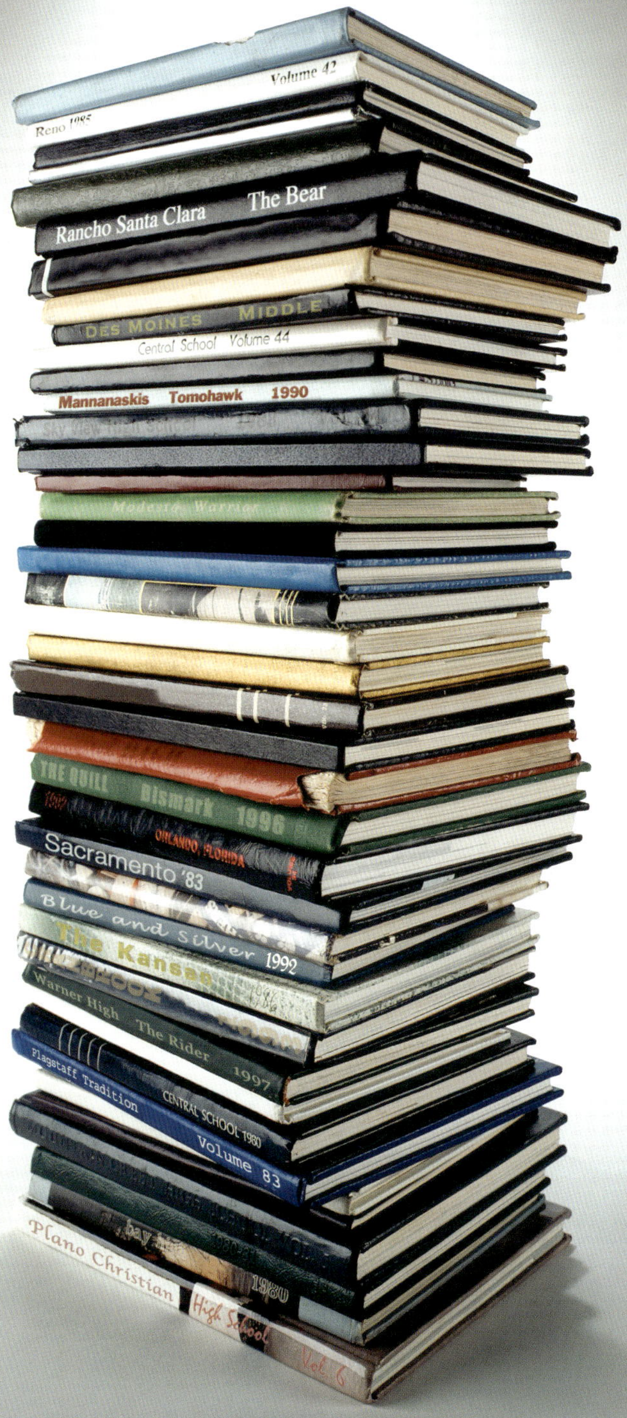
Volume 42
Reno 1985
Rancho Santa Clara
The Bear
Des Moines
Middle
Central School
Volume 44
Mannanaskis
Tomohawk
1990
The Quill
Bismark
1996
Orlando, Florida
Sacramento '83
Blue and Silver
1992
The Kansan
Warner High
The Rider
1997
Flagstaff Tradition
Central School 1980
Volume 83
1980
Plano Christian
High School
Vol. 6

3, rue Beautreillis 75004 Paris
phone (33 - 1) 48 87 07 09 - fax (33 - 1) 48 87 07 14
e-mail : disvoir@aol.com - website : www.disvoir.com

Ouvrage publié avec le concours

du Ministère de la culture et de la communication
Délégation aux arts plastiques
(CNAP)
Fiacre (aide à l'édition)

de la Fondation de France dans le cadre de son programme pour
le soutien au développement de l'histoire de l'art en France

du Centre culturel Canadien, Paris

du Centre Culturel français, Vancouver

ISBN 2-914563-07-8

PRINTED IN EUROPE